D1478863

The Local Merchants of Prato

The Johns Hopkins University Studies
in Historical and Political Science

117th Series (1999)

1. *The Local Merchants of Prato: Small Entrepreneurs in
the Late Medieval Economy*

RICHARD K. MARSHALL

Folio from an account book of the tailor Domenico di Jacopo.
Archivio de Stato de Prato.

THE   LOCAL

Merchants

OF   PRATO

Small Entrepreneurs in the
Late Medieval Economy

Richard K. Marshall

The Johns Hopkins University Press
BALTIMORE AND LONDON

This book has been brought to publication with the generous
assistance of the Karl and Edith Pribram Fund.

The Johns Hopkins University Press
2715 North Charles Street
Baltimore, Maryland 21218-4363
www.press.jhu.edu

Library of Congress Cataloging-in-Publication Data will
be found at the end of this book.
A catalog record for this book is available from the British Library.

ISBN 0-8018-6057-1

To my wife, Emily
Always helpful and patient

CONTENTS

*P*rato enjoys a very special reputation with the economic his-torians of late medieval and Renaissance Italy—but not for its prominence in the economy they study. In the fourteenth and fifteenth centuries the city was a provincial market, no more important than the several other smallish cities within the territorial state under the control of Florence. Its economy hardly extended beyond the region. It did not produce much for international markets, and although a few Pratese merchants ventured abroad to operate in the vast commercial and financial network built up by Italians throughout the Mediter-ranean and western Europe, the city itself was not on the map of this far-flung Italian system.

In the historiography of the economy of late medieval Italy, how-ever, one of these Pratese merchants who was active in the Florentine community abroad has brought his hometown well out of the shadow of Florence. This is Francesco di Marco Datini, perhaps the single most famous entrepreneur of the entire period before Cosimo de' Medici, whose career was just beginning when Datini died in 1410. Datini made his mark in history, not because of his notable success in business and certainly not because of the kind of accomplishments, such as art patronage and political influence, that mark the fame of some of his contemporaries, but because of the considerable patrimony he left be-hind. The bulk of his great wealth went to Prato for the founding of a charitable institution that is still functioning; and with this inheritance came a collection of personal and business documents that is, quite sim-ply, the most impressive archive of a single businessman anywhere in all of Europe, probably, before the nineteenth century.

These Datini materials consist of almost 600 account books and over 500 volumes of bound documents containing some 150,000 let-ters, deeds, insurance contracts, and other miscellaneous items (esti-

mated at well over a half-million pieces of paper). There are more business records for Datini than exist for all the other entrepreneurs of Florence together throughout the fourteenth century and the first decade
of the fifteenth; and his claim could probably be extended to include
the rest of Italy, if not also all of Europe, inasmuch as hardly any ledgers
at all survive for the merchants of the other two centers of the international Italian system, Venice and Genoa, for the same period, and
ledgers for the businessmen of the rest of Europe are extremely rare
well into the early modern period. Much of what we know about business practices during this early period is based on research in Datini's
archive. Its seemingly inexhaustible riches continue to attract economic historians to Prato from all over Europe and America, and every
year the city celebrates the importance of this material for the historiography of Europe in general in a week-long international congress of
the economic historians of late medieval and early modern Europe
sponsored by the Istituto Internazionale di Storia Economica
"Francesco Datini," now about thirty years old.

An enormous amount of work remains to be done in the Datini
archive, and in fact only now is a complete inventory being prepared
for publication. Yet, the hundreds of scholars of all nationalities who
have converged on Prato to look at this material—hopeful economic
historians on a research pilgrimage and dutiful students ordered there
to do a university thesis—have for all these years overlooked another
treasury of economic documents lying alongside the Datini papers in
the state archives. This is the collection of materials explored by
Richard Marshall in this book. It consists of approximately thirty account books kept by eighteen artisans, shopkeepers, and other small
operators of Prato—including a tailor, a mercer, a druggist, a butcher,
a cheese maker, a grain dealer, a stationer, a hostler, a small-time broker, a moneylender—all active during Datini's lifetime or earlier. For
all the modesty of its size in comparison to the Datini archive, this collection is in its way every bit as impressive, for it can make some of the
same claims. If a survey were made of all materials in Italian archives
that were generated by such small operators, it would probably reveal
that the Prato collection contains more ledgers of this kind dating before 1400 than exist for the rest of Italy taken all together. Moreover,

this claim, like that made for the Datini archive, can probably be extended to take in all of Europe. How many centuries forward would we have to go before we could accumulate as many as thirty ledgers of shopkeepers and artisans outside of Italy?

There is more than just rhetoric in this question, for it points to a historiographical void: precisely because of the rarity of such documents, historians have hardly studied the small entrepreneurs who operated in the local markets of late medieval Europe. In this sense, the collection of ledgers in the Prato state archives that is the foundation of Marshall's book is every bit as important as the Datini archives for widening and deepening our view of the economy of late medieval and early modern Europe. While a few scholars have made forays into this material to look at individual ledgers, Marshall is the first to use them to gain a comprehensive overview of the local market of Datini's Prato; and by extension this local study marks a new direction for the history of work and the working classes, one based on the documents of these small entrepreneurs themselves. In short, these records constitute the perfect complement to the Datini archive as a source for the economic life of the time; and for the rarity of such materials elsewhere in Italy, they put Prato's unique place in the historiography of the economy of late medieval Italy—indeed, of Europe—into even higher relief.

The traditional view of the working men of the medieval town is largely based on guild materials. The guild was an exclusive organization: within, it regulated the work of its members, it adjudicated disputes among them, and it controlled the training of young craftsmen; without, it protected its members from competition and it guaranteed the quality of their products. Moreover, the guild reached beyond the economic world to bind its members together through joint religious and civic activities, social welfare programs, and support of family craft traditions. Such an institution fits in well with our view of the corporate structure of medieval society. Indeed, guilds have been regarded as obstacles to the development of the free market associated with modern capitalism; and what we might regard as a "crisis" stage reached in the opposition of these two different economic systems is behind the recent formulations of "proto-industrialization" or "industrialization before industrialization," which economic historians have invented to characterize a major dynamic in the economic development of early modern Europe.

Virtually nothing of this corporate institutional structure so central to the traditional view of the history of working people in the Middle Ages emerges from the account books of the artisans and shopkeepers of Prato studied by Marshall for the writing of this book. Here we see these men as small entrepreneurs freely plying their trade in the marketplace, on the one hand unregulated by particular guilds and on the other assured of the sanctity of contract by a higher legal authority. Most striking is how well prepared they were to operate in a market economy. Not only were they literate and so able to keep a record of their activities, but they also had an expertise in accounting approaching that of an international merchant-banker, such as their famous contemporary, Francesco di Marco Datini himself. They organized their records using the standard formats and the professional jargon of the accountant. These accounting skills also enabled them to enter into the capitalist spirit of the marketplace: they thought about value in the abstract terms of a "ghost money" (as Carlo Cipolla has labeled moneys of account), and their ability to shift around debits and credits on paper freed them from the confines of a primitive market mentality geared to the concrete realities of barter and cash. Moreover, who is to gainsay that here, in the ability of these small operators to impose a kind of arithmetic order in keeping track of their economic activities, we find something of those deeper cultural foundations that historians have read into the correspondence between the extraordinary penchant of Florentine entrepreneurs for keeping accounts and their taste for the geometrical organization of space so characteristic of Florentine art of the Renaissance?

These ledgers document the daily lives of small operators at work in the marketplace. To set themselves up in business some of these men required capital investments, went into partnership, employed assistants, and entered into contracts with clients of various kinds. Their individual economic interests extended much beyond the narrow confines associated with the principal activity by which they defined themselves, and collectively they were all over the marketplace. The people they dealt with ranged from peasants from the countryside to Francesco Datini himself and included ecclesiastical institutions and the commune, and a great many women show up in their ledgers, both as customers and as fellow entrepreneurs. Some of these operators were continually borrowing money or lending it out to others, and through the offsetting of debits and credits on their own books they themselves performed a primitive banking function within the local market.

In all this, these men had virtually no recourse to the notary: their ledgers provided the written record they needed to be assured of the inviolability of the various contracts they entered into during the course of a day's work. Unseen in these ledgers but looming over all the relatively petty activities they record is the larger institutional structure that ultimately regulated the marketplace, and it clearly instilled into the modest operator of the kind we meet in this book that same confidence about his economic relations with others that underpins the capitalist system. Economic historians have long emphasized the importance of this confidence (*fiducia* is their term) in the growth and development of the forward sectors of the economy of late medieval and Renaissance Italy promoted by men like Francesco di Marco Datini; here, in this book, we see how deeply Italian capitalism had taken root even in the local market of Datini's provincial hometown.

In any event, the picture Marshall gives us of these Pratese shopkeepers and artisans is altogether different from the guild stereotype that dominates much of the traditional historiography. The two views are not necessarily contradictory, but it remains to be seen to what extent they do in fact overlap or what indeed were the frictions between the corporate mentality and the spirit of the marketplace. Recent work has pushed the boundaries of the history of the working classes in Italian towns during the late Middle Ages considerably beyond the older guild categories—with studies of wages, poverty, women, diet, spirituality, and welfare institutions, and with research into particular sectors, especially textiles, construction, and the visual arts—and now Marshall's book opens up yet another direction in taking a look at how the entrepreneurs among the working class confronted market forces in organizing their work. This is one of the central problems of the economic history of preindustrial Europe, and these small operators working away in provincial Prato are as unique a testimony as their more famous contemporary, Francesco Datini, to the development of capitalism in late medieval and Renaissance Florence.

Marco Spallanzani
Institute of Economic History
University of Florence

ACKNOWLEDGMENTS

Without the help and encouragement of Richard Goldthwaite, of Johns Hopkins University, this book would never have come to fruition. He acted as advisor and guide while the manuscript first took shape and made himself always available as friend and mentor throughout the years during which I sought to turn my research into this book.

The staffs at the Archivio di Stato di Prato and the Biblioteca Roncioniana in Prato were also of great assistance. Many friends read parts of the manuscript and offered valuable suggestions on ways to improve the text.

Dates, Weights and Measures, and Money

*A*ll dates have been converted into modern style unless otherwise indicated. The Pratesi used the same calendar as the Florentines, in which March 25 marked the beginning of the new year.

The tables at the beginning of volumes 1* and 1** (asterisks indicate
part number) of *Prato stori di una città* (ed. Giovanni Cherubini [Prato,
1991]), give a detailed list of the weights and measures used in Prato in
the late Middle Ages. Equivalents for those that appear in the present
work are as follows, according to A. Martini, *Manuale di Metrologia, os-
sia misure, pesi e monete in uso attualmente e anticamente presso tutti i popoli*
(Turin, 1883):

  1 staio = 24.36 liters = .686 bushels
  1 barile of wine = 45.58 liters = 12.03 gallons
  1 libbra = 339.54 grams = .74 pounds
  1 staioro = 5.25 ares = .1294 acres

Units of currency have been indicated as follows:

  lire: £
  soldi: s.
  denari: d.
  florins: f.

In the system known as *lira di piccioli,* 1 lira = 20 soldi = 240 denari.

The Local Merchants of Prato

Introduction

*T*raveling from Florence to Prato by train or car, one cannot easily see where the environs of one city cease and those of the other begin. The names of former villages such as Calenzano or Sesto Fiorentino persist, but these areas now are simply part of the urban sprawl between the two cities. Six hundred years ago this was not the case. Then, occasional small clusters of humble homes interrupted the forests and open spaces between the two urban centers; and only after passing through a gate in the third circle of walls around Prato would one find the shops of the druggist, the tailor, and other local tradesmen whose businesses and way of life are the theme of this study.

The numerous account books of these local tradesmen in the Archivio di Stato di Prato provide an unusual opportunity for such a study. One of the books, the 1285–86 ledger of the moneylender Sinibaldo, has been published by Luca Serianni, who discussed its contents as examples of the early Pratese dialect.[1] The others, dating back to the 1340s, have been largely neglected except in a few theses by students from the University of Florence.[2] The fortuitous survival of these accounts resulted from their preservation by the Hospital of the Misericordia and Dolce and by the Ceppo, a charitable organization for the poor,[3] where they had been left along with more substantial legacies to these institutions.[4]

Though only about twelve miles northwest of Florence, Prato was at that time and is still today a separate city. It has its own geographic features, including a river and bordering plain. The Bisenzio River was as important to Prato as the Arno was to Florence. Although too shallow for traffic, it was ideal as a source of hydraulic power for grain and fulling mills. Numerous natural and manmade tributaries provided water for irrigation as for various stages in textile manufacture. Flowing south from the Apennines, the river entered the broadening plain near the town of Vaiano, enclosed on both sides by mountains of moderate height. The land in this valley of the Bisenzio was fertile, yielding a variety of agricultural products—in particular, grain and wine, the staples of medieval life. The hills supplied wood, stone, and sheep-grazing terrain.

Geographical configuration is but one of the distinguishing features of the Florentine and Pratese districts. The citizens of Prato pride themselves, today as in the past, on a heritage distinct from the Florentine metropolis. They do not hesitate to blame some of their problems on their larger neighbor. It is as if the centuries of subjection to Florence still color the Pratese outlook, intensified by tragedies such as the month-long sack of Prato in 1512 by Spanish troops supporting the return of the Medici.[5]

Prato's passage from a feudal jurisdiction into a free commune that controlled the surrounding countryside proceeded in a unique way for Tuscany.[6] Whereas other free Tuscan communes in the twelfth and thirteenth centuries extended and consolidated power beyond their walls by following the boundaries of the dioceses of their resident bishops, Prato, with no bishop, had to encroach on the diocesan territory of other cities. Prato's urban center was under the jurisdiction of the bishop of Pistoia, but the neighboring countryside was a part of either the Pistoiese or the Florentine bishopric. On September 5, 1460, Pope Pius II confirmed the de facto status of the provostry of Santo Stefano as *nullius diocesis,* thus establishing that the district of Prato belonged to neither neighboring diocese. On September 22, 1653, Innocent X granted joint episcopal jurisdiction to Prato and Pistoia. Finally, on January 25, 1954, a pontifical decree allowed Prato to have its own resident bishop. Prato's territorial expansion and consolidation, therefore, was defined not by diocesan boundaries but by feudal jurisdictions that emanated from the Alberti counts and later the imperial vicars who resided in the urban center (in a castle at the location of the present restored fortress of Frederick II), and who exercised at least nominal authority over the surrounding area. By de facto usurpation of these rights, the communal jurisdiction replaced those of the feudal lords.[7]

Given its proximity to Florence, a city of growing power and expansionist policies, how could a minor commune like Prato avoid the same fate as Fiesole, which became a subject of Florence in 1125? Although Prato developed in the shadow of its larger neighbor, it managed to escape total domination until 1351.[8] Before the middle of the twelfth century the Alberti counts provided a buffer. Then the Alberti turned over their rights to the emperor, affording the city another protector, distant yet potent.[9] Toward the end of the thirteenth century, however, the emperor no longer represented an adequate shield; in fact, Prato's allegiance to him became an invitation to Florentine intervention. In 1280–81 Florence placed its own garrison in the fortress to prevent the imperial vicar from taking possession of it, and later, in 1312, the descent of Henry VII of Luxembourg provoked a similar response.[10] Consequently, in 1313 and again in 1326 the Pratesi looked south for a guardian, conferring overlordship first on King Robert of Naples and then on his son Charles, Duke of Calabria. These maneuvers preserved a measure of freedom for half a century but eventually proved Prato's undoing.

In 1350 Florence, as a consequence of a juridical dispute between the two cities, sent an army to Prato and forced the government to accept Florentine overlordship; and on February 23, 1351, at the instigation of the Florentine Niccolò Acciaiuoli, Grand Seneschal of the Kingdom, Queen Joanna sold all her rights over the city to Florence for 17,500 florins.[11] This was quite a bargain compared with other financial settlements that Florence made in the ensuing decades: 18,000 florins paid in 1361 to the heirs of Musciatto and Nicola Franzesi for the castle of Staggia and its jurisdictional prerogatives, 40,000 florins paid in November 1384 to the French for Arezzo, and 18,000 florins paid the following year to appease Siena.[12] The Angevines had had only nominal rights over Prato, but Florence took complete control. Its overlordship became far more than legal tenure: the authorities proceeded to incorporate Prato and its district into the Florentine state, and the political history of Prato became one with that of Florence.[13]

Yet Florence, consistent with its policies toward other subject areas, jus-
tified its expansion as a defense of republican liberty in Tuscany and allowed Prato a semblance of autonomy.[14] As long as it paid the required
taxes and in no way interfered with Florentine interests, Prato continued to elect its own councilors and priors to manage local affairs; however, final approval of all decisions remained in the hands of the Florentine *podestà* and the central government.

Perhaps it is more accurate to regard the official purchase of Prato
in 1351 as the final legalization of an accomplished fact. After the tri-
umph of the Black Guelfs in both cities at the beginning of the fourteenth century, Florentine influence shifted increasingly toward inter-
ference and, at times, exploitation.[15] The nominal lordship of the
South was in reality a meaningless facade masking Florentine designs,
for the royal vicars or representatives invariably were Florentines. Florence did not hesitate to use its own troops to garrison Pratese fortifi-
cations and to recruit additional manpower from the area; it did this
frequently, for example, during the years of its struggle against Cas-
truccio Castracani of Lucca.[16] Moreover, the Florentines obtained tax
exemptions for their exports without due compensation for those entering Florence from Prato. A proclamation by the council of Prato in
1307 to the effect that the authorities at Florence had the right to de-
cide "about the affairs of the land of Prato" makes the relationship
clear—Prato was a protectorate, almost a colony, subject to a delaying
action that, for fifty years, postponed the *legal* loss of autonomy but did
not limit the Florentine intrusion. Florence installed its own magis-
trate, the executor of justice, who usurped many of the functions of
Prato's "captain of the people." The relationship between the two cities
before and after the sale of Prato has never been studied in depth, although the impact of Florentine domination on subjugated areas has
received increasing attention in recent years.[17]

Limited in area and population, the district of Prato did not constitute a viable entity for the maintenance of an independent existence
against the trend toward large territorial states.[18] Enrico Fiumi's research on the demography of Prato, for which he used the tax records
of Prato and those of Florence after 1351, confirms the relatively sparse

population of the territory in the late Middle Ages.[19] By the end of the thirteenth century this area, with 6,500 households *(fuochi)* or about 32,000 inhabitants, reached a demographic height not to be equaled until modern times. Forty years later, in 1339, city and countryside counted only 4,548 households, or a population of 18,249—a one-third loss.[20] A few years later, the Black Death, disastrous in its toll, accelerated a process already well under way.

A complete census is not available for the years immediately following the plague of 1348. Some demographic information from 1351 and 1352, fragmentary for the city and more extensive for the district, has survived, published by Fiumi, who however drew no conclusions from it.[21] A comparison of this information with that recorded for the same areas in the comprehensive survey of 1339 reveals the effect of the Black Death on the population of one small section of Tuscany.[22] In the tax assessment of 1351, two of the eight divisions—Porta Fuia and Porta Capo di Ponte—counted only 439 households, a decrease of 31 percent from the 638 in 1339;[23] and a 1352 survey of households in the *contado,* conducted to determine how many oxen, carts, and olive presses each possessed, listed 1,017 households in forty-three villages, a loss of 37.4 percent from the 1,625 households in the same villages in 1339. While some villages show a drop of more than 50 percent, a few, surprisingly, increased their number of households despite the ravages of the plague (an increase undoubtedly to be explained by migration from one village to another).[24] Since numbers of households rather than individuals *(bocche)* are being compared, these percentages of 31 percent and 37.4 percent should be considered conservative estimates of the decrease in population. It seems highly unlikely that households in 1351 and 1352 still averaged 3.9 family members in the city and 4.3 in the country as they did in 1339.

Twenty years later the Florentine estimo of 1372 provides data as complete and reliable for demographic purposes as that of 1339.[25] Whatever gains may have occurred subsequent to the Black Death were far from sufficient to reach the 1339 figures. The totals for city and district again show a one-third drop from 4,548 households to 3,047, or from 18,249 inhabitants to 12,240.[26] The well-known Flor-

TABLE I
Population of Pratese Territory, 1300–1429

Year(s)	Households	Inhabitants
1300	6,500	32,000
1339	4,548	18,249
1372	3,047	12,240
1428–29	1,894	8,240

SOURCE: E. Fiumi, *Demografia, movimento urbanistico e classi sociali in Prato* (Florence, 1968), 83, 91, 111.

entine catasto of 1428–29 reveals a continuing decline in population; by then the area contained only 1,894 households, or 8,240 inhabitants (table 1).[27]

In summary, the average population for Prato and its district during the last three fifths of the fourteenth century and the first decade of the fifteenth—the period covered by this study—approached 12,000, about evenly divided between city and contado. As is often the case, the average family was larger in the countryside.[28] Judith Brown estimated that Pescia averaged about 1,900 inhabitants making it only one third the size of Prato.[29] David Herlihy concluded that the city of Pistoia had about 6,000 people, the same number as Prato; the countryside under the jurisdiction of Pistoia, however, encompassed a larger area than Prato's contado and had a population twice as large.[30]

By the twelfth century Prato showed the first signs of its future domination by the textile industry. A document as early as 1107 refers to a fulling mill on the bank of the Bisenzio River near Capo di Ponte, the later site of one of the gates of the city.[31] The river and its many canals *(gore)* provided locations for additional fulling mills, while the city supplied skilled labor for essential tasks such as dyeing and for other refinements of the cloth.[32] Prato and its district increasingly became associated with textiles—a commercial and industrial affiliation that has continued to the present day.[33] Florence imposed restrictions on the industry but without curtailing the continual development of this staple of the Pratese economy. Other industrial enterprises also developed, although none approached the importance of cloth manufacture. The green marble quarried on the slopes of Monteferrato gave a distinctive appearance to many churches and monuments in Prato, Florence, and other Tuscan cities. Its rarity is recognized today, and its use is restricted to repairs of existing structures. Ceramics also has an ancient heritage in the area, particularly at Figline, a small village close to Monteferrato. And some of Europe's earliest paper mills had appeared in this district by the fourteenth century, employing the same hydraulic energy as the fulling mills.[34]

Extant records from the guilds and the commune tell us little of the economic vitality of late medieval Prato. The Florentine estimo of 1372 and the later catasto of 1428–29 yield quite precise demographic information, yet both are woefully deficient in recording people's occupations. Only the official who compiled the 1372 list for Porta Gualdimare in Prato included the occupational categories of taxpayers—and what conclusions can be drawn from five blacksmiths, seven shoemakers, and three tailors in an area constituting only one eighth of the city, with no data at all for the countryside?[35] Two lists of gifts of candles for the collegiate church of Santo Stefano in 1396 and 1401 reveal that economic and professional activities at Prato were organized into twenty-one guilds, but no membership figures are provided.[36] Included are the Wool Guild and the Guild of Judges and Notaries, along with the guilds of artisans and shopkeepers found in most small Italian cities. The listing of an Arte del Cambio undoubtedly indicates something about the number of merchant bankers in the city at this time.

Other sources suggest that Florentine domination did not impede economic development in Prato. The unparalleled Datini archives (in the Archivio di Stato)[37] offer frequent glimpses of successful merchants and industrialists in the city, particularly those engaged in textiles. The famous international merchant banker Francesco di Marco Datini was not the only entrepreneur able to exploit the economic opportunities of the time to rise above the ranks of local operators.[38] The early fifteenth-century careers of the Marcovaldi brothers, sons of the doublet maker Marco di Sandro, whose register is a source for this study, further suggest that it is misleading to let Datini completely overshadow other Pratese entrepreneurs in historic accounts.[39] A community of Pratese merchants at Ragusa on the Dalmatian coast reached sufficient size in the first half of the Quattrocento to justify the election of its own consul. During that period the Pratesi living at Ragusa engaged in trade not only with their native city but also with communities in southern Italy and the Balkan interior. They formed partnerships with local businessmen to develop the cloth industry at Ragusa, and they further supplemented their incomes through moneylending.[40] At the same time, another Prato merchant was operating successfully in Hungary.[41] Despite the activity of Pratese merchants abroad, however, there is no study assessing the city's economy in the second half of the Trecento or the beginning of the Quattrocento.[42]

This study does not address the overall economy or the world of Prato's textile manufacturers and international merchants; it seeks instead to portray the way in which the local merchants of a small Italian town lived and worked. Although not comparable to the Datini records in extent and detail, the account books of Pratese artisans and shopkeepers are unique in European economic history for the documentation of a single local market. Notarial records undoubtedly would add valuable information to expand this study, but unfortunately that type of source—available in other centers such as Florence—is represented in Prato by only a few fragments. A number of account books of small businessmen have survived at Arezzo but, for the most part, they commence after the Florentine purchase in 1384.[43]

In spite of the wealth of the archives at Florence, only one fourteenth-century account book of a small Florentine businessman has been noted in the literature. In an article on the Ciompi Revolt, Gene Brucker mentions extant accounts of two comb manufacturers *(pettinagnoli)* from 1372 to 1378 who, in addition to selling loom reeds, bought, sold, and exchanged cloth and engaged in moneylending on a small scale.[44] Outside Italy the documentation is no better. Four French account books, or fragments of them, have survived that record retail trade in the fourteenth century.[45] In Germany two registers are extant, one of a family partnership of Nuremberg drapers (1304–7) and one of a Hamburg cloth merchant (1367–92); both businesses sold at retail.[46] Raymond de Roover's brief comments on the mercantile and financial aspects of these non-Italian records indicate business practices similar to these found in Prato;[47] but de Roover used no records of local tradesmen in Italy, limiting his examples of Italian accounting procedures to the records of prominent entrepreneurs. It is not unlikely that the archives of other communities, particularly in central and northern Italy, contain unexamined records of local tradesmen. If this author's experience in Prato is typical, descriptions in archival inventories do not always reveal the true contents of manuscripts. Some of the account books used in this study were discovered only by a check of all documents with dates falling within the time frame of the study; a similar procedure might be necessary in investigating the holdings of other archives of similar size.

In addition to the published fragments of the ledger of the thirteenth-century moneylender Sinibaldo, no fewer than forty-five books of seventeen different tradesmen provide the basis for this study. The earliest accounts, those of the cloth seller Giovanni di Spinello Viviani, commence in 1337; the last, belonging to the broker Matteo di Matteo Toffi, end in 1410.[48] Within this seventy-three-year period are included the records of three druggists, two cheese sellers or delicatessen operators, two cloth sellers, a tailor, a doublet maker, a grain seller, a secondhand dealer, a broker, a shearer of cloth, a family of innkeepers, and partnerships of butchers, wallers, and paper manufacturers. Seventeen of the books belonging to one family of innkeepers alone span the entire period from the middle of the fourteenth century to the middle of the fifteenth. For purposes of this study, these various economic operators all are classified as local tradesmen. A complete list is provided in the appendix.

In Prato as nowhere else—not even in Florence—it is possible to enter the world of small businessmen and to learn how they lived and plied their trades. For the most part, the world of artisans and shopkeepers in the late Middle Ages has received little attention, a primary reason being the absence of direct evidence of their activities.[49] In recent years economic historians have shifted their focus below the level of prominent merchant bankers and industrialists, but their studies, except for those on workers in the building trades,[50] have been limited to analyses of wages, estimations of daily and annual work periods, and descriptions of the general conditions of laborers.[51] In a recent article Marco Tangheroni discussed retail trade but failed to assess the significance of tradesmen's role in the local economy and of the advanced business practices they employed.[52] Although the shopkeepers at Prato occasionally sold in bulk to a fellow tradesman in the same business, their usual daily sales were small and went to customers representing all levels of society—clearly retail transactions. Tangheroni suggested possible sources for future investigation (without, however, mentioning account books) and emphasized the importance of fairs and markets in facilitating exchanges between urban centers and the countryside. Throughout Prato's history, fairs and markets operated there, as they still do today.[53] But hundreds of people from the contado bought directly at the city shops and supplied the shelves of the tradesmen with their products.

The small tradesmen of the late Middle Ages still await their historian. Recent studies of provincial towns, including Prato as well as Pescia, Pistoia, and Pisa, comment on local economies in the late Middle Ages but mention the local tradesmen only in passing.[54] None of these studies uses account books or any other records of the tradesmen themselves. In one study of a later period, A. Astorre employs as one of his sources the account book of a Florentine broker representing the druggists' guild. Astorre examines the broker's activities in 1483–85 and assesses the overall importance of apothecaries in the local economy of late Quattrocento Florence.[55]

The objective of the present study is to investigate how one local economy was organized and functioned in the late Middle Ages. De Roover stresses the need for such studies in his chapter on the organization of late medieval trade in *The Cambridge Economic History of Europe*. Explaining his failure to discuss local trade adequately, he writes, "The trouble is the organization of local trade has yet to be studied."[56] Two other chapters in *Cambridge Economic History* consider the effects of the economic policies of governing bodies on local economies and, in the process, describe the framework in which local trade and industry operated, particularly in attempts to safeguard basic food supplies.[57] A chapter by Sylvia Thrupp on guild organization and development discusses the practices of local tradesmen as revealed in guild statutes.[58] Yet guild statutes do not necessarily represent the reality of the marketplace, and Armando Sapori notes how "dangerous" it is to rely on them alone. De Roover's study of the records of a Florentine cloth firm points the way to a more accurate assessment of the city's cloth industry than that previously obtained by a study based almost solely on guild statutes.[59] The present study is intended to serve a similar purpose by illustrating the ways in which local tradesmen conducted their businesses as revealed by their own day-to-day records.

Part 1

The Local Marketplace

C H A P T E R

One

Way of Life

hough not as extensive as the business records of Datini, which also reside in the archives at Prato, the contemporaneous account books of tradesmen provide sufficient information to sketch their business life. No documentation such as the numerous personal letters of Datini, his wife, and his close friend Lapo Mazzei has survived for these tradesmen, and it is impossible to portray their way of life in as much detail as we have for Prato's most famous merchant. Yet information about their personal lives is not entirely lacking. The local tradesmen of late medieval Prato included more than business entries in their registers. These books also served as diaries, or *ricordi,* of important events such as births, deaths, and marriages, and of personal expenditures and other miscellaneous records. Although the information is limited, it permits some general observations on the standard of living and lifestyle of this middling class of urban entrepreneurs.

Diet and Cost of Living

The incomes of these men, being well above subsistence level, afforded a better than average diet.[1] But grain and wine constituted their staples as for most people in late medieval Italy, flour being used not only for bread but also for soup, polenta, and pap.[2] The book of the grain seller Stefano di Cecco shows hundreds of sales of grain and flour to people from all walks of life; and many pages in the other books offer details about the shipment of grain to the mill for grinding.[3] Not surprisingly in this period after the Black Death, entries for wheat far exceed those for the cheaper cereals such as barley, millet, rye, or spelt. There are innumerable entries for the purchase of wine, and the quantities are impressive: the doublet maker Marco di Sandro, for example, records the purchase of 58 1/2 barrels of wine in 1384 through October 2 and states that he has 48 barrels still at his house.[4] Although the type of wine or its provenance is rarely recorded, the varying prices per barrel, ranging from s.4 1/2 to s.70, must indicate something about differences in quality.[5]

We can learn about other foodstuffs that supplemented the basic diet from the books of the two cheese sellers Paolo di Ser Ambrogio and Giovanni di Paolo. They sold a variety of foods to a wide range of tradesmen and their wives, and many of these customers returned frequently. Leading the list of sales was cheese of all types, both local and imported. Second was olive oil, which apparently had then, as now, an important place in the Italian kitchen. Giuliano Pinto asserts that olive cultivation still was not widespread; olive oil was used by a restricted class, he says, and lard (lardo) was the fat (grasso) of common use. The frequent purchases of olive oil by tradesmen suggest that they can be included in Pinto's "restricted class," although they also purchased some lard.[6] These delicatessen storekeepers handled less meat and seafood, as one might expect in a town where there were many butchers; but they did make occasional sales of dried meat, lamb (castrone), pork, sausage, liver, herring, tuna, tripe, crayfish, and eels.[7] They also sold apples, oranges, pears, figs, and grapes but, curiously, no vegetables. Datini's accounts, however, mention onions, turnips, carrots, and leeks as some of the vegetables readily available in the local marketplace.[8]

In order to add a little flavor to the routine of this diet, local artisans and shopkeepers used spices, and the books of the three druggists examined in this study record many sales to them. The tradesmen also had frequent recourse to druggists for the purchase of miscellaneous laxatives (medicina da purgare) to correct what must have been recurring complaints.

What portion of his income did a man from this middling class of tradesmen spend on food for himself and his family? Giuliano Pinto's average price of a daily ration of bread, wine, and meat, calculated from

Florentine sources of 1395–1406, provides a comparative basis for estimating the cost of living in nearby Prato.[9] Pinto estimated s.2 for an adult and half this amount for a child; but his prices, derived from the wholesale purchases of the Hospital of San Gallo, do not reflect the retail market. Since we know from the tradesmen's books that their retail prices represented an average markup of about 25 percent,[10] the typical Prato tradesman, buying on the open market for a family of four, must have paid s.7½ (rather than s.6) daily. Total food costs at this level would add up to almost half of the average annual income for men of this status.[11]

The prices paid by institutions for bread and meat reflected other advantages institutions enjoyed over the private individual who bought in the retail market. (The wide range of wine prices, from s.4½ to s.70 a barrel, makes it impossible to arrive at a meaningful average for this third staple of the medieval diet.)[12] Most large institutions had their own millers and bakers to process grain into bread, whereas most individuals had to pay for the grinding if not also for the baking of bread. The grain dealer Stefano di Cecco recorded s.1 d.6 as the cost of grinding one *staio* (.686 bushels) of grain;[13] as this charge remained constant despite frequent fluctuations in supply and great differences in the quality of cereal, its percentage of the market price varied considerably. It amounted to 3 percent of the price Stefano di Cecco charged for wheat and 6 percent of the price he charged for rye during the eight months in 1389–90 when his book was open.[14] This charge for grinding to make flour is not included in Pinto's price of bread in his calculation of a daily ration.[15]

Stefano's prices for grain and flour, recorded almost daily from October 1389 to May 1390, indicate another serious problem for the individual consumer—a problem that often is overlooked in scholarly interpretations of grain prices derived from institutional records. Unless the individual tradesman was able to buy an annual supply at the opportune time, right after the harvest as an institutional buyer with large storage facilities undoubtedly could,[16] he had to pay greatly fluctuating prices over the course of a year.[17] Not only did the price of flour rise 43 percent from a low of s.42 per staio to a high of s.60 in 1389–90, but this increase occurred within a short time.[18] The price was s.44 ½ in October with a slight drop to s.42 in late November and most of December; by January, grain supplies were depleted and the price for flour began to rise dramatically. On January 9 the price was s.44; on January 15, s.45; on January 24, s.49; on January 30, s.51; on February 3, s.53 ½; and by the end of February, s.60. The price dropped slightly to s.58 in March, April, and May. To cope with this large increase, a customer could buy a mixture of wheat and some other cereal (Stefano's price for mixed grain was, however, only s.4 below that for pure wheat) or could buy one of the lower-priced cereals. These became more expensive during the winter months, however, as did wheat. The price of millet *(miglio)* rose from s.23 to s.38 per staio (65%); Italian or foxtail millet *(panico)* rose from s.18 ½ to s.30 (62%); and barley *(orzo)* rose from s.18 to s.24 (32%).[19] Only the price of spelt shows a much smaller increase, from s.14 to s.16 (14%).

The price of meat depended not on the time of year but on how it was sold. Wholesale suppliers sold the whole animal or a sizable portion of it, and local shopkeepers sold individual cuts of meat in small quantities; the price varied accordingly. Pinto's price series for pork, based on bulk purchases by a large hospital in Florence, averaged s.1 per pound near the end of the fourteenth century;[20] but the retail sales of the cheese seller Giovanni di Paolo in 1380–84 show that nearly all pork cuts cost much more than this, some more than twice as much (table 2). The comparison is based on the price of s.1 d.4 per pound that Pinto used in his calculation of a daily ration of meat.[21] When Giovanni made a few bulk sales, his prices, too, were much lower (s.1 d.10 per pound in two sales of pork *[carne di porco]*, one of 30½ pounds in 1381 and another of 49 pounds in 1384)—almost as low as the prices paid by Pinto's hospital.[22]

Although expenditures for grain, wine, and meat must have constituted the major portion of a food budget, tradesmen purchased many other foodstuffs. Table 3 lists the prices of some of these in the later years of the fourteenth century and the beginning of the fifteenth.[23] All were sold by the pound, except spices, which were sold by the ounce.[24]

As these tradesmen, on average, spent less than half of their annual income on food, they could afford to buy a variety of personal and

TABLE 2
Retail Prices of Pork Products 1380–1384

Type	Average Price per Pound	Low and High
Saddle (arista)	s.2 d.7	s.2 d.5 to s.2 d.8
Fresh ham (coscia)	s.2 d.2	(only one entry)
Leg (gamba)	s.2 d.5½	s.2 d.5 to s.2 d.6
Head, feet (capo, piedi)	s.1 d.3	s.1 to s.1 d.6
Head only	s.1 d.2½	s.1 to s.1 d.5
Feet only	s.1 d.7	s.1 d.6 to s.1 d.10
Sausage (salsicia)	s.3 d.6	s.3 d.5 to s.3 d.8
Pork fat (sugna)	s.3 d.6	s.3 d.6 (constant)
Liver (fegato)	s.9 (no wt.)	s.8 to s.10
Heart (paracuore)	s.5 (no wt.)	(only one entry)
Stomach (pancie)	s.10 (no wt.)	(only one entry)

SOURCE: Ospedale 810-F4 (for an explanation of references to manuscript sources, see "Abbreviations" at the beginning of the notes section).

TABLE 3
Retail Prices of Other Food, 1380–1414

Item	Average Price per Pound	Year(s)
Cheese (local)	s.3	1380–1414
Cheese (foreign)	s.4	1380–1414
Oil (olio)	s.20	1380–1410
Lamb (castrone)	s.2 d.11	1381, 1386, 1392–93
Eel (anguilla)	s.4	1382, 1384, 1406–11
Tuna (tonno)	s.4	1402, 1406, 1408–9
Sturgeon (storione)	s.4½	1409
Rice (riso)	s.1 d.8	1395
Butter (burro)	s.5½	1395
Apples (mele)	s.1 d.9	1393–94
Peaches (pesche)	s.28	1405
Pepper (pepe)	s.21	1392–96
Saffron (zafferano)	s.192	1392–93, 1395
Cloves (garofani)	s.90	1393
Sugar (zucchero)	s.34	1392, 1394–95

SOURCES: Ospedale 809-F3, 810-F4, 812-F5, 814-F5; Ceppi 1414, 1415 (for an explanation of references to manuscript sources, see "Abbreviations" at the beginning of the notes section).
   NOTE: If more than one year is given, the price is an average. The price of oil had a low of s.11 d.3 and a high of s.26 d.10 during the thirty-year period; the prices of the other foods varied little.

household items. Table 4 shows the prices of some of these items from 1392 to 1412. One could buy many of these items at lower prices from a secondhand dealer such as Taddeo di Chelli. For example, the price of a secondhand pair of socks ranged from s.10 to s.37, as compared with new ones for a child at s.23 or for an adult at s.45.

Tradesmen did not always depend on purchased goods. Many raised

TABLE 4

Retail Prices of Personal and Household Items, 1392–1412

Item	Unit	Price	Year(s)
Shoes (adult)	pair	s.13	1392, 1395, 1411
Shoes (child)	pair	s.10	1411
Socks (adult)	pair	s.45	1393–95
Socks (child)	pair	s.23	1394
Soap (white)	pound	s.3	1392–96, 1408–12
Soap (black)	pound	s.1 d.2½	1392–93, 1395–96
Glass (*di foggia*)	one	d.4	1403–6
Soup plate	one	s.1	1406
Candles	pound	s.4	1404–5, 1408, 1410–11
Bucket	one	s.10	1393
Lantern (new)	one	s.24	1405
Lantern (repaired)	one	s.8	1405
Strainer	one	s.11	1405, 1407, 1409
Scissors	pair	s.9½	1406, 1408
Chamber pot	one	s.1 d.5	1406–7, 1412
Rope (hempen)	pound	s.3½	1404, 1406
Paper (waste)	quaderno	s.2 d.8	1405
Paper (fine)	quaderno	s.7 d.3	1405, 1410
Comb (boxwood)	one	s.4	1406
Veil (fine)	one	s.42½	1410
Dog collar	one	s.4½	1411
Dice	pair	s.8	1410

SOURCES: Ospedale 809-F3, 810-F4, 812-F5, 814-F5; Ceppi 1414, 1415 (for an explanation of references to manuscript sources, see "Abbreviations" at the beginning of the notes section).

some of their own food. The cloth seller Giovanni di Spinello and the cheese seller Paolo di Ser Ambrogio mention kitchen gardens *(orti)* located on their city properties.[25] The broker Matteo di Matteo Toffi negotiated sales of houses to two druggists, one with a kitchen garden, the other with a dovecote.[26] An inventory of twenty small houses that Datini owned in Prato, in addition to his own spacious residence, provides further evidence of the use of urban property to supply food. Almost all of these small houses—rented to a baker, two cobblers, a tailor, and other artisans and shopkeepers—had small garden plots. Some had a threshing floor, one had an area for making wine, another had a few apple trees, and yet another had four big orange trees.[27] In addition, many tradesmen owned land in the country and obtained food from their farms, worked by a hired laborer or a tenant. The cheese seller Paolo di Ser Ambrogio, for example, rented part of his land for a payment of 18 staia of grain per year.[28] Frequent sales of grain and wine by the druggist Benedetto di Tacco indicate that these farms at times produced far more than was needed for the family. Another source of victuals was customers who made payments in kind. In these exchanges a wide variety of cereal products predominated; but wine, fruit, and meat were also traded.

Because the occupations of customers reflected the whole gamut of activities in the local economy, shopkeepers could satisfy many personal and household needs in addition to food through barter. Shoes, socks, dresses, coats, furniture, blankets, and kitchenware were just a few of the items obtained through this form of exchange. Occasionally, customers paid their bills in labor services. Digging, mowing, pruning, and other types of work on tradesmen's farms were the most frequently recorded,[29] but other labor services were offered: The baker Agnolo di Chele paid his bill by baking bread; the shoemaker Andrea di Greci mended shoes for Benedetto di Tacco's wife, Francesca; two women made partial payments in labor to the cloth seller Giovanni di Spinello, one by weaving, the other by spinning; Monna Sole di Bonaccorso contributed her labor three times to settle her account with the doublet maker, Marco di Sandro; and one customer loaned out his nag in lieu of payment.[30]

When a payment was made in kind, the tradesman always recorded the value of the commodity or service in a money equivalent, and often a debit or credit resulted from the transaction. Pucci di Migliore of the village of Casale paid for purchases from the druggist Paolo di Bonaccorso di Tano in goods and labor; in the end, when these added up to more than the value of his purchases, he received a payment of s.15.[31] Likewise, the shoemaker Andrea di Greci had a credit of s.5 after supplying new shoes and repairing old ones in payment for purchases from the druggist Benedetto di Tacco.[32] By contrast, two other customers of Benedetto's had debits of s.6 and d.6 after the druggist evaluated their payments in kind.[33]

While tradesmen satisfied many of their basic needs through barter, they had to pay cash or credit for prestigious and valuable items. In the accounts used for this study, there is no instance of bartering for luxury items, such as the cloak the grain seller Stefano di Cecco bought Monna Mattea for 8 florins,[34] or the silk, silver buttons, and squirrel

skins the druggist Benedetto di Tacco purchased for 11 florins and sent
to the tailor Stefano to make into a dress for his wife.[35]

Net Worth

The average income of Prato's local tradesmen was a comfortable living at the time, providing a family of the middling class a varied diet,
necessary household and personal articles, and a few luxury items. But
what do we know about the net worth of these small businessmen? A
citizen's tax assessment can suggest an approximate financial status, and
Enrico Fiumi used such records to ascertain the relative wealth of
Pratese families whose members he was able to link together through
common surnames. However, only one of the families of tradesmen
whose books have survived had a surname. The doublet maker Marco
di Sandro, who belonged to this family, is not included in Fiumi's list
drawn up from the information recorded in the Florentine estimo of
1372;[36] nor does a check of the assessments of the city and villages of
the district turn up his name although Marco's father (age sixty-five),
his brother Giovannino (age twenty-six), and his wife Agnola and four
children appear in the same household in Porta San Giovanni.[37] In the
same estimo, however, we can locate four of the other tradesmen and
review their tax assessments. Two of the four, the secondhand dealer
Taddeo di Chelli and the cheese seller Giovanni di Paolo, were just
commencing their business careers, and the assessors listed them as having no taxable possessions (nulla) after allowable deductions.[38] (The
designation nulla does not represent the lowest category; those with
this classification paid a modest amount while the citizens described as
nulla e miserable paid nothing.)[39] Of the two tradesmen listed with taxable assets, the druggist Benedetto di Tacco (age fifty), had an assessment of £100, and the tailor Domenico di Jacopo (age thirty), an assessment of £30.[40] Also recorded in the estimo was an assessment of
£50 for the father of the brothers Biagio and Giuliano di Giovanni
Bertelli, who later manufactured and sold paper at retail; in 1372 they
were mere children, eight and six years old.[41]

Such indications of financial status derived from official sources can
be supplemented by the information recorded in most of the account

books used in this study. From the books of one tradesman, the cloth seller Bonagiunta Zucassi, the data needed to draw up a balance sheet of the business have survived. When Bonagiunta died at the height of the Black Death in Tuscany in 1348, his widow Datina had an inventory made of his business assets and liabilities. The credits of £64 s.16, listed on one page, included receivables for the sale of cloth, grain, office furniture, and even s.5 for the sale of a servant's *(fante)* bed; but the liabilities of £84 s.11 d.11, recorded on the following two pages, left a debit balance of £19 s.15 d.11. In addition to numerous debts to suppliers, the widow owed unpaid rent on the shop, wages to the apprentice, and s.10 d.1 for the salt tax. In spite of what would appear to be a precarious financial situation, she added another debt of £2 so that friar Luca would arrange memorial masses for the soul of her husband.[42]

The cloth seller Giovanni di Spinello recorded the value of his business at one point in his career (January 1, 1341), when his assets amounted to £170. Three fifths of this was unspecified merchandise (£103 s.17 d.7), two fifths was customer debts (£66 s.2 d.5). He referred to these debts as collectible and listed the thirty-four debtors with the amounts owed;[43] he listed no liabilities. An undated, notarized inventory of Giovanni's personal assets recorded on a loose sheet inside the cover of the account book provides additional information about his house, furnishings, and other property.[44] His house was located in the section of Prato called Porta al Travaglio, and his two neighbors were a baker and the priest Ser Leonardo di Stefano. The building had a kitchen garden, and its furnishings included one bed *(sanzaltro)* with a feather mattress and one sheet, a large bench, a table with two three-legged stools, two cobbler benches, and two chests, much of this furniture in poor condition *(tristo).*[45] This house and its contents, however, represented only a portion of Giovanni's assets. At the end of the inventory he enumerated his land holdings in the country, consisting of five parcels about 6 kilometers west of Prato, near the stream Bardena. He does not give the value of this rural property of 26 *staiora* with vineyards; but with the price of land at about 10 florins per *staioro* (.1294 acre), it probably far exceeded that of his city house with its modest furnishings.[46]

Like Giovanni di Spinello, most of the petty entrepreneurs either rented or purchased land in the contado. Indeed, in their desire for country property they appear to have differed little from the more prosperous international merchants like Datini, who owned a farm south of the city, not far from the present church of the Madonna del Soccorso, and a villa to the north on the bank of the Bisenzio where the Villa del Palco now stands.[47] The secondhand dealer Taddeo di Chelli rented some land and paid part of the rent in grain; the paper manufacturer Biagio di Giovanni Bertelli rented a house with a farm near the village of Santa Lucia, a few kilometers north of Prato.[48] The accounts of these men also record land purchases; many local tradesmen owned more than one property.

The druggists had more land in the country than the others, perhaps because they were wealthier.[49] Paolo di Bonaccorso di Tano owned five properties totaling 94 staiora outside the city, one with a small house.[50] During the period from 1365 to 1378, Benedetto di Tacco acquired three land parcels for 80 florins; and in 1386, toward the end of his career when he was sixty-four years old, he purchased another farm. The properties he purchased all included orchards, vineyards, and olives. His exchange of land in San Giusto for another parcel in Santa Trinità owned by Bartolozzo di Bonaventura suggests that he preferred to own property closer to his residence in the city.[51] To ascertain the size of one farm before purchase, he paid s.8 to have it surveyed.[52] Florentine druggists also bought land in the countryside near Prato; the broker Matteo di Matteo Toffi arranged a purchase of a farm of 70 staiora near the village of Paperino for two brothers who had their business in Florence.[53]

The tradesmen did not limit their real estate investments to property outside the city walls. In 1371—during the same period that he purchased the above-mentioned three farms—Benedetto bought a house in the city from the baker Agnolo di Chele for 13 florins; so as not to waste his precious time ("senza lo sciopiaio mio") he paid the agent Niccolozzo £5 s.6 to take care of the purchase arrangements. He was apparently more interested in the site than in the house; within a year he spent £250, or about 77 florins, to have the house demolished and replaced by another.[54] The rents he recorded from 1365 to 1378 indicate that Benedetto also owned three other city properties.[55] Unlike most of these men, the cheese seller Giovanni di Paolo limited his purchases to the city, where he owned houses in four of the eight divisions *(porte)*. Around the turn of the century he bought nine urban properties at a total cost of 275 florins.[56] In one instance, he first bought half a house and then five weeks later purchased the other half. In recording one purchase he added in the margin that his wife Matalena had provided the full cost of £28. In another entry he recorded the purchase of a house for 30 florins and simultaneous rental of it to the former owner for 4 florins per year—a return of 13.3 percent on his investment.[57]

The tradesmen's records further show that at times they improved their properties. In 1405 the cheese seller Paolo di Ser Ambrogio spent £11 s.3 raising the wall surrounding the kitchen garden of one of his houses. He detailed the expenses involved as follows:[58]

1. 30 *some* of sand at d.6 per *soma*—s.15[59]
2. 10 *misure* of lime at s.6 per *misura*—£3[60]
3. For slaking the lime by a master—£2
4. 75 bricks—s.12
5. To transport the lime and bricks—s.6
6. Three days' work by a waller—£3
7. Three days' work by a laborer—£1 s.10

The daily rate of s.20 for the waller is far higher than the average of s.13 paid to the men who worked on the walls of Prato. However, the unskilled laborer's wage of s.10 was the going rate.

Another indication of financial well-being was the large amount of cash these small businessmen kept on hand. Although they used it principally to maintain the cash flow in their businesses, they occasionally spent it on real estate to avoid recourse to long-term credit.[61] The cheese seller Paolo di Ser Ambrogio paid 67 florins at settlement for one of his land acquisitions and the balance of 12 florins within a month; the tailor Domenico di Jacopo completed his payments in three months for 5 staiora of land, although his contract with the seller allowed him eight months to pay off the balance.[62] Many of the tradesmen put extra cash to work in the form of loans. Several large loans made by the cheese seller Giovanni di Paolo (for £200, 58 florins [£225], and £450) probably exceeded his annual income;[63] the records show

the largest loan made by the tailor Domenico di Jacopo as 70 florins
(£252);[64] the largest by the druggist Benedetto di Tacco was 20 florins
(£77).[65]

With incomes above sustenance level but not large, these tradesmen
would seem to have lacked the resources necessary for the numerous
properties they purchased and the sizable loans they made.[66] Inheritances from parents or relatives may have furnished some of the funds
for these investments, although the records offer no evidence of this.
One documented source of capital was the dowry. Like the rich, these
small businessmen received substantial dowries from their fathers-in-
law,[67] although the payments sometimes stretched over many years after the wedding. In 1345 the druggist Benedetto di Tacco received a
dowry of 200 florins; in 1378 the doublet maker Marco di Sandro received 340 florins.[68] The tailor Domenico di Jacopo made no record
of the dowry that Master Guardi gave him for Margherita, but at one
point he noted that his father-in-law had left the unpaid balance of £50
with the merchant banker Ser Jacopo di Neri.[69]

As their daughters grew up, these men themselves had to pay
dowries. The 225 florins paid by the cheese seller Paolo di Ser Ambrogio for his daughter's dowry in 1410 was higher than that received
by the druggist Benedetto di Tacco in the previous century. Although
Paolo recorded his dowry debt to Andrea di Giovanni on May 29, the
marriage was not consummated until a year and a half later when he
sent his daughter to her husband *(mandaila a marito)*.[70] These small businessmen could be as demanding as their patrician superiors in con-
tracting a daughter's marriage. A shoemaker who lived in Empoli revealed his approach to the matter in a letter he wrote to the cheese seller
Giovanni di Paolo. Addressed to (Giovanni di Paolo, basket maker on
the Piazza della Pieve in Prato) "Giovanni di Pagholo chorbelaio alla
Piazza della Pieve in Prato" and dated "Al nome di Dio ame, fatta a dì
27 Febraio 1395" (1396 in the modern calendar), the letter opens with
"greetings from Giovanni Aringo di Corsi shoemaker of Empoli." The
shoemaker wanted Giovanni di Paolo to determine the suitability of a
prospective husband for his daughter. The candidate was Leonardo di
Mone di Tozzo, another shoemaker who lived in Porta Santa Trinità.
What kind of person was this Leonardo, how was he doing in business,

what were his prospects for profit, and what dowry did he require? If Leonardo proved unworthy or too demanding, the shoemaker asked that Giovanni suggest other possibilities, on the condition that the dowry not exceed 100 florins.[71]

Few sons of petty entrepreneurs were able to change their economic and social status. However, the careers of two brothers illustrate the possibility of upward mobility in Prato. The doublet maker Marco di Sandro's eldest son, Sandro, born in 1379, and his youngest, Giuliano, born in 1386, achieved prominence as international merchants.[72] Their father, like Datini's a generation before, died before any of his children had reached majority; and their uncle Giovannino, also a doublet maker, became their guardian at the turn of the century.[73] Sandro remained in Prato and by his thirties was purchasing and exporting textiles to Giuliano, who for many years made his headquarters at Ragusa on the Dalmatian coast. Giuliano also maintained a lively trade in products from southern Italy and later engaged in moneylending at Ragusa. His clients included the Medici at Venice.[74]

It should be stressed again that, although all of the small businessmen of this study are described as belonging to the middling class, they do not constitute a homogeneous group. The income of one tradesman could be double that of another, and their assets and way of life varied widely.[75] The widow of the cloth seller Bonagiunta Zucassi may have inherited enough personal assets from her husband to offset the £19 business debit he left behind in 1348, but his net worth was only a fraction of that of the druggist Benedetto di Tacco or the cheese seller Giovanni di Paolo, both of whom had extensive investments in real estate and loans. The secondhand dealer Taddeo di Chelli, who recorded no real estate holdings or large loans and borrowed continually to finance his business, may have lived no better than the laborer Bartoli Firi, who was able to buy 9 staiora of land for 76$\frac{1}{2}$ florins (£306).[76] Such contrasts in economic and perhaps social status also existed among those in the same occupation. Jacopo di Bartolomeo Mati, the shearer of cloth *(cimatore)*, records numerous credits of more than £100, including one of no less than £2,018 s.18; but other shearers appear in the 1487 catasto with no taxable assets at all.[77]

The few comments historians have made about the economic status of the middling class have been based on sources other than the records of local tradesmen themselves. In his analysis of the relative wealth of those who possessed surnames based on the estimo of 1372, Enrico Fiumi reported the assessments of eight local craftsmen as ranging from £400 for the delicatessen operator Giovanni Giuntini to £25 for the blacksmith Lazzaro Franchini.[78] Giuliano Pinto's and Charles de La Roncière's studies of real wages in Florence, which together cover the period from 1280 to 1430, offer little information on petty entrepreneurs other than skilled wage earners in the building trades. De La Roncière concludes that adequate records do not exist to evaluate the incomes and standard of living of most independent artisans and shopkeepers.[79] However, he used assessments for forced loans in 1362, 1369, and 1378 to measure the well-being of men in eleven local trades against standards set by two categories: salaried masons and skilled workers in the cloth industry. According to his survey, in 1362 only tailors had an average assessment below both standards, and delicatessen operators were ranked below cloth workers but above masons; in 1369 only butchers were listed as less prosperous than both standards; in 1378 all tradesmen had assessments above the standards. On the basis of the average assessment, dealers in old clothes or secondhand dealers led the list in 1362, and druggists were at the top in 1369 and 1378.[80] However, a daily wage derived from the records of employers cannot always be used alone in calculating the total income of the masons in the construction industry. The three masons at Prato whose partnership is documented received wages of s.15 per day from the partnership for their individual work on the city walls; but because they had contracted with the commune for the total price of the job, they expected profits beyond their daily wage.

Religion

The small businessmen of Prato lived and worked in an environment of organized religion, and in fact the patronage of numerous religious institutions and their staffs was essential to business success. Without this clientele, some shopkeepers would have found their sales cut in half. In one two-year period (1356–58) the druggist Benedetto di Tacco made more than 85 percent of his recorded sales to the church of San Domenico and its fraternal affiliate (see chap. 2). Nevertheless, these religious customers received no preferential treatment in prices or in the time allowed for payment of their debts. When Sister Salvagia of the convent of San Niccolò died, her debt of £3 s.9 to the druggist Matteo di Matteo, who had numerous customers from the same convent and sold candles worth £8 s.18 1/2 for Sister Salvagia's funeral, was paid in full.[81] Some shopkeepers also bought commodities from religious and charitable institutions: for example, the cheese sellers Paolo di Ser Ambrogio and Giovanni di Paolo made many purchases from the Hospital of the Misericordia.

There is some slight evidence in these business documents for the extent to which religion governed or affected the personal lives of the local tradesmen.[82] Their legacies to the Misericordia and the Ceppo, which include the personal financial documents used in this study, indicate a financial commitment to religious and charitable institutions.[83] The grandson Antonio di Cambio di Ferro included the account books of three generations of innkeepers in his legacy to the well-known Chapel of the Holy Belt in the collegiate church of Santo Stefano. The treasurer of the opera of the chapel acted as the executor of his estate, arranging for the payment of funeral expenses, the collection and payment of debts, and the return of the £554 dowry of his wife Nana.[84] However, only the druggist Benedetto di Tacco, the cheese seller Paolo di Ser Ambrogio, and the broker Matteo di Matteo Toffi actually recorded charitable or religious donations in their accounts. Given the convention of using account books to record debts and credits rather than across-the-counter cash transactions, this paucity of references to almsgiving is not surprising. In 1371 Benedetto noted a gift of s.20 to the collegiate church of Santo Stefano; for the festival of the Virgin in 1372 he listed gifts of bread, cheese, meat, wine, eight dozen eggs, and £1 in cash to the brothers.[85] Paolo's books show that in 1405 he paid a priest £6 to officiate at the oratory of Sant' Ambrogio (still intact in the Piazza Mercatale), and that two years later he gave £5 to Ser Alesso di Ser Simone, the sacristan of Santo Stefano, for the feast of Saint Ambrogio (probably to honor his father).[86] When the broker Matteo arranged a land purchase in 1408 for the blacksmith

Benedetto di Manetto, he set aside d.1 for God out of his total commission.[87]

Can the religious invocations at the beginning of each account book be interpreted as anything more than adherence to custom? The opening of the book of the paper salesmen is typical: "In the name of God, the Virgin Mary, Blessed Saint Stephen, our protector of the land of Prato, and all the saints of paradise."[88] The tradesmen all used nearly identical words; only the druggist Benedetto di Tacco, on opening his book in 1382, went beyond the stereotypical formula and included a pope and the college of cardinals. In that year two popes, Urban VI and Clement VII, claimed legitimacy, and Benedetto presumably wanted to designate his preference for the Roman Urban—a preference that incidentally corresponded with that of the Florentine authorities.[89]

While they conformed to religious custom by opening their books with invocations to God, the Virgin Mary, and Saint Stephen (patron saint of Prato), the tradesmen showed little regard for guild and commune statutes prohibiting work on religious days, often keeping their shops open on Sundays, religious holidays, and even Christmas Day. Because the statutes of communes and guilds usually prohibited any work on Sundays or on the numerous religious holidays, many historians have concluded that the year contained approximately 260 workdays. Sylvia Thrupp, for example, concluded that "everybody's working time was curtailed by the Church's designation of more than a quarter of the year as sacred time."[90] In his study of the construction industry in Florence, Richard Goldthwaite used this number to calculate annual wages; Sergio Raveggi assumed the same figure for Prato in determining the number of artisan workdays and the days on which shops remained open.[91] Information from the wallers' accounts at Prato confirm the assumption that there were approximately 260 workdays in the construction industry.

Shopkeepers, however, did not close their stores on religious days. From March 1384 to the end of 1385, when the accounts of the wallers show no work on Sundays or religious holidays, Benedetto di Tacco's store was open on thirty-one Sundays and on many of the religious holidays, including Christmas Day, 1384.[92] A check of the records of

some of the other tradesmen shows shops open on Sundays, Christmas, and holidays, when the wallers did not work. For example, the
cheese seller Giovanni di Paolo worked twenty-five Sundays and three
Christmas Days, the tailor Domenico di Jacopo ten Sundays and three
Christmas Days, and the doublet maker Marco di Sandro eleven Sundays and four Christmas Days. From July 1408 to July 1410, the broker
Matteo di Matteo Toffi did business on eighteen Sundays and on numerous religious holidays. The doublet maker Marco di Sandro entered
more sales in his ledger on Sundays than on any other day.

In one respect religious concern influenced the tradesmen's accounting practices. No interest charge was recorded for direct loans or
for debts resulting from extension of credit for purchases. The position
of the church was clear: any interest charged for the use of money was
condemned, and entries in an account book would constitute evidence
of violation of this doctrine. Tradesmen recognized the threat of prosecution backed by governmental officials and were careful not to ex-
pose themselves. Their records nevertheless reveal these illicit activities, as is discussed in later chapters.

Local Government and Political Events

The account books reveal little more about the tradesmen's involvement in local governmental affairs than about religious events or religious and charitable donations. The druggist Benedetto di Tacco
recorded the days spent and the pay received for his guard duty in Prato and the salaries he earned for financial and administrative work for
the mayors of some of the surrounding villages (see chap. 2). Another
druggist, Matteo di Matteo, kept records as the treasurer of the village
of Pizzidimonte in 1392.[93] The innkeeper Cambio di Ferro became
supervisor of the debtors' prison in Prato for six months starting on
February 1, 1407; during his term of office he recorded the names and
debts of all prisoners, their release dates, and payments received.[94]

Only the cheese seller Paolo di Ser Ambrogio left a record of active
participation in city government. From September 1, 1399, to September 1, 1400, he served as mayor, treasurer, and collector of the salt
tax for Porta Gualdimare, receiving £8 for each of the first two posi-

tions and £4 for the last. In November and December of 1400 he served
as one of "the Eight," the highest elective office in Prato. Later, in 1406,
he personally repaid the loan of f.30 £33 that the officials of Porta Capo
di Ponte had received from the merchant banker Benedetto di Filippo
(making sure, however, that the officials guaranteed his loan in their
own names, not just as governmental officials ["i sindachi mi promi-
sero in loro propio e privato nome di conservarmi senza danno"]).[95]

The major events of the time passed almost unremarked in these
business records, including the struggle with Pisa in the 1360s, the War
of the Eight Saints, and the conflicts with Giangaleazzo Visconti and
later with King Ladislaus—all moments when one might expect businesses to have been affected by supply problems.[96] Only the tailor
Domenico di Jacopo recorded some political news, including a brief
description of the Ciompi Revolt at Florence, the takeover of Arezzo
by Florence in 1384, and the submission of Padua to Giangaleazzo Visconti.[97] This account of the Ciompi uprising by an artisan of a nearby town has remained unknown to the numerous historians who have
searched diligently for any documents referring to those momentous
events during the summer of 1378:

> On Tuesday, the 22d of June, 1378
> On the day above, the *popolo minuto* and the workers of the Wool Guild of
> Florence rose up in tumult and burned 13 houses of *grassi cittadini* of Florence,
> namely those of the *popolo grasso.* The same day they broke into the prison *(le
> stinche)* and all the prisoners came out. On Tuesday the 20th of July, 1378, the
> *popolo minuto* revolted a second time and burned 13 houses—in truth, palaces;
> and the city of Florence remained in tumult and under arms until July 22d, the
> feast of Saint Mary Magdalene; and on this day they deposed the priors who
> were in the palace and who did not complete their office, in which they should
> have remained through July; and the *popolo minuto* set up in the palace as gov-
> ernment a gonfalonier for the minor guild of workers of the Wool Guild. He
> stood alone in the Palace of the Priors, issued all the proclamations, and then
> all the priors were selected by hand. They ruled and stood in the government
> for all of July and August. Through a third uprising they were deposed, and
> the guilds of Florence and certain *popolari grassi* took over the government; one
> of those chosen by hand to be a prior was Giorgio degli Scali.[98] While I was
> writing this account, fear and trembling enveloped the city.[99]

Domenico's account reflects the conservative outlook characteristic of most artisans and shopkeepers throughout history, whose "great enemies were not the rich and the powerful, but the poor and lowly laborers."[100] Domenico di Jacopo did not welcome political change, for any threat to stable government at Florence endangered the security and tranquility that allowed him to go about his daily business as always. The other tradesmen undoubtedly would have concurred, for their world, like his, was the local marketplace of Prato.

The Conduct of Business

The shopkeepers and artisans of late medieval Prato operated in a fully integrated business environment. A thoroughly monetized local economy, complete with a money of account and extensive record keeping, provided the framework within which daily business flourished. Credit based on trust—that same *fiducia* that Federigo Melis so passionately insisted was the essential cement in merchant society at the highest ranks—sealed the close relations of these more modest operators with people of all walks of life, from the international merchants who were their suppliers to the most humble of their customers and employees.

Merchant bankers and brokers facilitated many of the purchases of these shopkeepers, particularly of imports from other regions of Italy and beyond. Although cheese of the local variety constituted the majority of sales by the two cheese sellers, more expensive types came from Parma, Pisa, Sardinia, Calabria, and Sicily. Much of the rope sold by a number of the tradesmen came from Bologna.

The cloth seller Giovanni di Spinello sold inexpensive cloth *(panno bigello)* called Romagnol. The more expensive cloths, identified only by color, that he and some other tradesmen occasionally sold could have come from many areas of Italy and beyond. Barrels of salted tuna and herring crossed coastal waters on both sides of the peninsula; one account book showed 2,500 Ragusan herring purchased by Matteo di Matteo Toffi for a local butcher in 1410. A variety of spices, sold by the three druggists, came from even farther—the Levant—by way of Pisa.

The customers of the local tradesmen were both men and women, and they came from both the city and the countryside. They included peasant farmers, unskilled day laborers, housewives, artisans, shop-keepers, priests, nuns, public officials, merchant bankers, and nobles. The international merchant banker Francesco di Marco Datini, prob-ably the most famous customer in the local market, recorded the many purchases he made there from comparatively cheap foodstuffs such as eggs, cheese, and meat produced locally to expensive imports such as salt, sugar, and all kinds of spices; from the coarse cloth for a maid's cos-tume to the rich material to make a dress for his wife Margherita; from locally produced wine to supplement that from his own farms, costing only a few lire a barrel, to fine, imported varieties costing twenty-five times as much. Of the many local tradesmen Datini dealt with, only the cheese seller Paolo di Ser Ambrogio is a subject of this study; Pao-lo's accounts note a number of sales to, and purchases from, Datini.

These small entrepreneurs can be divided into four general cate-gories: (1) true retailers, such as cheese sellers, cloth sellers, and grain dealers, who bought their products wholesale and made profits through resale at a markup; (2) producer retailers, such as tailors, doublet mak-ers, and druggists, who in addition to purchasing products for resale, added their labor to the process of production of some items (e.g., clothing, candles, and medicines); (3) artisans, such as members of the building trades, who sold their labor; and (4) providers of services, such as brokers and innkeepers. Virtually all of these men needed some working capital, for plant, equipment, or inventory, or merely to main-tain cash flow to pay expenses and salaries. Only the broker Matteo di Matteo Toffi needed no organizational capital of any kind for his work, as it consisted solely of bringing together buyers and sellers.

Like local artisans and shopkeepers of today, those of fourteenth-century Prato organized their businesses for the most part as sole pro-prietorships. Although at times some tradesmen employed the first-person plural when referring to a transaction *(ci de' dare),* their account books supply no evidence of an active partner. Nevertheless, to help finance their businesses these sole proprietors sought outside capital. At times the funds were called loans, with the rate of interest and ma-turity clearly specified. For example, in 1389 the tailor Domenico di

Jacopo received loans of 10 and 12 florins at 30 percent interest, with maturities of one year and thirty-one months, respectively (see chap. 6 for details). At other times the funds were called investments, which the investor or "silent partner" contributed in exchange for a share in the profits or losses; however, in many cases the return on the "investment" and the conditions recorded suggest that the funds were in reality loans. For example, in March 1337 Messer Spinello Dicamanti gave the cloth seller Giovanni di Spinello 40 florins with the stipulation in a notarial document that he would share in the profits and losses of the business on a pro rata basis. The following year Giovanni recorded the year's profit as exactly 4 florins, paid Spinello Dicamanti 44 florins, and had the notarial document cancelled. These arrangements suggest a veiled loan at 10 percent interest rather than an investment.[1] An even more obvious case was the £200 that the cheese seller Giovanni di Paolo gave to another cheese seller in 1383. Giovanni stated that, although he would share in the profits and losses of the other's business, the profits must equal £24 for one year and the £200 must be returned in full—a loan at 12 percent.[2]

Only four of the businesses studied were clearly partnerships: two butcher shops, a paper manufactory, and a team of three wallers *(muratori)*. The single small journal kept for the two butcher shops identifies one business on its cover and opening page: "Lorenzo Cosi and partners, butchers of Prato." In the first 4 folios Lorenzo recorded sales of meat to the Hospital of the Misericordia; later sales of meat to the hospital were recorded by another butcher, Peruzzi di Lotto.[3] Peruzzi's brother Piero is named as a partner a few pages later.[4]

The term *partner* is not found in the account book of the paper manufactory of the brothers Biagio and Giuliano di Giovanni Bertelli, who sold the paper they made at retail; but information in the book indicates that they in fact operated as partners. The title on the cover reads, "book of Biagio and Giuliano di Giovanni Bertelli," and the first entry states that Biagio will keep the accounts of "all those creditors of Biagio and Giuliano di Giovanni Bertelli of Porta Gualdimare." Furthermore, the abbot of the monastery of San Salvatore at Viano wrote in Biagio and Giuliano's book that the rental agreement for mills *(le gualchieri)* between the two parties was with the two brothers.[5]

The partnership of the three wallers was established for work on the city walls of Prato. Its books supply more information on the nature of the business. The three partners shared administrative tasks such as supervising and paying employees and acquiring building materials from suppliers and haulers. They made immediate purchases from suppliers but also entered into contracts for future deliveries over periods of weeks and months; often a supplier required a down payment to seal the contract. Each partner also worked on the job as a skilled artisan. Of the many teams of masons mentioned by Goldthwaite in his study of the construction industry in Florence, none is described as a formal partnership *(compagnia)* with a fixed capital. However, the records of this Pratese partnership refer occasionally to a capital fund *(corpo)* to which the partners assigned credits from their wages rather than paying themselves entirely in cash. When in 1384 one of the partners, Niccolò Guardi, was asked to contribute £24 s.18 d.8 to the fund to bring his investment up to the level of the others, he paid this not in cash but in work over the next two months; in June of the next year he had an additional £5 s.18 d.10 of his wages posted to the partnership's capital account. When another partner, Chimenti di Ghino, earned £16 for $21\frac{1}{3}$ days of work in May and June of 1385, he took out £4 s.11 d.6 in cash and left the balance of £11 s.8 d.6 as a credit on the capital account.[6] The fund probably consisted of working capital needed to meet operating expenses (which could be considerable if the masons had to pay for equipment and, especially, building materials) and to maintain cash flow between periodic payments from the commune. Because the fund was continually depleted, the partners presumably had to hold back part of their own wages on occasion, until they could replenish the fund on receipt of payment from their client; meanwhile, their unpaid wages accumulated as credits on the capital account.

Two other Prato businesses may have been partnerships. The first, a grain supply business, was operated for the most part by Stefano di Cecco; but his brother Jacopo also participated throughout the eight months covered by the account book. Jacopo made sales, received installment payments from customers, and sometimes recorded debits and credits in the ledger.[7] The second possible partnership was the retail cloth shop of Giovanni di Spinello. Vimano Gherardi, who frequently collected debts for the cloth seller (see chap. 5), helped finance Giovanni's entry into business. On January 1, 1337, Vimano gave Giovanni 25 florins "to engage in the cloth business" *(per fare l'arte di bigelli),* and over the next three years Vimano received 50 florins as his share of the profits *(utile).* Vimano also paid a portion of the entrance fee to the Wool Guild and on one occasion made a rental payment for the cloth shop ("casa dove facciamo l'arte di bigello").[8]

Of all the tradesmen in this study, only the wallers had a large workforce, which included some craftsmen like themselves and numerous unskilled laborers. Most of these employees lived in Prato or its district, but a few came from as far away as Rome, Todi, and Como.[9] Two laborers are identified as Germans.[10] For both unskilled and skilled workers the pay scale varied widely; the unskilled received from s.6 to s.14 per day (s.10 on average),[11] the skilled from s.11 to s.15 (s.13 on average).[12] The three partners always paid themselves the top rate of s.15.

These wages approximated those for construction workers in the nearby capital city of Florence. Moreover, the work was steady because the job was a large one financed by the communal government; it required nearly five years to complete.[13] No reduction in pay took place during the winter months, and bread and wine at times supplemented the wages.[14] Both skilled and unskilled laborers occasionally received advance wages. On one occasion a master named Antonio di Giovanni used his total wages of £13 s.10 to repay previous advances.[15] After only a few days on the job the unskilled laborers Antonio and Domenico di Lippi borrowed 3 florins; when after a month of work the wages withheld had not yet covered the loan, they repaid the difference (s.25) to the company.[16] Another employee who borrowed 1 florin on his first day of work did not stay with the company long enough to repay the loan; he left the partners with a debit of s.15.[17] A former employee received a loan when he was no longer employed by the company and repaid it without having gone back to work during the intervening time.[18] Numerous entries for individual loans and frequent references to a book of loans *(libro delle prestanze)* suggest that much closer personal relationships existed between companies and employees in

Prato than in Florence a century later, where Richard Goldthwaite found few advances to construction workers.[19]

There were, however, some unfavorable work conditions that led a number of employees to leave the job. Perhaps most troublesome were the frequent delays in payment of wages; sometimes months elapsed before an employee was paid wages already earned and calculated.[20] The partners had a cash flow problem. The commune, by making its payments in random and widely separated installments, at times left the company without sufficient funds to meet its obligations. For example, a delay in the payment of the commune's fifth installment was the reason given for failure to pay the skilled worker Antonio di Giovanni on time. After waiting five months for back pay of £10, Antonio left the job, even though he was the brother of the partner Biagio di Giovanni and had worked for the company for more than a year, keeping his own roster of laborers *(bastardello)*.[21] On another occasion, an unskilled laborer waited a year to be paid the small sum of s.1 d.8.[22] Reductions in wage rates and irregularity of payment may have contributed to turnover of labor. Marco di Michele of Rome left the job soon after his wages dropped from s.12 to s.11 in the month of August.[23] Another worker was incorrectly paid at the rate of s.10 for seven days; even after the company changed the rate to s.12 and paid him an additional s.14, he quit.[24] A third employee, not identified either as a master or a laborer, wrote on a loose scrap of paper (preserved inside the cover of one of the company's books) that the company owed him £3 s.4 ("lo Domenicho debo avere . . . sono in tutto l.iii s.iiii"). No entry in the account book reveals the outcome of his claim.[25]

Unlike the wallers with their large payroll, the other tradesmen of Prato had few, if any, employees. If they needed assistance in their business, they usually hired an apprentice at a very modest salary. Only the moneylender Sinibaldo in 1285 and the druggist Paolo di Bonaccorso in 1394 employed a cashier; neither described the duties of the job or gave the salary.[26] Some historians have suggested that in addition to apprentices, the wives of local tradesmen often assisted their husbands in the business. Yet in the sources for this study only the cheese seller Giovanni di Paolo records the fact that his wife Madalena made a few

sales and loans.[27] The grain seller Stefano di Cecco mentions a Monna Mattea who occasionally made sales and received installment payments from customers, but does not identify her as his wife. His purchase of a cloak for her for 8 florins suggests, however, that she was his
wife or a member of the family.[28]

Women did take an active part in the economic life of Prato as business operators, artisans, moneylenders, and frequent customers of all
the tradesmen. Women business operators included four bakers,[29] two
kiln operators,[30] a delicatessen operator,[31] a furrier,[32] and sellers of
kitchenware,[33] pots,[34] leather goods,[35] and corsets (ventraiuola).[36] Account book entries reveal how three women ended up managing their
own businesses. On April 23, 1394, Monna Giovanna is identified by
the cheese seller Giovanni di Paolo as the wife of Leonardo, a kilns-
man; in a subsequent entry on June 3 of the same year, she appears as
a widow operating the kiln and making sales to Giovanni.[37] Another
woman, also named Giovanna, succeeded to the ownership of a delicatessen on the death of her husband but ran the business only a short
time—a year later she is identified as the wife of Zanobi, the new owner of the delicatessen.[38] A third woman, Monna Agnola, handled the
family grain business after the death of her husband; throughout the
eight months covered by the register of the grain seller Stefano di Cecco she continually sent him cereal products to be sold.[39] Among the
women working as artisans were the weavers who paid for purchases
from the cloth seller Giovanni di Spinello by doing work for him,[40]
and Monna Margherita from Florence, who made leather shoes or san-
dals (galigaia).[41] Other women were identified merely as laborers. One,
a customer of the cheese seller Giovanni di Paolo, was called a chu-
randaia, a woman who washes raw wool.[42]

In a recent study David Herlihy described the participation of
women in the urban economies of preindustrial Europe as undergo-
ing a profound transformation between the thirteenth and fifteenth
centuries.[43] In the thirteenth century many women were artisans or
shopkeepers, but by the fifteenth century their participation in the
workforce had greatly diminished. Herlihy's evidence for the earlier
period comes from notarial cartularies and guild statutes; for the later
period, from fiscal surveys. In both cases the numbers cited are very

small, and in the later sources the whim of the particular assessor seems to determine whether occupations are included in the redactions. For example, from the city survey in Bologna in 1395 only fourteen or fifteen women appear with an occupation; and except for one retailer of old clothing, they are all spinners, servants, or menial laborers of other kinds. At approximately the same time, a far greater number of women turn up among the artisans and shopkeepers mentioned in the Pratese account books.

Women in Prato also made loans to tradesmen and, at times, lent more than a modest sum. The widow Lappa lent the tailor Domenico di Jacopo 3 florins in 1379 and was repaid five months later; Monna Lisa, who lived at the monastery of San Fabiano, lent Domenico 7 florins in 1385 and 2 florins in 1391.[44] Women were frequent customers, of course, but not to the extent suggested by a speaker at a recent conference in Prato on the role of women in the industrial European economy:[45] The speaker asserted that they constituted more than 90 percent of the purchasers of basic necessities and therefore had a significant impact on local economies by influencing the demand for products and the prevailing price levels.[46] However, the account books of the two cheese sellers, the three druggists, the two cloth sellers, and the secondhand dealer—the Pratese tradesmen whose products were most likely to be purchased by women—do not support this assertion. Women represented closer to 10 percent of the customers for cheese, lard, dry meat, thread, buttons, small pieces of cloth, and other similar items whose cost rarely exceeded s.10. Unfortunately, no account books have survived for a baker or greengrocer, whose records might have provided more significant evidence for the percentage of women among family shoppers in fourteenth-century Prato.

As is to be expected, Prato's local economy was not highly specialized. Tradesmen sold a wide variety of products and performed services beyond those suggested by their occupational designations. The brothers Biagio and Giuliano di Giovanni Bertelli, who primarily manufactured and sold paper at retail, also sold candles, sugar, and spices, and at times were referred to as druggists.[47] Benedetto di Tacco, in addition to performing the pharmaceutical services expected of a druggist, such as concocting laxatives, poultices, and various ointments, acted as a funeral arranger. He not only supplied the great numbers of candles needed for the masses, but also paid the grave digger, the pallbearers, and the priests, brothers, and members of religious fraternities who took part in the funeral.[48]

Indeed, an occupational designation did not always indicate the primary business of a tradesman. The business activities of two tradesmen both called secondhand dealers *(rigattieri)* illustrate how divergent these activities could be. Taddeo di Chelli, whose register has survived, made the usual sales and purchases expected of a secondhand dealer: shoes, stockings, goblets, hammers, and anything that could be sold. His individual sales rarely exceeded a lira. Antonio di Lapo di Simone was always called a secondhand dealer, but the sixty-three entries for his transactions in the register of the broker Matteo di Matteo Toffi depict a business far different from that of Taddeo.[49] Antonio's purchases and sales through the broker usually exceeded £10 per transaction. Sometimes he employed the broker to buy and sell one commodity on the same day. On January 23, 1408, he instructed the broker to buy 318 pounds of Sardinian cheese at £9 per hundredweight, then to sell it for £10 s.10—turning a profit of more than £3 after deducting the brokerage fees.[50]

For two years, from January 1356 to January 1358, the druggist Benedetto di Tacco greatly restricted the products he sold and the number of his customers, and thereby achieved a sales volume greater than in previous or later years. During this period he sold only candles, and only those manufactured with his own wax or with wax supplied by the customer. Of his 152 sales during the two years, 69 were to an institutional purchaser, the monastery of San Domenico and its fraternal affiliate. A comparison of sales volumes in this period and in an earlier two-year period (1344–46) highlights the extent to which specialization increased Benedetto's receipts. In the earlier period his receipts totaled £137 for 947 sales of a wide variety of products—candles, spices, sugar, saffron, medicine, and thread, to name just a few. In the later period, although the number of sales dropped to 152 and candles were the only product, his receipts increased to £264. Of this, £227 (86%) came from large sales to the one institutional buyer, San Domenico and its fraternal affiliate. Unfortunately, Benedetto's account book for the seven years following 1358 has not survived; by 1365, as can be seen in the second extant book, he had returned to his earlier practice of selling a wide variety of products in small transactions with many customers.[51]

The amount of profit from sales depended on the markups on merchandise, but these are not recorded in any of the account books. Some markups can be calculated, however, by comparing the purchase and resale prices of specific commodities. The books of the two cheese sellers and two of the druggists provide this kind of information. The products involved in these calculations are identified in the same way; all calculations are based on the price per pound *(libbra)* except in the case of glasses, which are priced individually. For the cheese sellers, four markups on candles *(di sena)* averaged 25.9 percent;[52] three on eels, 26.5 percent;[53] three on oil, 28 percent;[54] five on glasses *(di foggia)*, 28.2 percent;[55] and ten on cheese *(di forma)*, 28.7 percent.[56] For the druggists, the markups on four products frequently sold by medieval apothecaries were 12 percent on white cotton *(brambagia bianca)*;[57] 23 percent on strong pepper *(pepe sodo)*;[58] 29 percent on saffron *(zafferano)*;[59] and 41.3 percent on white sugar *(suchero bianco)*.[60] Although the markups on the cheese sellers' products, including nonfood items, vary only slightly and those of the druggists vary widely, the average markups for the two trades differ by just 1.2 percent (the druggists' average markup was 26.3 percent, compared with the cheese sellers' 27.5 percent).

A markup of 27 percent, when applied to the annual sales of a cheese seller, druggist, or other tradesman, represents the gross profit of the sales *recorded* but not the total profit from the business. The books are incomplete records of sales. Cash sales were sometimes indicated, but the main purpose of the books was to record credit sales. For example, in 1395, 1404, and 1410 (some of the years in which markups of the cheese sellers were calculated), Paolo di Ser Ambrogio recorded only one cash sale (in 1410).[61] Furthermore, lapses of more than ten days frequently separate credit sale entries in all of the books.

Profits from unrecorded cash sales were not the only other source of income for a tradesman. The druggist Benedetto di Tacco's ledger and journal for the year 1370 show how numerous and varied the additional income sources could be. In addition to sales he recorded sixty-one large loans for a total of £55 s.10 in his ledger and twenty-nine small ones totaling £6 s.7 d.2 in his journal.[62] If he charged 25 percent interest on the combined total of £61 s.17 d.2, his annual return on moneylending would exceed £15.[63] In addition, he performed various services to increase his income. As a craftsman, he received £14 for manufacturing candles from wax supplied all or in part by his customers.[64] As a pharmacist, he undoubtedly charged for concocting laxatives, poultices, and ointments, although he did not specify fees. For these medicinal items he apparently did not use his own formulas; he noted that a Master Alberto or Master Salimene provided them.[65] As a funeral director, Benedetto would have earned a total of £2 for the two funerals he arranged in 1370 if he charged the same fee that the druggist Matteo di Matteo did some twenty years later.[66] Also during 1370, Benedetto fulfilled his obligation to serve guard duty seven times, receiving s.21 altogether, or an average of s.3 for each tour of duty.[67] Though he did not always specify the nature of his employment, he also received £9 in connection with his roles of tax collector and treasurer of the village of Gherignano, tax collector of the village of Mezzano, and collector of the *gabella* on wood with Chello Pucci, the *sindico* of that guild.[68] Like many other tradesmen, he owned property in the country, and in 1370 he sold grain and wine from his farms for a total of £18; one of his customers (for 2 staia of grain at s.42 per staia) was the Hospital of the Misericordia.[69] Benedetto also collected rents from his real estate holdings: in 1370 he received annual rents of £3 s.15, £5, and £10 from his urban properties.[70] Benedetto was the kind of businessman who never missed an opportunity to pick up some cash. He once rented his donkey to Nino di Stefano Nini for s.5;[71] occasionally he took advantage of customers by adding a few denari to their accounts.[72] In 1370 Benedetto received income in excess of £78 from these supplementary sources.

Some of these tradesmen had still other sources of supplementary income. The cheese seller Paolo di Ser Ambrogio worked as an assessor for the commune;[73] the cloth seller Giovanni di Spinello received s.20 as one of the consuls of the Wool Guild;[74] the tailor Domenico di Jacopo once recorded a credit of s.3 for cleaning a pale blue cloak;[75] Domenico also rented part of his own residence for £5 per year.[76]

What were the annual incomes of these men and how did they compare with those typical of other occupations? Again, Benedetto di Tacco's earnings in 1370 can serve as an example. His profits of £59 from recorded sales of £220 (a markup of 36.6%) plus £78 from supplementary sources totaled £137, but this does not include profits from unrecorded cash sales. On the basis of the large number of days for which his books contain no entries, one might propose a figure five times the total of recorded sales as a minimum in calculating annual profits from unrecorded cash sales. This would add £295 to Benedetto's recorded income to make a total gross income of £432—more than three times the £130 of an unskilled construction worker and two and a half times the £169 of a skilled one.[77] Thus calculated, Benedetto's income would fall below that of Sinibaldo, who earned £452 from interest charges for the ten months covered by his ledger, or more than £540 per year; and this does not take into account the very considerable inflation that occurred.[78]

It appears that Benedetto, with his numerous real estate investments and other sizable expenditures, enjoyed a financial position near the apex of the heterogeneous group of tradesmen who are the subject of this study. The shearer Jacopo di Bartolomeo Mati perhaps earned more, for his records include numerous credits greater than £100, including one for £2,018 s.18.[79] The secondhand dealer Taddeo di Chelli certainly earned much less; he mentioned no real estate holdings or other investments, his sales were all very modest, and he resorted to credit for most of his purchases. The gross incomes of the smaller operators in the group probably fell between £200 and £500, averaging around £300.

Whether income came from a tradesman's principal occupation or from supplementary sources, expenses of various kinds could reduce his take-home pay. Although shopkeepers sometimes recorded the costs of transportation and municipal duties *(gabelle)* separate from those of merchandise, they included all costs in the total to be passed on to the customer.[80] Expenses such as an apprentice's salary, rent, dues to a guild, and interest on loans for operating capital had to be paid out of profits from sales. There is no evidence of accrual accounts to anticipate these expenses or of any systematic schedule of payments for a fixed expense such as rent. The tradesmen fulfilled their obligations, whether for a few soldi or many lire, whenever they had the money on hand.

The cost of apprentices is well documented in these business records. Throughout his fifty-year career the druggist Benedetto di Tacco continually relied on this reservoir of cheap and apparently readily available labor. On November 1, 1345, he hired Domenico, the son of Piero Leonardi, for two years at an annual salary of £8. Off and on during the year the druggist paid portions of the salary in cash and other portions in kind; most payments went to Domenico's father, a few directly to the son.[81] Before the two years expired, Benedetto hired another apprentice at a lower rate of £7, either as a replacement for Domenico or for additional help.[82] Before the second apprentice completed his two years, Benedetto hired a third, the son of the tailor Bartellino, for only £1 s.10 per year. Perhaps because this salary was so low, the druggist asked the father to include in the contract an assurance that the son would always do the job required of him. This apprentice's salary increased in stages to £8 by 1352–53,[83] but despite the increase he quit. The following year Benedetto was paying a higher salary of £9 s.10 to another apprentice, also the son of a tailor.[84] In 1368 he paid an apprentice £11 s.2; in 1370 he paid 4 florins (£13).[85] The seemingly inflationary trend in these salaries may reflect variations in the age and experience of apprentices. In 1388 the cheese seller Giovanni di Paolo paid his apprentice £20; in 1398 the other cheese seller, Paolo di Ser Ambrogio, paid his only £10.[86]

The accounts also include many entries for rentals, but because most of these are isolated payments the trend in rents cannot be traced. Two annual rents paid by the doublet maker Marco di Sandro show how wide the range could be for different spaces: he rented a shop in 1376–77 for one florin (£3 s.13) and another four years later for £12.[87] Only Benedetto di Tacco, around the middle of the century, recorded a series of rents for a single property;[88] but from this record it is possible to gauge the deflationary effects of the Black Death on rents at Prato. For three years, beginning August 20, 1345, Benedetto paid Ser Arrigo Sementucci an annual rent of £8 s.10 for his store on the corner of the piazza.[89] When Benedetto negotiated a new rental agreement on September 1, 1348, two months after the height of the Black Death, the situation had changed drastically. Ser Arrigo had died, and the new contract with his heirs called for an annual rent of £6, almost a 30 percent decrease.[90] By 1353 the heirs had sold the property, but Benedetto continued paying £6 to the new landlord, Ser Lotto di Ser Rodolfi.[91]

There is little information on other expenses that reduced the gross profits of a shopkeeper. No tradesman recorded guild dues. Only one recorded a matriculation fee: the cloth seller Giovanni di Spinello, at the beginning of his career, opened an account to the Arte della Lana guild with a debit entry for a £5 matriculation fee and a salary payment of £1 to himself as one of the consuls of the guild in the same year.[92] The tradesmen rarely recorded the costs of borrowing operating capital, although these were sizable if the 30 percent interest paid by the tailor Domenico di Jacopo for loans of 10 and 12 florins represented the going rate.[93] The druggist Benedetto di Tacco included among his debits an incidental expense common to most shopkeepers: 31 pounds of wastepaper, purchased at s.2 per pound from the salt tax officials, which he and his apprentice undoubtedly used to wrap purchases.[94]

The wallers recorded little but expenses in their books. In the opening pages of the first book Jacopo d'Agnolo, the company bookkeeper, recorded purchases made by each of the three partners in preparation for their large job for the commune.[95] These included shovels, trowels, donkeys, carts, and other essentials. Expenditures for wine far exceeded all others; Jacopo bought it by the barrel[96] and at a tavern, in his own name alone or with a partner or friend. On one occasion the partners entertained two inspectors of their work. Once the partner Biagio di Giovanni submitted a bill of s.13 for a frog and a capon along with his beverage.[97] The bookkeeper also recorded some general operating and office expenses. He noted purchases of paper for £1 s.4 and a pair of book covers for s.7 that were used to make two books; he had the books bound but did not note that cost.[98] Another necessary expenditure was s.5 to obtain a letter from Florentine officials to the notary of the podestà of Prato for approving the contract for the work on the walls. The bookkeeper also was careful to enter his own salary of 4 florins. Once the job began, most of the wallers' recorded expenses were itemized labor costs; other entries detail the large and ongoing expense of materials such as stones, gravel, and sand, purchased for the repairing or building of the city walls.[99] Professional vendor haulers supplied these essential materials,[100] except on one occasion when the partners took advantage of some reconstruction work at the church of San Francesco to buy leftover stones. The agreement required the assistance of the friars in digging up, hauling, and unloading the stones.[101]

In order to conduct their daily business, the tradesmen of Prato needed a constant flow of merchandise to stock their shelves. As any long interruption of supplies would have deprived them of business, some reference might be expected to events such as the War of the Eight Saints or the years of conflict with Giangaleazzo Visconti, which at times must have diminished imports into Florentine territory. But the three druggists recorded no interruption in the supply of spices and medicines that came from beyond Italy by way of Pisa; and the cheese sellers and cloth sellers continued to buy products such as Sardinian cheese and Romagnol cloth.

To ensure a steady flow of products, tradesmen sometimes made long-term contracts with suppliers. For example, the cheese seller Giovanni di Paolo, to maintain his supply of local-style cheese, entered into a joint venture with Lippo di Dinuccio of the village of Montemurlo for a few years. Giovanni purchased some sheep, and Lippo tended them and provided the cheese. The two men agreed to share equally in the profit or loss on the cheese, the lambs, and the wool ("mezzo proe e mezzo danno").[102] Four years later, in 1384, Giovanni contracted with a farmer from the village of Sofignano to supply him every Saturday with all the cheese the farmer's sheep produced at a price of s.1 d.6 per pound. The cheese seller sealed the agreement with 1 florin as earnest money, and the arrangement continued for a number of months, during which the farmer delivered the cheese more than once a week.[103] A tradesman could establish an ongoing relation with a nearby supplier without entering into a formal agreement. For instance, for a number of years the druggist Paolo di Bonaccorso di Tano purchased supplies on credit from a firm of Florentine druggists.[104]

Information about incomes, expenses, and supply sources helps to characterize the local business life of fourteenth-century Prato but fails to convey the casual atmosphere of that marketplace. The relaxed and somewhat nonchalant conduct of daily business can best be seen in the settlement of debts. In the late summer of 1384, the hauler Biagio di Giuliano brought thirty-six loads of gravel to the work site of the wallers at s.5 per load for a total price of £9 but received no payment after final delivery. A few days later, one of the partners lent him 7 florins—almost three times what the company owed him. During the next three years the hauler reduced the balance of his debt by making additional deliveries of gravel and, on one occasion, by furnishing wine valued at £5. Finally, in June of 1387, he paid the remaining balance of £5 s.18 d.8.[105] The cheese seller Giovanni di Paolo, after waiting two years to be paid by one of his customers, cut the debt in half; eight months later, still having received no payment, he sold his debtor some roof tiles on credit. Yet another three months passed before the customer finally canceled his debt by curing some pork for Giovanni.[106]

In the informal business environment of late medieval Prato, local tradesmen found time to do a variety of favors for their customers. On one occasion, a client of the broker Matteo di Matteo Toffi left some stockings with a Pratese artisan for repair and returned home to Borgo San Lorenzo. As a favor, Matteo contacted the artisan to make sure the work would be done by the following Saturday, when the client again visited Prato.[107] The cheese seller Giovanni di Paolo arranged for two large purchases of oil for the priests and brothers of San Fabiano and paid the bill, but had to wait a number of months for reimbursement.[108] The druggist Benedetto di Tacco, after accepting a deposit of £2 s.15 from a customer from the village of Cafaggio, later paid a fine to have the customer's son released from prison.[109] Benedetto also provided a free and informal notarial service by recording the agreements or contracts of his customers with third parties (sometimes with witnesses). These agreements included sales of grain, the renting of a house, and a detailed sharecropping arrangement between two parties.[110] Customers probably sought Benedetto's free "notarial" services because of the legal recognition of entries in account books in those areas under Florentine jurisdiction.

It appears, however, that Benedetto was not above taking advantage of his customers, unless we read the evidence as mere bookkeeping errors. As already noted, he increased the debt of one customer in posting the amount from his journal to his ledger.

On another occasion it appears he padded an account in his own favor but was detected. Monna Lotta, wife of Bruno, made some purchases on November 1, 1369, totaling s.1 d.4. From the second entry of her account it is evident that she remitted s.2 d.4, or s.1 in excess of the correct amount. The third and final entry of the account shows a corrective payment to Bruno of s.1 d.1.[111] Did Benedetto add a little extra to the refund in order to soothe Bruno and avoid bad publicity? In the next account on the same page he had also entered an amount larger than it should have been; however, in small figures above the inflated sum he inserted the correct amount.[112] Thus he was in a position to show the potential complainant that he had corrected an unintentional error and was merely awaiting his return in order to make the refund.

The tradesmen of Prato appear somewhat lax, if not inept, in the way they managed their business affairs. Yet they achieved success over many years, and some made substantial investments in real estate both in the countryside and in the city. They were not Datinis, but they represented a strong and vital component of the late medieval economy.

Three

An Independent Broker and a Family of Innkeepers

For most of their stock and raw materials, local tradesmen could buy directly from nearby suppliers. But to acquire products such as spices that originated at a distance, in Italy or beyond, they often used middlemen. While the merchant banker was ideally suited for this role—he could arrange purchases through his network of contacts and make payment as well, with either cash or credit—he was not alone in providing the nexus of an expanding market. The *sensale,* or broker, also played a prominent role in bringing together purchasers and suppliers, in addition to arranging personal transactions such as dowries and marriages. From the thirteenth century forward, the somewhat shadowy figure of the broker appears repeatedly in a variety of Italian documents. (One even appears in the accounts of a Florentine firm operating around 1300 at Salon in southern France.)[1] There are occasional references to brokers in the account books of the Prato shopkeepers. For example, the broker Stefano di Francesco arranged a sale of a large amount of cloth for the cheese seller Giovanni di Paolo in July 1397.[2] Why Giovanni engaged in an operation involving more than £265 and certainly outside his normal business is nor revealed. Earlier in the century, in 1346 and again in 1347, the sensale Ser Ugo purchased cloth from the cloth seller Giovanni di Spinello, although not in the capacity of broker.[3]

The only sources that document the activities of individual brokers in some detail are from the second half of the fifteenth century. In his monograph on Botticelli's Adoration of the Magi" the art historian Rab Hatfield outlined the career of the broker Guasparre dal Lama, the patron of the painting; Guasparre served as broker for the Arte del Cambio and, in Hatfield's account, was expelled from the guild for fraud.[4] Richard Goldthwaite cited brokers of the same guild in his study of the local bank of Bindaccio de'Cerchi, describing them as an important source of the bank's business. He identified the brother of Botticelli as one of the brokers who referred clients to Cerchi for loans and speculative investments.[5] Astorre was able to detail the activities of the broker Girolamo di Agostino Maringhi, who worked under the jurisdiction of the Guild of the Druggists, by means of entries in his account book (1483–85). Astorre was also able to locate many of their shops in Renaissance Florence.[6]

In Prato, as in many other cities, most information about the operations of brokers in earlier periods has come from guild statutes. The statutes identified brokers as guild members who arranged transactions only for other members of the same guild.[7] The earliest Pratese guild statutes, those of the Arte della Lana (1315–20), indicate that its brokers were under the jurisdiction of guild officials and played an indispensable role in the sale of cloth. No buyer could make a purchase from a Pratese cloth merchant without a duly designated broker present to record all the details of the sale.[8] Yet some brokers apparently operated outside the jurisdiction of guilds and arranged transactions for a wide variety of commodities. The statutes tell us nothing about the activities of these independent brokers, at Prato or elsewhere.

Fortunately there has survived—not in the Archivio di Stato but in the Biblioteca Roncioniana in Prato—a precious source that illuminates the operations of an independent broker in the first decade of the fifteenth century.[9] This is the account book of Matteo di Matteo Toffi, which runs from July 1, 1408, to July 21, 1410 (the last date readable). Described as a *quaderno* containing all his *senerie*, the book consists of 92 folios and is in excellent condition except for a tear at the end, which has eliminated the dates of the last four entries. Matteo brokered numerous commodities, including cheese, soap, grain, eels, alum, saffron, tuna, and rope; he even brokered cloth, despite the prohibition on its sale by anyone other than a guild broker.[10] He also acted as a real estate broker for land and houses. It seems improbable that he was a member of all the guilds that regulated these activities; if the restrictions of the Arte della Lana guild were typical, he would have needed to join most of the guilds of Prato. However, his business may have been subject to communal statutes enacted in the interest of the public.[11]

Matteo usually followed a pattern in recording his brokerage transactions. He always gave the names of buyers and sellers and the quantities and prices of the numerous products sold. His fees, which he occasionally recorded for commodity sales, averaged 2 percent. For real estate sales, however, he recorded a range of commissions, averaging .5 percent on land and 2.5 percent on houses. His entries for real estate include far more information than those for commodities: he always recorded the price, the exact location with reference to adjacent property owners, and a detailed description of the property, giving the size in staiora and the price per staioro and specifying the agricultural use of the land (as a vineyard, for example). When buyers made only partial payment, Matteo noted the fact and specified the terms for payment of the balance. All sales were notarized with witnesses (usually including Matteo himself). On one occasion he acted also as broker for a rental: he arranged for the merchant banker Giovanni to rent a piece of land near the village of Mezzano for £9 per year, but did not record his commission for this service.[12]

Matteo's clients represented a broad spectrum of society, within Prato and beyond. Heading the list were petty tradesmen, most of them from Prato but some from beyond the district, such as the cheese seller Simone di Luchese, from Pisa.[13] Of the 291 accounts entered in Matteo's register, 186 show buyers and sellers who were either artisans or shopkeepers: druggists, blacksmiths, bakers, shoemakers, butchers, dyers, and a host of others, making a total of twenty-two occupations. Some are mentioned just once, others frequently. The secondhand dealer *(rigattiere),* Antonio di Lapo di Simone, appears sixty times as a seller and three times as a buyer. The retailer Monna Giovanna appears in connection with ten separate purchases for her delicatessen shop.[14] Certainly Matteo's wealthiest—and most famous—client was Francesco di Marco Datini and Company of Florence. The company's

purchase of cloth worth 130 florins from a Pratese merchant was the
largest sale Matteo ever negotiated.[15] The unskilled laborer Bartolo
Firi employed Matteo in purchasing 9 staiora of land from the daughter of the late Marchetto di Giunta; the price he paid—8½ florins per
staioro for a total of 76½ florins, or 306 lire—belies his modest social
status.[16]

Matteo's clients also included Florentines who, after the purchase of
Prato more than fifty years earlier, were extending their real estate
holdings into the territory of their neighbor. In five transactions
arranged by Matteo, Florentines purchased one house and four land
parcels from Pratese residents; one of the buyers of land was the silk
merchant Bartolomeo di Stefano, son-in-law of Francesco di Marco
Datini's close friend Lapo Mazzei.[17] Matteo also represented the Florentine sellers of two houses, one of which was sold to a Pratese, the
other to a Florentine. One of the joint sellers of the latter house was a
member of the famous Rucellai family.[18]

The cheese seller Paolo di Ser Ambrogio, one of the chief subjects
of this study, also used Matteo as a broker on numerous occasions, and
the pertinent entries in the broker's ledger provide information about
Paolo not found in his own registers. Whereas Paolo called himself a
cheese seller *(chasciaiuolo),* the broker called him a delicatessen operator *(pizzicagnolo),* a designation that more accurately reflects the wide
variety of products he handled. Matteo brokered and recorded the purchase by Paolo of a 7-staiora plot of land in the outskirts of Porta a
Corte, a holding that is not listed in Paolo's books.[19] Matteo's ledger
also tells us the location of Paolo's store: in an entry describing a land
sale he brokered, for which Paolo served as a witness, Matteo wrote
that the transaction took place "on the piazza of the Commune of Prato opposite the shop of Paolo di Ser Ambrogio, witness to the above
sale."[20]

Matteo's records of brokered transactions do not indicate which of
the parties paid his fee or whether it was divided between them; but
this can be determined from a number of instances for which we also
have the records of one of the parties—the cheese seller Paolo, who
was involved in ten sales arranged by the broker.[21] A comparison of
the two men's accounts suggests that in recording a transaction Mat-

teo always named the party that paid the commission first, whether buyer or seller. In nine of the ten transactions Paolo was the buyer: his accounts show no payment of a commission, and he is not named first in Matteo's entries. In the one transaction for which Paolo paid the commission, he was the seller; and Matteo named him first in his entry. The commission, however, is not explicitly stated. The entries in both registers bear the date of January 24, 1409, and record the sale of 170 net pounds of cheese at £15 per hundredweight for a total price of £25 s.10.[22] Paolo's entry states that the buyer must remit the £25 s.10 "in cash" to the broker, not to Paolo, the seller; but subsequent entries show that Paolo received only £24 s.17 from the broker—the difference of s.13 representing Matteo's commission.[23] As this is the only transaction for which Matteo named Paolo first, it might be concluded that the broker's practice was always to name first the parties who paid the commission.[24] These were usually sellers. For all of the real estate sales that Matteo arranged, he named the seller first;[25] and he named the buyer first for only 6 of his 217 commodity sales.

Matteo recorded his fees for a number of brokerage transactions. Hence a scale of average commissions can be calculated. The averages are .5 percent for land, 2 percent for commodities, 2.5 percent for houses. From July 1408 to July 1410, the two-year period covered in his register, the income from his brokerage business amounted to £346 s.5, or an average of £173 s.2½ per year—about 43 florins. During this period he received commissions totaling £190 s.18 for commodities, £84 s.10 for land, and £70 s.17 for houses.

Brokerage fees did not represent Matteo's total income, however. One entry in his register lists four loans that he made personally to Luparello di Verzoni, without any mention of interest rates or maturities as with other loans recorded in his book, in which he was not a party.[26] If Matteo received the same interest of 30 percent that is shown for these other loans (discussed in chap. 6), he earned about 8 florins on the 24 florins he lent, assuming maturities of one year. This amounts to one fifth of the average annual income from his recorded brokerage operation! In another entry Matteo records that at the beginning of 1409 he served along with Ser Giovanni di Ser Jacopo as a procurator in order to recover the dowry of Monna Nicola di Matteo Brunetti; presumably, he received compensation for this service, although no fee is mentioned in his itemization of expenses.[27] We learn, too, from the accounts of the cheese seller Paolo di Ser Ambrogio that in July 1407 Matteo sold him some barley, worth more than £7, which probably came from his own farm. This is the earliest known reference to Matteo, recorded a year before the opening of his extant account book.[28]

Matteo earned additional income from his services as an official assessor of property. Information about this activity comes not from his brokerage ledger in the Biblioteca Roncioniana but from two other books of his accounts that turned up by chance in the Archivio di Stato. The archive's inventory lists these books as belonging to Matteo Fossi of Prato, but the name on both books is Matteo di Matteo Toffi. Neither of the books records any of Matteo's brokerage activities, and both indicate that he worked as an assessor. One contains an inventory of Ser Lorenzo d'Agnolo Ridolfi's estate, which Matteo drew up in July 1411 at the request of the executors.[29] The inventory apparently remained unfinished: on fol. 60r is a heading for liabilities, but no entries are recorded; nor is any fee recorded for Matteo's services. Matteo opened the other book on August 1, 1410 (immediately after closing his brokerage ledger), to keep a record of assessments that he and three colleagues were commissioned to make for the commune of Prato at the request of the podestà and his court.[30] Twenty-two folios contain evaluations of real estate, business and household possessions, grain, cut wood, a horse, and other miscellaneous items. These were assessed to determine the assets of people who owed money for taxes, debts, returns of widows' dowries, and damages to property. (The properties damaged were a vineyard, by oxen, and a forest, by *bestie* [small livestock].)[31]

One entry notes an assessment performed for the heirs of Francesco di Marco Datini and his former business partners.[32] In November 1410, a few months after the death of Datini, his heirs and partners obtained a levy by seizure *(slaggimento)* against Stefano di Nicolozzo Chini for nonpayment of £6 s.10 for the dressing *(conciatura)* of cloth. As Stefano's assets were evaluated at 6 florins for an old oxcart and £80 s.15 for grain and cloth, the creditors presumably had no trouble collecting their claim. Matteo and his colleagues received s.44 for this work.

The fees recorded for the fifty-two assessments in the book[33] totaled £112 s.9 d.8, but this had to be divided among Matteo and his three colleagues. On a loose folio without a date Matteo listed his compensation as £26 s.5 d.10, along with that paid to two of the other three evaluators.[34] On the same sheet he noted that the treasurer of the commune owed £5 s.2 d.2 for expenses, but it is not clear whether these were his own expenses or those of all four. Matteo therefore received payment in excess of £26, or more than 6 florins, for his work as assessor from August 1410 to January 1411.

Like other tradesmen at Prato, Matteo earned money from a variety of sources. The brokerage business provided a base income of £173 s.2½, on average. To this he added interest from loans, profits from sales of his own produce, and his fees as an assessor and possibly as a procurator. A reference to Matteo as the sensale for a purchase of cheese by Paolo di Ser Ambrogio in October 1410 indicates that he continued his brokerage business while working as an assessor.[35] His annual income probably reached £300, or about 75 florins—the average estimated for the shopkeepers of Prato.

Another service business, different from the broker's in that it required considerable capital to establish and operate, was the Stella Inn. Fourteen account books and three books describing the legacies of the grandson Antonio di Cambio detail the operations of a family of innkeepers from the middle of the fourteenth century to the middle of the fifteenth. In one entry the inn is described as containing seventeen rooms; in another, twenty rooms.[36] (At the death of the grandson in 1450, each of seventeen rooms was described in the book, and the rental of the inn to Biagio di Bartolo for £60 per year was noted. In 1454 a list was made of the contents of twenty rooms.)[37] Ferro di Cambio, the first owner whose records we have, did not indicate in his books whether he inherited or purchased the inn. In addition to providing board and lodging, the three generations of owners also sold bottled wine at retail. One account book, covering the years 1372 to 1391, shows wholesale purchases of red and white wine from the countryside, the gabella charged, and the retail sales.[38]

Most customers bought meals at a fixed price, similar to the tourist

meal of today, paying s.10 for themselves and s.8 for a servant. Some of
the more prosperous guests ordered à la carte and were treated to del-
icacies such as a capon (for 1 lire), nuts, fruits, cheese, and the best wine;
their bill could come to many lire. Purchases of wine by far outnumbered all others: people drank it in the morning, in the afternoon, at
dinner, and before going to bed. Many items that would be included
in the bill today had a separate charge: for example, candles at dinner
and after dinner (s.3), and warm water (d.2 for one person). For *fuo-
co*—a place by the fire?—one paid s.2. A bed for one night cost s.1; a
bed in a private room cost £1. Later, in 1445, a room with two beds was
rented for £7 per month, another with one bed for s.44.[39] In one entry for a guest designated only as a Jew, the charge was s.2 for the bed,
not the usual s.1. Travelers from outside Prato customarily came on
horseback and, if they were merchants, sometimes had a mule or donkey carrying their goods; in such cases the innkeeper increased his receipts by charging for stabling and fodder.

    Who were the customers of the inn and where did they come from?
The guest roster mirrors the society of that time. Guests included a laborer, a mule driver, a barber, a trumpeter, a student, a druggist, a cas-
ket maker, a doctor, a wool merchant, a linen salesman, a banker, a broker, a bishop, and the mayor of Prato. The Pratese district and all of
Tuscany were well represented, including urban centers such as Pistoia,
Pescia, Lucca, Pisa, Florence, Arezzo, and Cortona. Surprisingly, guests
from Empoli, particularly merchants, outnumbered even those from
Florence. Southern Italy was represented by only three ambassadors
from Naples, who spent one night at the inn. Some of the central Italian cities listed are Urbino, Rimini, and Ancona; among the northern
cities are Venice, Genoa, Milan, Padua, Parma, Ferrara, and Modena.
Most travelers from beyond the Alps came from Germany, which supplied the majority of non-Italian workers on the city walls. One guest
came from Geneva, one from Catalonia, and one from Portugal. A
group of ambassadors from France stayed for two nights.

    In most cases it is not possible to determine whether travelers had
Prato as their primary destination or were merely spending the night
on their way to somewhere else. When a merchant from afar stayed at
the inn for four or five days, however, it appears likely that he had busi-

ness in Prato and was not just passing through. Probably this is also true when an entry lists the dinner companion of the foreigner as Pratese. Sometimes it is evident that a guest had a destination other than Prato. For example, one entry states that a merchant was on his way to Lucca; two weeks later, on his return trip, he again spent the night at the inn.

Many customers delayed payment for days, weeks, or even months. For the most part, credit was extended only to local customers. When a traveler from beyond Prato was granted credit, the innkeeper usually had a local citizen guarantee payment, and did not hesitate to call upon the guarantor if necessary.[40] In addition to extending credit for their services, the innkeepers made loans to customers and to other people not named in the books as guests. For the most part these were small loans, although a few were in florins.[41]

It is impossible to estimate reliably the profits generated by the operation of the inn. For four months in 1407, the total receipts from customers for meals, lodging, and the feeding and stabling of animals were as follows:

July   £125 s.5[42]
August   £156 s.4[43]
October   £76 s.10[44]
December   £80 s.19[45]

These figures do not include receipts for the sale of wine at retail, which were recorded separately. The accounts for operation of the inn occasionally show outside sales of food products and wine, but these are too small to matter. Only two entries show employee wages, one for Iacopo di Cicilia at the end of 1395 for £3 per month, and one for Simone in March 1396 for £2 per month.[46]

The extant records document a highly successful operation, a family enterprise that lasted close to one hundred years.

Part II

Business Practices

Bookkeeping

*D*atini thought very little of the recordkeeping of the Pratesi. Iris Origo quotes him as saying that his fellow townsmen kept books only in their heads, "like the carriers who reckon up their accounts twenty times along the road. . . . And God knows how they do! For four out of six of them have neither book nor ink-well, and those who have ink have no pen." Yet he complimented them by adding, "Just for that reason, they call things to mind better after 30 or 40 years than most men would after a month!"[1]

Widespread use of credit for sales and purchases in a thoroughly monetized economy nevertheless required accurate records—not just a good memory—and the survival of the records of so many Pratese tradesmen allows a rare glimpse into the accounting practices of some small medieval entrepreneurs. Few comparable account books from other Italian towns, including Florence, date back to so early a time, and in any case these have been little studied. The numerous contributions of Federigo Melis and Raymond de Roover to the history of accounting have dealt almost exclusively with the accounting practices of prominent merchants and industrialists.[2]

All of the account books studied, except two, present characteristics of a principal record of a business operation. But their disparate content prevents any meaningful classification as a group; all will be referred to as ledgers, although they employ single-entry rather than double-entry methods. Some show only credits in the form of receivables from customers and payables to suppliers; some also include cash receipts and disbursements; some contain personal and patrimonial accounts as well as business records.[3] The earliest, that of the thirteenth-century money lender Sinibaldo, was used for business purposes only, to record loans and subsequent repayments. Perhaps they are best described as financial memoranda *(memoriali).*[4]

Though not approaching the sophistication and precision of the accounting systems used by Datini and many other merchant bankers of the same period, the records of these artisans and shopkeepers appear to have served their purpose. Overall, the handwriting is legible except where the tradesman crowded in an additional entry at the bottom or side of an account. The rarity of grammatical and spelling mistakes attests to their high level of literacy. (Often, what at first appears to be a spelling error proves to be a local form.)[5] Moreover, a modern accountant would find little fault with these tradesmen's dexterity in mathematical calculations. Time and time again the addition in accounts of more than twenty entries proves correct to the denaro, even when sales and payments are randomly intermingled throughout. Where mistakes occur they appear to be intentional in most cases. For example, an entry for an amount smaller than that actually owed may plausibly suggest that the tradesman recognized this was all he would receive or that he saw no point in keeping the account open for just a few denari.[6] Not surprisingly, errors in favor of the seller predominate. Such errors in the posting of a summation from one page to another suggest that the petty entrepreneur was not averse to padding an account.[7] Corrections in one of the wallers' accounts were made for a different reason. Someone other than the original accountant, as indicated by the different hand and the color of the ink, apparently checked the monthly pay record of the partnership and corrected two entries concerning the laborer Matteo di Lenzo. Credit for a full day's work was changed to one third, and "not here" was written beside another entry (for September 12), where he was recorded present. Matteo's pay for the month of September, recorded on October 2, reflected both alterations.[8]

The similarity in format and terminology of all the books of the Pratese tradesmen suggests that they either had some formal training in accounting procedures or had learned traditional practices as assistants or apprentices.[9] Most of the tradesmen divided their ledgers into two sections according to standard practice: the front of the book contained sales (debits to customers), the rear contained purchases (credits to suppliers). This division did not always prevail, however, and debit and credit accounts sometimes were entered in the same section. Throughout the books, entries always were made in chronological order, and a set format and formulaic language (accounting jargon) were employed. Each account opened with the name of the customer or supplier, followed by either a debit *(de'dare)* or a credit *(de'avere)*. Payments intermingled with purchases and sales. Invariably, the tradesman would leave vacant a space between accounts in order to record later entries. The length of the blank space varied, perhaps in accordance with expectations of activity in the account. This determination often proved erroneous, however, and unused areas alternated with overcrowded ones, some overflowing at the end or side of the page. When it was impossible to squeeze in any additional entries, the tradesman would post the balance to a later page. Usually that page number was noted, and the opening entry of the new page indicated the earlier page from which it had been posted. In an account with numerous debits and credits the tradesman sometimes recorded the outstanding balance and then, in a final entry, the amount due before posting. Similar summations in the body of an account appear in the books of the moneylender Sinibaldo in the thirteenth century. Indeed, in every respect—except for minor differences such as the use of the singular *de'dare* instead of *deono dare* with a plural subject—Sinibaldo's entries read the same as those recorded one hundred years later.

The artisans and shopkeepers of Prato used money of account for most amounts recorded in the body of the entry and always for totals written to the right in columns. All but one of the tradesmen used *lira di piccioli* (£1 = s.20 = d.240). The exception—the shearer Jacopo di Bartolomeo Mati—used *fiorino a fiorino* (f.1 = s.29), following the guild-imposed practice of his customers, textile entrepreneurs who operated at a higher level in the business world. In some registers (especially those of the cheese seller Paolo di Ser Ambrogio), entries in the right column have subdivisions in lire, soldi, and denari di piccioli, an approach that Goldthwaite calls "the florin + lire money of account."[10] In all of the books studied, roman numerals predominate over arabic numerals and spelling-out of numbers;[11] with very few exceptions roman numerals are used for money of account summations to the right, a practice that can be explained by the roman numerals' lesser susceptibility to alteration.[12]

If a prize were awarded for neatness and accuracy, Paolo would be the winner. Last place would go to Taddeo di Chelli, the secondhand dealer. His accounts are full of sloppy writing and erroneous calculations; at times he made a mistake even in transferring a single amount in the body of an entry to the right column.

There is no indication that these artisans and shopkeepers relied on their records for more than a chronological history of sales and purchases and a system for keeping track of receivables and payables. They apparently had no interest in ascertaining their financial health by means of a balance sheet listing assets and liabilities or an income statement showing profit or loss. Occasionally, however, they took stock of outstanding debts and attempted to consolidate and collect them. On a number of occasions the druggist Benedetto di Tacco drew up separate lists of debtors and amounts due; one such list of four pages contained the names and debts of 106 persons.[13] The cloth seller Giovanni di Spinello went further in appraising his assets by recording on the first page of his book (dated January 1, 1341) an evaluation of his stock on hand and a list of the debts he judged collectible.[14] In chapter 5 we shall return to this "asset sheet" of Giovanni di Spinello and discuss in detail its significance for the extension of credit in the local economy.

When buyers paid in full at the time of sale, there was no need to enter their names in a register; but, because many customers of the tradesmen bought on credit, adequate identification of the debtor became a necessity. Part or all of the following information was recorded, depending on how well the tradesman knew the customers:

1. Christian name (e.g., Francesco).
2. Patronymic (e.g., Francesco di Paolo or Francesco Paoli).
3. Place of origin (a village or a precinct of the city[15] and sometimes the street, lane, or intersection).
4. Surname (e.g., Francesco di Paolo Migliorati).
5. Title (e.g., Ser or Messer).

6. Occupation.

7. Nicknames.[16]

8. Relationship to a known person (e.g., son, brother-in-law, mother, or godparent) or geographic location of customer's residence in relation to a known person.

9. Female designation (*monna* preceding a woman's name, with *donna di* [wife of] added as further identification if applicable; for a widow, *che fu di* was added).

10. Religious identification (status as a priest, brother, friar, or sister and the church or monastery to which the person was attached, either in one of these roles or as a lay employee).

11. Further aids to memory (e.g., designation of the person for whom the purchase was made, such as a wife or daughter, or the name of the individual who picked up the item if different from the buyer).

Sometimes a note was added describing the circumstances surrounding the sale. This elaborate system of identification confirms the importance the tradesmen attached to entering essential information in their records. Without some record of each debtor's identity and of amounts owed and payments made, often over a period of years, these small businessmen could not have operated.

Two businesses had supplementary books that resembled the ledgers in many ways. The butchers' supplementary book had a clear-cut purpose: it served as a journal of individual sales of meat to one institution, the Hospital of the Misericordia. Its supplementary nature in the hierarchy of accounting is also clear: at irregular intervals, the sales were totaled and posted to a ledger (no longer extant).[17] The opening accounts name as purchasers the rectors Stefano di Cone and Francesco di Matteo; farther into the book, the names are omitted and only *rettori* (rectors) is used.

The druggist Benedetto di Tacco also had a supplementary book. Its purpose and its relation to his ledger can be determined with some precision because the ledger, too, survives. The *vacchetta,* which Benedetto identities as a *libriciuolo,* does not represent a true secondary book in a hierarchy of accountancy. Although some of its transactions are posted to the ledger, others are not, and for the latter the supplemen-

tary book is the only record. For example, twenty-nine of the numerous loans recorded in the supplementary book, totaling £6 s.7 d.2, are
not posted to the ledger. Sometimes Benedetto identifies an entry in
the principal register as a posting from the *libriciuolo;* but many postings are not so identified, and the notation of posting *(posti a libro)* appears only in the supplementary book, with a date to allow for locat-
ing of the posted entry in the ledger. In some cases information
recorded in one of the two corresponding entries clarifies incomplete
or imprecise wording in the other. On June 3, 1369, Benedetto recorded in his supplementary book a sale to Giovanni di Lenzo of sheepskins *(carte di pecora)* for s.1 d.4, with a notation of posting to the ledger;
the purchase appears in the ledger with the same date but without any
reference to the supplementary book.[18] And it is the ledger that details the exact nature of the sale and provides clarification of the low
price of s.1 d.4: what had been sold was not sheepskins but one piece
of sheepskin *(uno pezzo di carte di pecora).* On the opening page of the
supplementary book Benedetto wrote that he would allow his apprentice to make entries therein; perhaps he regarded this book as a
kind of training ground, reserving for himself the task of posting transactions that he felt were important to show in the ledger.

Benedetto treated a sale or purchase entered in the supplementary
book in one of three ways: by closing the account upon payment of
the amount owed, by forwarding a balance due in the same book, or
by posting the transaction to his ledger. An analysis of the first fifteen
accounts, starting on fol. 1v and continuing through fol. 2r, illustrates
these procedures. (However, two accounts on fol. 1r are impossible to
read because of faded ink.) Nine accounts are settled on the same page,
four are posted to a later page, and one is posted to the principal register. A note attached to one account tells us that the balance due is to
be posted to the account of the purchaser's father, but without indicating which book contains that account. Of these fifteen accounts,
six include references to previous purchases from a supplementary
book—an indication that this book was one of a series.[19]

Benedetto also made entries starting from the back of the supplementary book, but these appear to be no different from those in the
front. There is no sign of any overall format. Debits, credits, and *memo-*

riali intermingle throughout, including such casual notations as "I sent oil home" *(mandai l'olio a casa)* without an amount, price, or date.[20] In keeping with the general inconsistency of the book is a lack of precision in the recording of payments. Sometimes Benedetto closed accounts carefully, noting payments and their dates, or stating that he had been paid *(anne dato* or *sono pagato);* sometimes he simply canceled an account with two diagonal lines. Although he designated this book on the first page as containing small credits *(credenze minute),* the amounts are by no means all small. Sales and other expenses for the funeral of Nicolozzo di Fede, which fill a whole page (fol. 5r), exceed £.30; and the third account on fol. 22v records Benedetto's purchase of a house for 13 florins and his subsequent payments.

Later in his career the druggist occasionally used a "blackboard" ("tavola gesata"), on which he recorded some sales.[21] The innkeeper Cambio di Ferro referred to "loose folios" as the source of many of his ledger entries; perhaps these sheets were used at the time of sale, then collected and copied in his permanent record.[22] Benedetto's postings to accounts for wax ("alla ragione della cera"), for candles, for saffron, and for the rental payments of his store ("della pigione della bottega") are not found in his ledgers and must have been recorded in another book or books now lost.[23] He also refers to a book of the guard ("posti a libro della guardia") that is no longer extant.[24] Postings to and from lost records also appear in the three ledgers of the wallers. They refer to a book of accounts for the haulers ("veturali") who brought stone and gravel to the worksite; a book of loans ("libro delle prestanze") for employees of the company; and waste books ("bastardelli") kept by each of the partners and some of the other masters to record the work hours of their crew of unskilled laborers.[25]

A World of Credit and Trust

The local economy of fourteenth-century Prato functioned in a world of credit and trust. And, unless the Pratese community at that time was unique in its makeup and circumstances, other towns and cities of central and northern Italy must have manifested a similar economic environment. Yet prominent economic historians—Armando Sapori, who contributed so much to our knowledge of the economic and business history of Florence in the first half of the Trecento,[1] Federigo Melis, who did similar work on Pisa and even Prato itself in the second half of the Trecento;[2] and the many others who preceded them or followed in their footsteps—have missed this prevalence of credit in daily transactions.

Sometimes our eyes turn only upward, to the higher levels of society—in this case, to the merchant bankers and industrial entrepreneurs. That seems to be where the real action was, not in the daily exchanges of artisans and shopkeepers. Only when a petty entrepreneur managed to break his bonds and rise into the upper world of commerce and manufacture did he become a candidate for study. Datini offers the best example—an orphaned son of a tavernkeeper who rose far above his family's social and economic milieu. To trace the broad evolution of business and even to assess the local economy of a city or region, historians typically have focused on the economic movers: the Bardis or the Albertis. This preference cannot be explained entirely by the paucity of documentation for the activities of local tradesmen in contrast with the far more abundant sources for merchant bankers and industrialists.

Despite his considerable contributions to business and economic historiography, Melis serves as an example of one who failed to investigate local economies and their possible influence on the economic development of an age. In April 1972, at a yearly seminar held in Prato by the Istituto Internazionale di Storia Economica "F. Datini," Melis delivered a significant paper entitled "La grande conquista trecentesca del 'credito di esercizio' e la tipologia dei suoi strumenti fino al XIV secolo."[3] He concluded that in the second half of the fourteenth century, banks began to grant a line of credit (*credito di esercizio*) to merchants, based on trust (*fiducia*); and that this line of credit laid the foundations of modern deposit banking. He dismissed the world of the artisans and shopkeepers of that period, saying that when the owner of a small business needed a loan, it could only be a "consumption loan" because "the environment of local business did not offer opportunities to obtain financial aid from others. The money lying idle in his cashbox, even if modest, was always sufficient for the acquisitions and other needs of his business, which was based on tradition."[4]

Although Melis was speaking here in the context of the rise of bank credit for businessmen, his remarks convey a view of the local economy that is not supported by the available evidence. The "consumption loans" that he thought were the only loans possible at the lower levels of society could have come only from pawnbrokers. Yet the archives at Prato, where Melis spent so many years of his later life reordering and probing the wealth of the Datini records, contain documents that show a completely different picture. These are the registers of shopkeepers and artisans, and they can very much illuminate the actual functioning of the local economy. They invalidate Jacques Bernard's contention that local trade left no traces as daily transactions were conducted either in cash or by barter.[5]

Credit—short-term and long-term—was a way of life in fourteenth-century Prato. People bought on credit and they sold on credit. Going through the account books of these small businesses, the reader enters an environment of six hundred years ago that is not, in fact, so remote from the credit world of today. Some payments were remitted the same day, some the following day or week; but frequently they extended over a period of months or years, sometimes more than ten years. Advance payments to suppliers are also recorded. For example, on January 16, 1385, the wallers paid two haulers more than 3 florins to bring stones to the work site; a month later the wallers received a partial delivery and repayment of £3 s.16 d.6 in lieu of additional deliveries.[6] Advance payments were rare, however, and the wallers often delayed their payments to suppliers for months.

Sales on credit were not an occasional practice in fourteenth-century Prato; they predominated. The register of the cloth seller Giovanni di Spinello provides the earliest examples. During the two-year period from January 1337 through December 1338, Giovanni extended credit on recorded sales of £484.[7] In a later two-year period, from April 1382 to April 1384, the druggist Benedetto di Tacco extended credit of £475.[8] Because the Prato tradesmen apparently did not use their records as a means of analyzing past performance in order to maximize future profits, they had no need to enter cash sales.[9] They needed a record of money owed, however; therefore it is not surprising that their books show mostly credit sales. Nevertheless, the magnitude of the record of indebtedness substantiates the importance of credit as essential to their operations. Giovanni's and Benedetto's reliance on credit typifies the operations of all of the shopkeepers.

Members of all social and economic classes, from inside the city walls and beyond, in virtually all of the forty or so villages constituting the district of Prato, bought on credit.[10] The podestà himself, Messer Bonchi, purchased paper and candles twenty-one times and settled his account with one payment five months after the opening of the account in March 1377.[11] Even the communal government bought on credit: in 1375 the city treasurer bought eleven two-branched candlesticks from the druggist Benedetto di Tacco "to illuminate the precious belt of our Lady for Easter."[12] (This revered relic, which the cathedral chapel was constructed to house, was displayed by the bishop five times a year from the exterior pulpit.) In 1369 Giovanni di Bartolomeo Saccagnini, a son of the wealthiest family in Prato, charged a small purchase of only d.8.[13] Other presumably worthy candidates for credit included the mayor of the village of Castelnuovo, whose account opened in October 1366 and was never settled, although it ran for more than sixteen years;[14] the rector of the Hospital of the Misericordia, who purchased cloth worth £14 from the secondhand dealer Taddeo di Chelli and settled the account a month later;[15] and the prior of San Domenico, who bought a pound and a half of tuna from the cheese seller Paolo di Ser Ambrogio and waited till August to pay.[16]

The well-known Datini was not above buying from shopkeepers on credit and taking his time in remitting. In 1407 this wealthy merchant made purchases amounting to s.12 from the cheese seller Paolo di Ser Ambrogio and waited a year before finally paying the bill.[17] Datini's debit balance for items purchased from the cheese seller in 1408–9 was not cleared until September 20, 1414, four years after Datini had died; Paolo received s.7 in final settlement of the outstanding account.[18] Armando Sapori would have welcomed these examples to buttress his characterization of Datini as a miserly merchant, so different from the mercantile "heroes" of the first half of the century.[19]

Customers whose recorded occupations identify them as artisans or shopkeepers, or as poor people living at or near subsistence level, also received credit. As early as the first half of the Trecento, the cloth seller Giovanni di Spinello Viviani recorded numerous purchases on credit by textile workers and others designated simply as laborers.[20] He identified a few of the textile workers as having done work for him, in which case the extension of credit can be construed as an advance on wages. In Giovanni's book and those of the other tradesmen, the identifying information on borrowers provides a fairly comprehensive catalogue of the artisans and shopkeepers who operated in Prato at that time. Moreover, hundreds of customers outside the urban center, some even from Florence and its countryside, charged their purchases. One of these customers, the dyer Piero—who took seven months to complete his payments for pork—was from faraway Siena.[21]

Women are not excluded from this world of credit. For example, during a two-year period from April 1382 to April 1384, the druggist Benedetto di Tacco extended credit to twenty-nine women. In addition to listing a woman's name at the opening of the account as an indication that she, not her husband, was responsible for payment, Benedetto made an occasional notation that the husband had picked up (portò) the purchase or made a payment for her.[22] The wide range of the women's social and economic classes is indicated by their occupations (e.g., weaver, baker, washerwoman)[23] and by the status of their husbands, ranging from *messer* to laborer.

Whether repayment was delayed by a few days or a few years appears to have made no difference to the tradesmen; they continued to grant credit even to a customer who had made no payment on a prior debt. Rarely did a borrower remit in full within the term specified. (In studying sixteenth-century documents of the Medici in the Selfridge collection at Harvard University, Florence Edler de Roover made a similar observation: "Payments made according to the terms agreed upon are hard to find in the ledgers.")[24] It was a casual regime in which time was not yet calibrated, a world of business free from the host of collection devices employed today to exact payment of outstanding debts. Time was not yet money.

The vast majority of credit customers apparently provided neither security nor verification of the debt. The account book entry sufficed, and it generally included only the customer's name, the goods purchased, and the value of the transaction. When either security or verification was demanded, the requirement was explicitly noted: it could take the form of a pawn, a notarized document, the guarantee of a third party, or the testimony of a witness.

Only rarely did a customer deposit a pawn *(pegno)*, the surest device to secure a loan. The pawns recorded include a wide variety of objects—clothing, tools, even weapons.[25] Some of these secured only a small debt and for a short time. One customer from the village of Cafaggio needed a pledge to assure payment of a s.5 balance, even though he had paid s.28 d.9 in cash for Romagnol cloth that cost s.33 d.9.[26] Another customer deposited a pawn and retrieved it the same day. (This was Coro, the servant of the greengrocer Jacopo Simoni, who bought small candles worth s.7 d.2 from the druggist Benedetto di Tacco, paying nothing and leaving his coat and hood as security. Later the same day—December 13, 1347—he returned with the money and repossessed the coat and hood.)[27] It is impossible to know for sure if the value of a pawn always exceeded the amount of credit extended. The tradesmen did not indicate the value of pawns; even when they kept a pawn after failure of the customer to pay, they usually closed the account without recording either profit or loss on the transaction.[28]

On one occasion, however, when a priest from the contado of Pistoia failed to pay his debt, the druggist Benedetto di Tacco sold the small notebook left as a pledge. He charged s.20, the exact amount of the debt; and the buyer agreed to sell back the notebook for the same s.20 if the priest settled the account.[29]

Of all the Pratese tradesmen, only the cloth seller Giovanni di Spinello resorted to notarial documentation to protect a debt, and he did this only twice, in 1338.[30] The practice was rare because, in the Florentine area, entries in account books had been recognized as prima facie evidence of debt since early in the Trecento. By contrast, during a ten-month period in 1285–86 the Pratese moneylender Sinibaldo required each of his 175 borrowers to execute a notarial document, regardless of the size of the loan, and to reimburse him for the notary's fee, usually s.1. One loan recorded in his notarial documents was as low as £1, and two others were for only £2. Sometimes Sinibaldo granted additional small loans to the same borrower, usually without requiring another notarial verification; occasionally, however, he required a second notarial document, which could be redacted by a different notary than the one who had drawn up the first loan.[31] He used four notaries extensively,[32] but hired thirty-four others for at least one contract each. When one notary took out a personal loan of £7½, Sinibaldo had him draw up his own notarial contract.[33]

Though not as reliable as a notarial document, a personal guarantee from a third party was the most common method of securing a loan. Guarantors were noted in all of the tradesmen's registers. Sometimes the name was included in the opening entry of the debit account, sometimes it appeared in a later entry—perhaps after the tradesman had become a little apprehensive about a customer's intentions. Most guarantors were not called upon to make good on an unpaid debt. But if the borrower defaulted, the guarantor usually proved as reliable as Monna Lipa, who sent her son with the £2 s.5 in order to complete the payments she had guaranteed for a miller from the village of Carteano.[34] However, the cloth seller Giovanni di Spinello Viviani failed to collect from three different guarantors whose names appear in successive accounts.[35]

The testimony of a witness was the least formal device used to verify a credit transaction. Usually the shopkeeper himself entered in the account the names of those who were present at the time of the sale, but sometimes he would have one or more of the witnesses themselves write the pertinent information. Lando Spinelli's large debt of £70 s.8 d.6 undoubtedly prompted the tailor Domenico di Jacopo to ask three witnesses to write in his ledger that Lando owed this sum and would pay within one month; in spite of this verification, however, a portion of the bill remained outstanding a year later.[36]

The tradesmen's books do not reveal their criteria for deciding which method—if any—to use to secure a loan. The magnitude of Lando's debt may explain why Domenico di Jacopo wanted three witnesses, but why security was required in other cases is not clear. Why a pawn for a relatively small debt of s.7, a guarantor for a moderate one of £2 s.5, and a witness for a sizable one of £4 s.17?[37] Factors such as customers' financial status or their distance from a shopkeeper's place of business are plausible criteria, but each convincing example is contradicted by many others. Ultimately, the likely criterion was a tradesman's personal judgment of a customer's reliability. Some witnesses may have been used simply because they happened to be in the store at the time of sale.[38]

Not surprisingly, the problem of defaults arose. If a debtor had provided security for payment and then failed to remit, the shopkeeper could keep the pawn or call on the guarantor to pay. In the former instance no loss occurred since the value of the pawn usually exceeded that of the debt; likewise, when the guarantor happened to be a creditor of the tradesman for an amount in excess of his guarantee, the tradesman could assure himself of payment by an offset of what was owed by the debtor. The failure of the wool merchant Guiccio da Lesso to pay a debt of £30 s.5 d.10 prompted the cheese seller Paolo di Ser Ambrogio to debit the account of the guarantor, the banker Lodovico di Ser Jacopo, whom Paolo owed more than this amount.[39] Otherwise, having a guarantor did not necessarily assure repayment.

In the absence of a pawn or guarantor as security, tradesmen resorted to other means to collect their money. Only one attested method of debt settlement is found in all the ledgers: arrangement for payment of less than the amount due. The reduction could be considerable. Mat-

teo from the monastery of San Fabiano made seven purchases from the
cheese seller Giovanni di Paolo between November 2, 1396, and August 5, 1398, totaling £5 s.16 d.4.[40] Almost two years later Matteo had
made no payments, so Giovanni agreed to settle the account for £2
s.3—less than half of what was actually due. The reduced amount was
not paid immediately, however, and Giovanni allowed this customer to
charge another purchase in the meantime, before the adjusted balance
was finally remitted.[41]

Evidence of a more aggressive approach to the perennial problem
of collecting debit balances is found in the account book of the cloth
seller Giovanni di Spinello Viviani. In December 1343 Giovanni and a
man named Giunta di Meccoluccio, undoubtedly another tradesman
who had collection problems, jointly obtained a notarial document to
secure payment from a certain Francesco and his wife, who owed Giovanni £2 s.2. Despite this resort to legal action, Giovanni received only
s.15 the following August.[42]

Giovanni apparently had his own bill collector, who may have been
a silent partner. In five out of six of the opening accounts in the ledger
that was begun on January 23, 1337, Vimano Gherardi made payments
for customers who were in debt to Giovanni;[43] and over the next four
years Vimano's name appears on every other page, on average, in the
capacity of payor for one of Giovanni's customers.[44] Of the 376 accounts opened during this first four-year period, 54 (14.36%) have a
credit entry for Vimano; and during the last six years in Giovanni's
ledger (fols. 61v–81r), a period of greatly lessened activity, Vimano
continued to make payments for his customers. At no time did Giovanni designate Vimano's occupation; but the records suggest that he
was a moneylender who took over accounts assigned to him by the
tradesman, paid the amounts due, and then proceeded to seek reimbursement. Additional evidence in an account headed by Vimano's
name, beginning January 23, 1339, and continuing over 4 folios, supports such an interpretation.[45] Many entries in this account bear the
same type of information: a debit for Vimano that offsets the amount
owed by one of Giovanni's customers. In the first entry Vimano
promised to pay the s.38 debt of the laborer Rosono Pacinini;[46] on
Rosono's account (fol. 3r), Giovanni wrote in the corresponding cred-

it entry; "Vimano has given to us for him the s.38 on 16 January." For Giovanni, apparently, a promise by Vimano was as good as payment; Giovanni credited Rosono's account with the s.38 on January 16, but did not receive the money from Vimano until January 23. Debit entries on Vimano's account for his purchases from Giovanni and even for some loans suggest that the cloth seller was helping to finance Vimano's business operation.

In the small businesses of Prato, as in any business where credit is the basis of a substantial portion of sales volume, the loss ratio on outstanding debts determined to what extent losses reduced profits. The rudimentary balance sheet that Giovanni di Spinello Viviani drew up before opening his shop provides a starting point for an investigation of this key factor for determining profitability (see chap. 1). On the first page of his ledger, bearing a date January 1, 1341, Giovanni listed thirty-four debit balances, totaling £66 s.2 d.5, that he considered collectible assets.[47] He failed to collect £6 s.12 d.8, or 10 percent of this amount. Given that some of these debts were two years in arrears, his 90 percent collection rate certainly is acceptable.[48]

Yet Giovanni did not include the debts of all of his customers as receivables. In addition to the thirty-four borrowers on the collectible list, thirteen others still owed him a total of £20 s.14 d.4. One can guess why Giovanni omitted some of the thirteen from his list of good debtors. Although the brothers Paolo and Cone Nardobaldi were the only two of the thirteen to pay their debt, they allowed nearly four years to elapse without a payment—a plausible explanation for Giovanni's belief that their debt of s.18 was noncollectible.[49] And there is little doubt why he excluded from his collectible list the debts of Francesco Dini, Carlo di Giunta, and Vieni Bonnemetti, whose accounts follow one another.[50] There had been a guarantor for Dini's debt of £3 s.11 and two witnesses to the original transaction, but Dini was himself the guarantor of another bad debtor on Giovanni's list, Carlo di Giunta, whose debt amounted to £2 s.1. And Carlo di Giunta, in turn, had guaranteed the full amount of Vieni Bonnemetti's debt. Clearly, Giovanni had misjudged not only his debtors but their guarantors, and he could hardly include these three deadbeats on his list of collectible assets.

Giovanni's lists of collectibles and noncollectibles provide an unusual opportunity to view one tradesman's appraisal of his credit operation. They do not, however, indicate his overall collection rate or answer the more important question of the effect of extensive credit on profits. An examination of the early years when Giovanni's business was at its height (considered in two-year periods) and of the last six years when his business slackened (considered as one period) will better provide meaningful collection ratios than considering the ten-year period as a whole. From January 23, 1337, to December 15, 1338 (fols. 1r–28r), Giovanni opened 188 accounts, many of which included more than one sale, and he extended credit of £484; five accounts contained uncollected sums totaling £5 s.10 d.9. Thus he failed to collect only 1.2 percent of what was owed him. Needless to say, this collection rate of 98.8 percent is remarkable for any period in history, including the present with all its modern devices for evaluating risk and aiding collection. Entries for the second two-year period, from December 15, 1338, to December 22, 1340 (28r–61v), show a lower, yet acceptable, collection rate of 93 percent.

During the last six-year period, from January 1, 1341, to February 7, 1347 (fols. 61v–81r), only 138 accounts were entered in Giovanni's register, totaling £135 s.10 d.5, or less than one-half the total sales volume in either of the first two-year periods. The collection ratio fell to 84 percent, but the drop is explained by the default of just one customer: Lorenzo di Petruccio, whose debt amounted to slightly more than half (£12 s.14 d.7) of the total sales of £22 s.14 d.3 for that year.[51] If we subtract Lorenzo's debt from the unpaid total of £20 s.9 d.1, the remaining £7 s.14 d.6 for the six years yields a respectable collection rate of 95.5 percent. Giovanni achieved this ratio at a time of greatly reduced activity in his business—and at a moment when Florence presumably was rocked by the disastrous collapse of its most prominent international bankers.

The collection rate of the other shopkeepers corresponds to that of Giovanni. The credit data of the druggist Benedetto di Tacco, who did business through most of the latter half of the century, provide a basis for comparison with Giovanni's collection rate before 1350. During his first two years in business (1344–46) Benedetto had more customers than Giovanni had at the beginning of his career—291 to Giovanni's 188—yet Benedetto's sales amounted to only £137 compared with Giovanni's £506.[52] Although Benedetto's credit operation involved far more customers and a smaller average sale, he achieved a collection rate of 97 percent during this period, only slightly lower than Giovanni's 98.8 percent in his first two years.[53] An analysis of a later two-year period at the beginning of Benedetto's second register—June 1, 1365, to June 3, 1367—yields a 97 percent collection ratio. For a like period at the beginning of the last register—April 8, 1382, to April 10, 1384—the ratio is 98 percent.[54]

Other tradesmen proved equally successful in the collection of their debts. The cheese seller Paolo di Ser Ambrogio extended credit of £411 from January 8, 1405, to January 2, 1407; twenty-six purchasers failed to pay a total of £13, which amounted to only a little more than 3 percent uncollected debt.[55] It is unlikely that a survey of all the other account books would appreciably change these extraordinary percentages. The reliability of those who purchased on credit in late medieval Prato would arouse the envy of many of today's storekeepers. Perhaps the small-town atmosphere of Prato explains the difference, in part: people knew one another, and no one wanted a bad reputation. Another factor undoubtedly was the severe judicial penalties for defaulters, which included mutilation, torture, and imprisonment. An example appears in one of the books of the innkeeper Cambio di Ferro, in which he recorded the names of prisoners when he supervised the debtor prison at Prato. From this record we learn that a petition of the butcher Lorenzo Cosi (one of the tradesmen studied here) resulted in the imprisonment of two men: Stefano di Lazaro for an unpaid debt of £8 and the mayor of Porta Fuia for failing to pay 270 florins.[56]

While the tradesmen of Prato had a large proportion of their own assets tied up in customer debit balances, they also sought and received credit from their suppliers. This widespread extension of credit by the suppliers of the small businessman contradicts Melis's assumption that only the "money lying idle in his cash-box" or a "consumption loan" could provide necessary funds. Most of the ledgers offer evidence that the tradesmen financed their purchases at a debt level comparable to that of their customers, although the number of debits entered is understandably far lower than the number of credit sales. A debit account of the secondhand dealer Taddeo di Chelli, starting on May 20, 1393, ran for almost three years, intermingling purchases and partial payments, some in products.[57] From 1339 to 1346 the cloth seller Giovanni di Spinello used credit to purchase cloth and wool as well as to pay artisans such as dyers, carders, and fullers for work they performed for him.[58] Although the vast majority of his purchases involved credit, for two larger ones of £45 and £75 he paid in full on the day of sale.[59] Often Giovanni would offset his debt with a purchase by the creditor or with the payment of an obligation of the supplier to a third party.[60]

Even in this earlier period, credit was sometimes granted to geographically distant parties. For example, Mazzio di Puccio of San Miniato and his partner Jacopo supplied Giovanni with 389 pounds of wool on September 16, 1344; in November the parties made an agreement for payment of the balance due, and in January 1345 Giovanni rendered his final remittance. He saw fit to have two witnesses verify this payment of £4 s.16.[61]

Fortunately, while most of the tradesmen's registers focus on customer sales, one of the two extant account books of the cheese seller Paolo di Ser Ambrogio contains mainly his payables. This book, which runs from January 10, 1390, to May 31, 1412, allows for a more complete and systematic study of one tradesman's reliance on credit.[62] The size and frequency of the purchases did not discourage suppliers from allowing Paolo to buy on credit and to take his time in paying. A typical example appears at the beginning of the ledger, where a whole page records Paolo's purchases from Giovanni di Bartolomeo, another cheese seller. On January 10, 1390, Paolo opened the account with a purchase of 135 pounds of cheese for £12 s.10. He continued to buy on credit from Giovanni, although some partial payments were intermingled with these purchases. Not until three years later, on January 20, 1393, did he finally clear the account.[63] Some of his purchases were larger than the initial debt of £12 s.10, yet he obtained credit for the full purchase price. Another example is Paolo's purchase of 1,617 pounds of oil from Piero di Chele on February 15, 1393, for which he owed £123 s.10. He waited until December 1393 to make a first partial payment of £9 s.10.[64]

Like the cloth seller Giovanni di Spinello, Paolo bought on credit not just locally but from outside the Pratese district. Distance alone apparently did not entail stricter terms: Paolo paid a supplier in Pistoia in three weeks[65] but kept one in Florence waiting almost six years before completing payment on merchandise worth £7 s.18.[66] The close relation between Paolo and another Florentine supplier named Rosso Ferrovecchio is evident in the account: no currency changed hands, and an offset of a purchase by Rosso seven months later settled the Pratese's debt.[67]

It would be natural to assume that sales or purchases on credit involved interest and that the almost complete absence of any reference to it in the tradesmen's books was due to the fear of prosecution for usury. Indeed, Raymond de Roover has pointed out a plausible reason for this absence. In 1311–12 the Council of Vienne under Clement V not only took an unequivocal stand on the prohibition of all usury but also specifically cited account books as bona fide evidence for conviction.[68] An examination of documents in Arrigo Castellani's *Nuovi testi fiorentini del Dugento* lends credence to de Roover's hypothesis. In the entries for the Florentine firm of the Fini brothers, which operated in France at the close of the thirteenth century, and in many other records reproduced in this collection, the rate of interest is explicitly stated.[69] The Pratese moneylender Sinibaldo also recorded the interest charge for all loans that he made in 1285 and 1286. But in the Trecento and beyond, tradesmen's records tend either to disguise interest charges or to omit them altogether. Of course, it cannot be assumed that extensions of credit always entailed a charge for interest. The tradesmen undoubtedly were influenced by popular preaching about usury and the contemporary debate in scholastic, and especially Franciscan, circles on the subjects of interest and credit instruments. A vast literature on these subjects is available for the Florentine area in the late Middle Ages.

Even after the prohibition, some interest charges are clearly indicated in the books of the Pratese tradesmen. The cloth seller Giovanni di Spinello paid interest on two large accounts for the purchase of supplies on credit. One account shows that during the two years from January 1337 to January 1339, he bought cloth three times from the same wholesaler for a total of 65 florins. He did not record the total interest due, but in October 1339 he noted a debit of 10 florins for the portion still unpaid. The second account reveals an exact interest rate. On March 1, 1337, Giovanni purchased cloth from another supplier for 40 florins; one year later, on March 4, 1338, he recorded payment of 4 florins in interest for the past year. On February 20, 1339, he paid both the principal of 40 florins and the interest of 4 florins—a two-year loan at 10 percent interest.[70]

In all of the ledgers in this study, only one other entry for a sale explicitly indicates an interest charge; and only a few entries contain even a hint that interest might be involved. On May 23, 1384, Giovanni di Paolo sold cheese and dried meat to another cheese dealer at a price of £365 s.14 d.9. Two witnesses verified the sale, which had a term of two years for payment. On the back of the folio detailing the sale is the record of payments. The last entry—£35 paid on October 9, 1386—brings the total to the full amount of the sale; but an additional remittance of £60 is noted, indicating an annual interest of about 10 percent.[71] Incidentally, Giovannni's occasional stipulation of a term of one month for payment did not mean—in contrast to the practice of many retailers today—that failure to pay on time resulted in an interest charge. For example, at the beginning of March in 1389, Monna Vanna made a purchase from the cheese seller for £3 s.3 and agreed to remit the full amount by the end of the month; but she paid no penalty for neglecting to settle the account until May 8.[72]

Whether debtors had to pay interest or not, a day of reckoning for payment of the bill eventually arrived—weeks, months, or years later, or even after death.[73] Except for the occasional use of barter (see chap. 1), customers settled their accounts in specie, and all payments were recorded in moneys of account. Like the international merchants, these petty entrepreneurs—and those in Florence studied by Goldthwaite—"thought" in the current money of account, the lira di piccioli. They were continually called upon to convert the variety of specie in use into this system of accounting. Only rarely did a tradesman record the denominations of coins in local use or of foreign coins in which a payment was made. In Paolo di Ser Ambrogio's record of the remittance to a hauler who delivered some cheese from Pisa, he valued the *bolognini tredici vecchi* at £1 s.8 d.2.[74] For another purchase of cheese from Pisa,

Paolo quoted the price in Florentine currency but specified that part of the payment consisted of Florentine quattrini rather than Pisan specie.[75] Two entries in Giovanni di Paolo's ledger in 1383 value 3 grossi at s.16 ½ and 5 quattrini at £1 d.8.[76] Thus it is clear that, although foreign coins circulated in areas under Florentine hegemony, Florence's own mint provided the basic specie. These small businessmen, involved in repeated and daily exchanges, must have had little difficulty in translating the values into money of account. It also seems likely that the commune of Prato minted a few petty coins and, earlier in the century, a *gigliato pratese* in honor of its Angevin overlord.[77] Prato's Via Zecca, which survives to the present day (it runs from the Via Santa Trinita, a little south of the Piazza San Francesco, to the Via Cicognini), supports the view that Prato minted coins. Further support comes from two references in the latest of the ledgers studied (1408–10), where the broker Matteo di Matteo Toffi specified that a settlement in two land transactions was "a misura pratese e a moneta pratese."[78]

In addition to the foreign money and local silver and billon coins that appear in these records, gold florins abound. Of all the account books surveyed, not one lacks numerous entries involving this prestigious coin. Two ledgers of the druggist Benedetto di Tacco illustrate the extent of their use: thirty-two accounts from 1365 to 1377 and forty from 1382 to 1392 mention florins, many for payments amounting to more than one florin.[79] Almost every time the tradesman made or received payment in gold, he entered the price of the florin in lire, soldi, and denari.[80] From this record it would be possible to construct a series of the price of the florin (i.e., its value in lire di piccioli), year by year and almost month by month, from about 1340 to the end of the century. In some entries the price of the florin is noted twice, both in the text of the entry and in the column to the right.[81] In others the number of florins is noted without a price in the text, but the total value is stated in lire di piccioli.[82] Only rarely are amounts entered in florins without any equivalence in lire di piccioli.[83] Yet the gold florin also appears to have been held somewhat in awe, as was our own gold currency at the turn of the century; sometimes it was used as a pawn (see chap. 6).

The extent to which florins circulated in the various levels of society has been a subject of debate. A few years ago Richard Goldthwaite, on the basis of his research on the Florentine building trades in the fifteenth century, was able to assert that "gold, far from being confined by the social barriers scholars have erected around it, commonly passed through the hands of ordinary men."[84] His statement applies to the fourteenth century as well, even in a "backwater" center like Prato.[85] Carlo Cipolla's view that in Florence the clothiers, bankers, merchant houses, moneylenders, doctors, lawyers, and big landed proprietors were virtually the only ones to handle florins needs reevaluation. Also open to question is his assertion that the two parallel monetary systems caused widespread tension and unrest between the classes.[86]

Numerous references in the account books of the artisans and shopkeepers of Prato clearly establish their familiarity with gold florins, but who were the customers making payments in gold? When Messer Niccolò di Cambioni bought a robe for his wife, he made one of his payments to the tailor Domenico di Jacopo with 2 florins; Francesco di Marco Datini gave the cheese seller Paolo di Ser Ambrogio a florin to pass on to the hauler who had brought him some skins from Lucca.[87] Such payments in florins by the well-to-do were not out of the ordinary. More surprising are the payments of 2 and 3 florins for a feather mattress by the baker Nanni.[88] And most surprising—one of many recent indications that gold coins circulated at even the lowest level of Pratese society—is the payment of florins by the construction partners to the unskilled laborers Bartolomeo and Duccio as loans or advances.[89]

Evidence from the few published accounts of medieval tradesmen in France and Germany suggest that the extension of credit to customers and the securing of debts were not confined to the more highly developed Italian economy. A list of debtors from fragments of an unknown draper's accounts at Lyon, running from 1320 to 1323, shows sales on credit to local customers and the occasional use of a guarantor to secure a debt.[90] Ten years later (1330–32) in the small town of Forcalquier in Provence, another draper, named Ugo Teralh, extended credit to his customers and required guarantors, acknowledgement of the debt in the borrower's own hand, and occasionally a notarial deed.[91] In 1340–41, while Giovanni di Spinello sold cloth on credit at

Prato, Jean Saval did the same at Carcassonne, often indicating the amount still owed after a partial payment.[92] Far more extensive records of credit operations were found in two account books of the Bonis brothers at Montauban in Languedoc, running from 1345 to 1368.[93] The brothers sold cloth, spices, and pharmaceutical products locally and also engaged in banking and moneylending on the side; at the end of ledger C they recorded a total of more than 551 *livres tournois* in receivables from customers.[94] In Nuremberg the account book of the Holzschuhers, a family of drapers, shows credit sales as early as 1304–7,[95] often including the names of witnesses to verify transactions. Apparently the family confined their credit sales to nobles, clerics, and burghers, for no peasants or laborers are recorded. Later in the century (1367–92) at Hamburg, the merchant Vickos von Geldersen, who kept his accounts in both Latin and German, combined an import-export trade in cloth with local credit sales of a variety of commodities.[96]

While these few examples of the use of credit in France and Germany suggest that it played some role in the local economies of those countries, the operators are in a far different class from the tradesmen of Prato. The Bonis brothers and Vickos von Geldersen clearly were international merchants, even though they made some retail sales—as did many of the large international firms in Florence. The other French and German tradesmen all were engaged in the cloth sector of the economy and operated on at least a regional as well as local level. At Prato, however, the petty entrepreneurs confined their business to local customers; and credit, as illustrated by the accounts of all the tradesmen, was widely used in exchanges of all commodities at the local level, including victuals. All members of society were enmeshed in a vast network of credit relations.

This widespread extension of credit in Prato, and presumably in other areas of central and northern Italy, leads one to question some of the assumptions previously made by economic historians. Far from operating on a primitive basis of barter or modest cash exchanges, the Pratesi plied their trades in a fully developed market economy. At the lower end of the economic spectrum, the wage earner could shop for food before payday. At a higher level, the petty entrepreneur was far more integrated into the world of the wealthy industrialist and merchant banker than previously imagined. Credit provided a ready means of exchange between classes, just as the florin circulated at all levels. The inability of the state at times to supply enough specie for the marketplace presented no acute problem because charge account "money" was widespread. A temporary financial setback did not necessitate recourse to a pawnbroker. Deferment of payment—even for years—was a readily available alternative. The roots of our modern credit economy extend deep into the society of fourteenth-century Tuscany—even into the lower ranks of provincial towns like Prato.

CHAPTER

Six

Loans

It is generally believed that pawnbrokers provided the majority of small loans in late medieval society and that these were largely distress loans for consumption, while larger loans for business purposes came from merchant bankers and affluent individuals. In Prato the *recordanze* of Bartolo di Lapo contain entries for loans to many private parties from 1346 to 1369.[1] The earliest evidence of moneylending in Prato comes from the accounts of the professional moneylender Sinibaldo. His surviving records from June 1285 to April 1286 consist exclusively of entries for loans and for subsequent repayments, without any explanation of the reasons for the loans; he used a notarial document as security for each loan rather than accepting pawns (see chap. 5 for Sinibaldo's use of notaries, even for small loans). A manifest usurer, he explicitly stated interest charges ranging from 10 to 40 percent. During the ten-month period of the extant records he made 175 loans for a total of £2,260, or about 1,256 florins; the amount per loan averaged £12 s.18, or 7.17 florins.[2]

The evidence from the sources in Prato substantiates the importance and prevalence of small loans in the local economy but suggests that shopkeepers, not pawnbrokers, were the principal moneylenders. Although pawnbrokers operated in the Pratese district during the second half of the fourteenth century and the first decade of the fifteenth, references to them are few. Guido Pampaloni cites the pawnbrokers Benedetto and Tommaso in 1366, Niccolò in 1384, and Biagio in 1390;[3] Enrico Fiumi mentions a certain Toringello among the 120 Florentines living in Pratese territory in 1361;[4] and both note Salomone the Jew and Benedetto di Filippo Amadori, *tavoliere di Firenze,* at the beginning of the following century.[5] Benedetto, however, probably was not classified as a pawnbroker in the Pratese terminology of the time, which distinguished between lending *(prestatore)* as a pawnbroker and as a banker *(tavoliere* or *banchiere).*[6] This Benedetto di Filippo is likely the merchant banker who is mentioned many times in the shopkeepers' account books at the end of the fourteenth century and the beginning of the fifteenth.[7]

Without providing any documentation other than the names of the people cited above as moneylenders, Pampaloni and Fiumi generalize on the importance and widespread activity of pawnbrokers in the Pratese district. After stressing the Jewish presence, Pampaloni concludes that it is "logical to think" that Christian pawnbrokers were also active, although they are rarely mentioned in the documents because they had to hide these activities to escape condemnation for usury.[8] While Fiumi also assigned to the Jews a predominant position in moneylending in the city, he adds that the Florentine Christians preferred to ply their trade in the Pratese countryside, which offered larger profits and fewer restrictions.[9]

A few more pawnbrokers *(prestatori)* who are so identified in Prato in the fourteenth century can be added to the list of those cited by Pampaloni and Fiumi. The pawnbroker Piero made payments twice in 1378 for clients of the doublet maker Marco di Sandro.[10] The son-in-law of the pawnbroker Sozzo appears in an entry of the grain seller Stefano di Cecco.[11] The pawnbrokers Niccolò and Bindo di Bartolo (probably brothers), who came from the village of Calenzano, visited the inn of Ferro di Cambio in 1376.[12] Two years later the pawnbroker Michele Dagliagli stopped by; and in 1407–8 Ciapelano, described in the inn's accounts as someone "who loans on pawn," was twice a guest of Ferro's son Cambio di Ferro.[13] In the books of other tradesmen, four more pawnbrokers show up in entries for loans made by the tradesmen. Three of these loans were made to people who needed to pay off their debts to pawnbrokers. The cheese seller Paolo di Ser Ambrogio lent a customer s.14 in order to pay the pawnbroker Checco.[14] In 1372 the druggist Benedetto di Tacco lent £2 s.4 to a customer so that he could retrieve a pledge from the pawnbroker Andrea di Matteo.[15] And in 1390 the cheese seller Giovanni di Paolo paid the pawnbroker Gherardo £2 s.4 so that Monna Buona di Gianni, from the village of Schignano, could repossess the bell she had left as security.[16] The fourth loan, for £40, was made by Giovanni directly to the pawnbroker Agnolo Giannini, who repaid it in two installments: f.10 on February 8 (the year is uncertain) and s.10 a week later, on February 15.[17]

The moneylending activity of local shopkeepers, however, went far beyond the four loans cited above. In fact, the prominence of moneylending in their business activities would almost lead one to believe that there was no need for pawnbrokers in the Pratese district. The use of terms such as the verb *prestare* and the nouns *prestito* and *prestanza* leaves no doubt that a loan has been granted; and where, infrequently, another verb such as *avere* or *accettare* is used, the context clearly indicates a loan. Throughout the second half of the fourteenth century and into the first decade of the fifteenth, loan entries turn up in all of the shopkeepers' account books, and these entries number in the hundreds; even the wife of one shopkeeper granted loans.[18] Other tradesmen also lent money, although less often. The grain seller Stefano di Cecco made loans to his customers as well as to other people who appear in entries only as borrowers; during the eight months covered by his register he made forty-six loans.[19] The partners of the walling company made frequent loans to their employees, both skilled and unskilled, although these perhaps can best be characterized as advances on salary (see chap. 2).

The number of loans on some pages in the account books of the druggist Benedetto di Tacco seem almost to suggest that he was a moneylender, not a retail druggist. In his earliest ledger Benedetto made loans to at least sixty-four customers, many of whom received more than one loan while their accounts remained open.[20] Throughout Benedetto's fifty-year career (1344–93) moneylending played an important part in his business activity. His ledger from June 1365 to August 1378 and his supplementary journal from May 1369 to September 1376 show 933 loans.[21] For one two-year period, from 1371 to 1373,

almost 50 percent of the 231 accounts in his main register include at
least one loan.[22] His last register, which follows 215 accounts from
April, 1388, to April, 1390, has loan entries in 51 accounts.[23]

The size of tradesmen's loans and the time allowed for repayment
varied widely. Many loans remained outstanding for as long as two
years; others were repaid within a few days, or on the next day or even
the same day.[24] Their sizes ranged from d.8 to an unusually high £450;
but loans larger than a few lire were rare.[25] The average size of the 177
loans in the earliest ledger of the druggist Benedetto di Tacco is only
s.15, and his loans in later registers are equally small.[26] The 14 loans that
the cheese seller Giovanni di Paolo made from September 1380 to September 1381 averaged s.18 d.8; the 142 loans made by the tailor
Domenico di Jacopo from 1385 to 1409 averaged only £1 s.17, including 19 that were made in florins.[27] A closer look at the extent and size
of the loans granted by Benedetto di Tacco, who recorded more loans
per year than any other tradesman, illustrates the nature of these
moneylending activities. During the ten-year period from 1345 to
1355, when the average size of Benedetto's 177 loans was only s.15,[28]
the largest was for £6 to the baker Agnolo di Chele, and 27 were for s.2
or less.[29] Benedetto lent an average of only a little more than £13 per
year during this period. In some later years he engaged in far more extensive moneylending. For example, in 1370 alone he made 90 loans
for a total of £61 s.17 d.2 (see chap. 2); yet the average loan still was
smaller than a lira.

The borrowers represent a cross section of Pratese society. They
came from all walks of life and from the city as well as the countryside.
The druggist Paolo di Bonaccorso di Tano lent £2 to a fellow druggist
in Pistoia. The tailor Domenico di Jacopo made five loans to Friar Bartolomeo of Poggibonsi.[30] A laborer from the country borrowed £1 s.4
in 1384; a meat cutter named Gherardo, s.2 d.8 in 1366; the blacksmith
Jacopo, 3 florins in 1396; a priest from the collegiate church of Santo
Stefano, s.5 in 1387; Giovanni di Bartolomeo Saccagnini, a member of
the wealthiest family in Prato, s.5 in 1369.[31] The range and variety of
the borrowers' occupations suggest a workforce typical of small Italian
cities and their environs in the fourteenth century. In addition to those
named so far, the borrowers included an apprentice to a druggist, a

farmer, a weaver, a potter, a miller, a baker, a shoemaker, a greengrocer, a wool merchant, a rector of a hospital, a constable of the podestà, a mayor of a village, and so forth. Even the commune of Prato borrowed f.2 from the druggist Benedetto di Tacco in order to pay servants *(fanti);* the communal treasurer repaid the loan within a month.[32]

Women appear as borrowers throughout the entire period studied. Fifty-eight, or approximately 3 percent, of the borrowers were women, and some took out more than one loan. Shulamith Shahar holds that married women by law could not borrow money,[33] but such a prohibition, if it existed at Prato, did not deter these women. Monna Buona di Gianni obtained a loan of £3 s.10 on September 9, 1390, and another of s.18 on September 19, 1391, both from the cheese seller Giovanni di Paolo.[34] The abbess of the convent of San Marco borrowed f.4 from the tailor Domenico di Jacopo in 1387; the tailor settled the debt two years later for only f.1 £3.[35] Some twenty years earlier, four married women borrowed from the druggist Benedetto di Tacco.[36] When women are identified only by their given names, determination of social, economic, or marital status presents a problem. Monna Jacopa, mother of Ser Meo, who borrowed £1 from the cheese seller Paolo di Ser Ambrogio, undoubtedly was a widow as her husband's name is not included.[37] Pietà di Santa Trinita, whom Benedetto di Tacco lent s.7, may have been single, married, a nun, or a secular employee of the convent.[38]

To secure or verify loans, the tradesmen employed devices similar to those used in the granting of credit. Unlike the moneylender Sinibaldo in the previous century, they never used notarial documents to secure their loans. By this time entries in an account book represented legal evidence in the Florentine territory. Some borrowers of all classes deposited pawns as security for their loans: a laborer left a knife, a potter a red coat, Messer Guccio di Roldolfo a belt.[39] The term *pegno* (pawn) was customarily used to describe such transactions, but sometimes the term *segnale* (marker) appears, or the object alone is mentioned in order to indicate that something of value has been given.[40] Typical pawns were tools, household utensils, and clothing; and the value of the pawn appears always to have exceeded the amount of the loan. The only luxury items left as pawns were a necklace of twenty-two pearls and a breviary, both accepted by Benedetto di Tacco for loans of 1 and 6 florins respectively.[41] He must have had second thoughts about the breviary, however. After his apprentice Cristofano had picked it up at the home of the borrower, Monna Castella, but before she had made any payments, Benedetto returned it to her at his house.[42]

A somewhat different kind of pawn was the gold florin. In Benedetto di Tacco's accounts, the florin was used as a pawn far more often than all other objects combined. It appears throughout his fifty-year career, used always for loans smaller in value than the florin.[43] At no time did Benedetto describe these florins, nor, apparently, did their value in moneys of account vary from the actual exchange rates as we know them from Florentine records. Even laborers offered florins as security for their loans: in 1384 a laborer from the countryside borrowed £1 s.4 from Benedetto, left a florin as security, paid the £1 s.4 a month later, and got back a florin.[44] The phrase accompanying the account entry—"as a pawn"—clearly indicates that Benedetto regarded the florin as security for the loan, not a credit to be drawn on.[45] In some of Benedetto's accounts, however, florins did function as credit, on which the borrower could draw for additional loans or purchases as long as he did not overdraw his account. The concluding entries in these accounts show that Benedetto returned the florins when customers paid the total owed.[46] In one instance the entire operation was negotiated in one day: Cione from the village of Castelnuovo borrowed s.20, left a florin, paid the loan "the said day," and received the florin back "the said day."[47] In other accounts the function of the florin changed with time: after being called a pawn in the opening entry, the florin served as a deposit on which the customer drew credit for further loans or purchases, eventually receiving the balance in cash. On July 20, 1376, Giorgio Martini borrowed £1 s.10 and left a florin as a pledge. After two more loans increased his total indebtedness to £2 s.10, he received £1 s.3 d.4, the balance of the florin's value.[48]

As an alternative to a pawn, tradesmen could require a personal guarantor to secure a loan. This method proved equally reliable only when the guarantor was a creditor of the tradesman in excess of the amount he had guaranteed. In one instance, the guarantor was a corporate body rather than an individual: Antonio d'Andreotto borrowed one florin from the doublet maker Marco di Sandro and pledged the trust of his company ("la sua fede di compagnia") to assure repayment. Even so, the debt was never repaid. What the doublet maker may have presumed to be a more reliable kind of guarantor proved otherwise.[49]

In the absence of a pawn or a personal guarantor, shopkeepers sometimes recorded the name of one or more witnesses to verify a loan. Like, those who verified credit transactions, these witnesses came from all walks of life, some apparently chosen because they happened to be present. When the two rectors of the well-known Hospital of the Misericordia borrowed 20 florins from Benedetto di Tacco, he noted that a third rector, Ser Filippo di Messer Tedaldo, and the baker Berto were present as he handed over the money.[50] A tradesman usually wrote witnesses' names himself, but sometimes, particularly when a large loan was made, the witnesses signed their own names.[51] On one occasion the tailor Domenico di Jacopo went into detail to describe how he and his wife Margherita happened to provide written verification of a debt transaction. They were having dinner at the home of Filippo in the nearby village of Figline, when Filippo paid a florin he owed to Monna Cristofona, another guest at the dinner. Domenico and his wife signed a statement confirming the event and giving the year, month, and day.[52]

Rather than asking for third-party verification, the shopkeeper sometimes requested a written receipt from the borrower—a practice not found in the granting of credit for purchases. A written receipt, however, was used only for larger loans. The ledger of the tailor Domenico di Jacopo includes two loans in 1373, for 7 and 10 florins, both entered in the handwriting of the debtors together with a date for reimbursement. As so often happened when a maturity date was designated, the borrowers failed to meet the deadline: the 7 florins were repaid a month late, the 10 florins five months late.[53] A receipt that the cheese seller Paolo di Ser Ambrogio obtained from the rector of the Hospital of the Misericordia for a smaller loan was written on a small slip of paper. It reads, "I, Stefano di Cone, rector of the Hospital of the Misericordia, was told by Paolo di Ser Ambrogio that he paid to Lorenzo di Giovanni, £2, and to Giovanni Martini, £3."[54] From the corresponding entry in the hospital's account book we learn that Paolo made both these payments on behalf of the hospital for guard duty the two men performed. In Paolo's ledger, however, the payments are reversed: Lorenzo is said to have received £3, Giovanni £2. Paolo also noted that his credit of £5 had been entered in the hospital's book.[55] He similarly confirmed some of his other credits by reference to a debtor's account book.

Tradesmen's own written records of the circumstances in which loans were granted may sometimes have served as verification, or at least as a prompt to the memory of a borrower. If someone other than the borrower came to pick up the money, the tradesman recorded that person's name in the entry; if the borrower received the money in person, the lender might add the phrase "in his hand" (*in sua mano*) to emphasize this circumstance. The location where the transaction took place was specified in a number of entries, for example, the lender's or borrower's store or house, a tavern, the palace of the podestà, the communal square, or the square of the collegiate church of Santo Stefano. Other personal information occasionally was included. The tailor Domenico di Jacopo, after indicating the date and location of his repayment of a loan of 3 florins from Monna Lapa, added that she was at the time suffering with a sore mouth ("quando avea male nella bocca").[56]

The most common way of identifying a loan was to give the reason for it. As a result, the tradesmen's books reveal many of the needs of borrowers at that time. Payment of taxes, direct and indirect, heads the list;[57] everyone but the well-to-do must have found it difficult to keep on hand the necessary cash to meet these fiscal obligations, even when the amount was quite small. In other areas of Italy, Jewish moneylenders apparently fulfilled the function of assuring the availability of cash for the tax coffers. Reinhold Mueller has documented this service by Jewish moneylenders in Venice toward the end of the fourteenth century, and Anthony Molho describes the successful efforts of Arezzo city officials of the same period to obtain permission from the Florentine authorities for Jewish moneylenders to settle there.[58] In Prato the ubiquitous salt tax was mentioned most frequently as the reason for a loan. Everyone except the very young was required to purchase a certain amount of salt from the state at a set price, even people who lived at a bare subsistence level.[59] Other taxes given as reasons for loans were the estimo, or *libra,* and the indirect gabella.[60]

A list of reasons for loan requests would fill many pages. A few examples will illustrate their variety. Giovanni di Messer Guido needed £2 s.17 to pay the wages of two laborers from Porta Santa Trinità.[61] Filippo of Figline needed 6 florins (which he borrowed from the tailor Domenico di Jacopo) to buy land and pay the transfer tax.[62] Two carders needed s.4 d.6 each, representing the price of a pair of combs in 1348, to purchase the tools of their trade.[63] Typical of consumption loans were s.3 to purchase millet, £4 for a little pig, and £8 for wine.[64]

As recorded, only a small fraction of the loans granted by the tradesmen of Prato involved a pawn, guarantor, witness, signed receipt, or any additional identifying information. The vast majority—far more than 75 percent—were entered in the books with only a name and an amount, apparently granted on simple verbal agreement, whether the borrower was a *messer* or a laborer. Borrowers on trust represented the whole gamut of occupations.[65] The pawnbroker Agnolo Giannini himself, who surely would have required ample security before lending to any of his own customers, was able to get a loan of £40 from the cheese seller Giovanni di Paolo without any accompanying security or verification.[66]

The collection rate for these loans exceeded the average 95 percent rate for the debit balances of purchases on credit (see chap. 5). Of the seven account books analyzed for loans, only one, that of the cheese seller Giovanni di Paolo, shows a collection rate lower than 98 percent. Giovanni made 190 loans for a total of £820 s.14 and collected all but 12 of these, worth £41, making his collection rate 95 percent.[67] Of the 71 loans made by the doublet maker Marco di Sandro, which averaged £4 s.5 per loan (larger than the average size of any other shopkeeper's loans), only 4, totaling s.87, proved uncollectible—a collection rate of 98.5 percent.[68] The tailor Domenico di Jacopo failed to collect only s.5 from loans totaling £262 s.3—a rate close to 100 percent.[69] The druggist Benedetto di Tacco had a collection rate higher than 98 percent on loans from 1344 to 1393.[70] In two of the books covering 1365–78, only one loan of s.5 in his ledger was unpaid, and the daily journal (1369–76) recorded no unpaid loans.[71]

Some tradesmen may have refrained from charging interest on credit for purchases because these transactions involved a profit margin in any case. But it is highly unlikely that the large number of loans made by most shopkeepers were interest free. That only an occasional hint of an interest charge is found in the loan accounts must be attributable to the usury doctrine. The expression *per grazia e per amore,* which the cheese seller Paolo di Ser Ambrogio used with three of his loans, was a standard formula to imply that interest was not involved when usually the opposite was the case.[72] The lowering of a debt for one of his customers who repaid in advance of the maturity date (to £.1 less than the amount due) may represent a reduction in an interest charge.[73] Raymond de Roover lists various euphemisms the shopkeepers employed to refer to interest: *prode* (yield), *costo* (cost), *guadagno* (gain), *dono* or *donamento* (gift or gratuity), and *merito* (reward).[74]

Like Sinibaldo, however, the tradesmen occasionally spelled out interest charges in special entries, generally designated as *memoriali.* These entries were set apart from an individual's day-to-day accounts to keep track of large loans with all the conditions. In light of the decree of the Council of Vienne declaring that account books constituted evidence of usury, it is surprising that the tradesmen kept such potentially damaging records. These *memoriali* include both borrowing and lending by the tradesmen and sometimes reveal how interest was camouflaged.

In one *memoriale,* dated June 6, 1385, the tailor Domenico di Jacopo recorded a loan of f.70 to Marco di Pino from Figline but added that Marco had given him written receipt for a loan of f.90, not the f.70 he actually received—a device often employed to camouflage interest.[75] This subterfuge had a long history. Toward the close of the Duecento, a borrower of the Florentine Gentile de'Sassetti received 60 florins and promised in a letter obligatory to repay 67 florins;[76] in 1333 in Santa Maria Impruneta a moneylender confessed in his will that he was owed 90½ florins and 37 staia of grain but had lent only 68 florins and no grain;[77] in 1401 a wool manufacturer made a loan of 20 florins but had it notarized as 22 florins;[78] in 1450 Francesco di Matteo Castellani signed an agreement in a banker's book to repay a loan of 110 florins when (as he tells us in his own accounts) he had in fact borrowed only 100 florins.[79] In other words, what the official record stated, regardless of the form it took, was what the borrower paid, not what he actually received—the difference being the interest charge.

Domenico di Jacopo followed this procedure for the loan to Marco di Pino but ended up exposing his false receipt by including in the same entry a reference to the interest. The charge on the seven-month loan of 70 florins was 14 staia of grain, or about 15 percent interest at the current price of grain.[80] In another *memoriale* Domenico mentioned interest again, indicating the rate charged for money he himself borrowed in July 1389. This was a loan of 12 florins for a term of thirty-one months, made in the presence of three witnesses and with a cheese seller acting as guarantor. When Domenico returned the 12 florins in February 1392, he paid an additional 9 florins as *pro,* or interest of about 30 percent per year.[81] Finally, on the page where that loan had first been recorded, Domenico referred to interest in connection with a third loan, on which the charge was reduced for early repayment. The interest on that loan of 10 florins—borrowed for a year at a charge of 3 florins, was reduced to f.2 £1 s.17 when he remitted two months early, reflecting an annual rate of about 30 percent adjusted to the period of ten months.[82]

Additional evidence for interest-bearing loans is found in the register of the broker Matteo di Matteo Toffi. When he recorded loans to which he was not a party, but rather a witness providing a written record, he included the rate of interest and the terms of the agreement (including, in one case, his lack of a commission fee).[83] For nine of the ten loans of this type that he recorded, the borrower paid 30 percent interest; for the other, the borrower paid 25 percent.[84] In contrast, when Matteo recorded his own moneylending activity, he avoided any mention of interest.[85]

Large loans like those recorded by Domenico di Jacopo and Matteo di Matteo Toffi are not found in the other account books of the Pratese tradesmen. The books make it clear, however, that small cash loans and extension of credit for purchases were readily available from all the tradesmen and for all members of society. These arrangements facilitated sales and increased liquidity in the marketplace. Far from primitive, this local economy possessed a certain modern sophistication and diversity. The following chapter, which considers banking activities in Prato, further explores the multiplicity of financial services on the local level.

Seven

Banking and the Local Economy

$\mathscr{D}$uring the last years of his life Federigo Melis devoted much of his research to the early history of modern deposit banking. Although other business historians, such as Raymond de Roover, have studied in greater detail some of the credit instruments essential to present-day financial institutions,[1] Melis was the first to probe the Tuscan sources in order to discover the elusive origins of modern banking. In keeping with his view that local tradesmen had no access to credit beyond an occasional loan from a pawnbroker, Melis believed that it was unnecessary to include local economies in his story.[2] A brief review of the steps he outlined for the evolution of banking will set the stage for considering whether the widespread use of credit by local fourteenth-century tradesmen should be included in the history of banking. Since it was the latter half of the fourteenth century, in Melis's view, that produced the essential ingredients of modern banking, the abundant available sources on Prato provide contemporaneous data for addressing this question.

Melis first established the function of credit as the linchpin of modern banking. He then enumerated the three successive forms of credit that underlie this financial institution: (1) credit that provides the original capital for the formation of businesses, (2) credit that allows for enlargement of capital to expand businesses, and (3) the "line of credit" *(credito di esercizio),* or availability of cash flow, that allows businesses to operate flexibly and smoothly. The first two Melis found present by the thirteenth century within the operations of partnerships. Melis also recognized that additional capital needs beyond the investments of the partners could be satisfied by outsiders, whose contributions were of a long-term, fixed nature—time deposits similar to modern bonds. In his view, however, it was not until the second half of the fourteenth century, when lenders began to employ a line of credit based on trust *(fiducia),* that all the conditions necessary for the functioning of modern deposit banking were present. Certainly, the emergence of the line of credit was an essential step in the development of banking and the rise of capitalism, even if Melis overstated its importance.[3] An investigation of this third stage in the use of credit will tell us whether Melis erred in excluding the local operators from any role in the development of deposit banking.

Surprisingly, Melis failed to probe for an answer to the fundamental question of the antecedents of credito di esercizio and why it arose in the second half of the fourteenth century. He sidestepped the issue and turned to a somewhat intuitive explanation: "The businessmen of the second half of the fourteenth century could not fail to comprehend through their ever more penetrating comprehension of business methods the inconvenience inherent in both long-term or too short-term financing by loans, one of which would lead to money lying idle, the other to not enough money to accomplish their purpose."[4] Such a statement, though true enough, adds little in a quest for origins. He proceeded to compare the need for a line of credit to similar needs for more efficient transportation and for the protection afforded by insurance.[5] Such comparisons fail to illuminate the origins of credito di esercizio. Melis planned to devote a subsequent volume to the history of banking and perhaps would then have given a meaningful explanation for the development of credito di esercizio. The scholars who have followed in his footsteps have also failed to confront this omission.

Though the modern line of credit, based on trust in the reliability of the borrower, embodies most of the aspects of Melis's credito di esercizio, a search for its roots requires identification of the essential elements that distinguish this type of loan from others. With a line of credit loans are granted (1) automatically, (2) for any required amount (with a probable maximum cap), (3) for a flexible period of time, and

(4) with no security required. Melis further specified in his definition of credito de esercizio that the grantor of the loan should be a third party set up formally as a "banking" institution.

Purchases through credit by businesses to meet defined business needs clearly were characteristic of the local economy of Prato (see chap. 5). Numerous entries in the account books of Giovanni di Spinello Viviani (1337–47) and Benedetto de Tacco (1344–58) confirm the widespread use of credit even before 1350,[6] and the practice appears in all the subsequent registers surveyed. Paolo di Ser Ambrogio's debit ledger, devoted almost exclusively to his purchases of cheese and other products for his store, presents a detailed and comprehensive portrayal of his continual and frequent use of credit granted by his suppliers during the last decade of the fourteenth century and the first decade of the following one. Not only did a climate of *fiducia* prevail in Prato before the mid-fourteenth century, but the extension of credit to local tradesmen included all of the characteristics of a line of credit enumerated by Melis except the presence of a third party as the grantor. When making their purchases, petty entrepreneurs for the most part did not pay the full amount at the time of sale; just as they extended credit to their customers, they "automatically" obtained from their suppliers unsecured loans with no fixed schedule of return payments. Repayment could stretch over months or years, whichever was convenient.

During most of the fourteenth century the supplier himself granted credit to the tradesmen, but toward the end of the century references to a third party begin to appear: a merchant banker, intervening as middleman for the local tradesmen in their purchases. Why did a third party become necessary? Even today, when businesses can easily obtain a line of credit from a bank, many tradesmen turn directly to the wholesale supplier for their financing. The retailer can order the amount he needs and remit on predetermined terms; he has recourse to a bank only if he desires inventory from a supplier who is unable or unwilling to extend credit to him. This modern analogy provides insight into what may have happened in the second half of the fourteenth century. When a supplier could not provide financing and the shopkeeper either lacked cash or preferred not to tie up too much of it, new solutions became necessary. Local suppliers usually granted credit, but suppliers at a distance from Prato for the most part did not.

Some records of the cloth seller Giovanni di Spinello showing products he bought at a distance from Prato illustrate the limits on the credit during the first half of the fourteenth century. For supplies from a Florentine merchant in 1338, Giovanni paid the whole price of £75 the same day; in September 1344 he paid another Florentine supplier a total of £24 s.4, half on the day of sale and the rest only two days later.[7] A month later he purchased 389 pounds of wool from the partners Mazzio and Jacopo of San Miniato, about 25 miles away, at a price of £48 s.12 d.6. He paid £20 in cash the same day and £23 s.16 d.6 within five days, and then waited a few months before remitting the small remaining balance of £4 s.16 on January 10, 1345.[8] Similarly, in 1380 the cheese seller Giovanni di Paolo made sales to a Florentine cheese seller without extending credit, in spite of the removal after 1351 of any legal obstacle to the collection of debts. (Before 1351 Prato would have constituted, at least de jure, a separate city-state; but with complete Florentine hegemony, recourse to legal authority to collect a debt was the same at Prato as at Florence.) Giovanni sold the Florentine 106 pounds of dried meat for 11 florins and collected in full on the same day. He continued to supply this Florentine, but each time the hauler delivered the products he picked up the cash in full for Giovanni.[9] Similarly, when Paolo di Ser Ambrogio went to Pisa in 1390 with Francesco di Mazzeo to purchase cheese, he had to borrow cash from his companion to pay the hauler, who apparently was reluctant to extend credit.[10] In 1396 Giuliano di Giovanni Bertelli, one of the brothers in the paper manufacturing firm, paid for supplies from a Pisan firm on the day of purchase.[11] These examples reveal a more circumspect approach on the part of suppliers when dealing with buyers at a distance or from a separate jurisdiction. This is not surprising; the business environment of long-distance transactions was not the same as in a local marketplace where most tradesmen knew each other and a single set of laws and customs prevailed.

The apparent reluctance of suppliers to extend credit to a tradesman who lived at a distance could create problems. Unless the prospective purchaser had anticipated the need and accumulated the required cash, he was forced to look elsewhere for the funds for wholesale purchases, the size of which substantially exceeded individual retail sales. He needed a middleman—a source of credit similar to that granted by his local suppliers, who provided funds for purchases and then allowed him sufficient time to repay the loans. There was at hand just such a middleman, the local and often familiar merchant banker, who mingled financial endeavors with commercial interests. The entrepreneur had the funds to pay for purchases in full or the requisite *fiducia* to obtain credit from the distant supplier. For fulfilling this essential role, he then could expect from the local tradesman a proper remuneration in the form of interest for the loan he had granted. As long as the tradesman had the reputation of living up to his financial obligations, the local merchant banker would have no hesitation in allowing him the same convenient payment terms that local suppliers customarily offered.

Near the close of the fourteenth century, this apparently is what happened. The tradesmen began to turn to merchant bankers to obtain their supplies on credit. The ledger of the cheese seller Paolo di Ser Ambrogio provides numerous examples of the services of a merchant banker. On March 1, 1391, Paolo purchased 116 pounds of Bolognese eels at a price of £20 s.6 through the agency of the merchant banker *(tavoliere)* Lodovico de Ser Jacopo. Ten days later he paid Lodovico £16, and on April 3 he extinguished the debt by paying £4 s.6.[12] The following year, between May and August, Paolo again employed Lodovico for three separate purchases of cheese. He made a partial return payment in June to Nanni di Ser Jacopo, the brother and partner of Lodovico; on October 14 he settled the major part of the obligation by means of an offset of more than £30 that a wool merchant owed him and which Lodovico had guaranteed.[13] Lodovico and his brothers were not Paolo's only bankers, however.[14] In 1392 Paolo employed the services of the banker Lapo di Turingo to purchase a barrel of cheese and took five months to settle the account.[15] About the same time, the druggist Paolo di Bonaccorso di Tano began calling upon Lodovico and Nanni for credit; he used overdrafts on his current account with the bankers in order to make payments to suppliers.[16]

By the last decades of the fourteenth century, the Pratese tradesmen used local bankers for many services in addition to a line of credit. For example, bankers sometimes paid debts for their clients, made loans on their behalf, or transferred funds directly from one person's account to another's. The earliest reference to one of these new services was recorded on July 2, 1366, in the account book of the tailor Domenico di Jacopo; the previous October Domenico had loaned £44 to a doublet maker to buy a house, and the book shows that the repayment in July of £42 came from the banker Ser Jacopo, "come aparisce in su libro di Ser Jacopo, tavolieri" (as it appears in the book of Ser Jacopo, banker). Domenico gave no reason for closing the account before the reimbursement was complete (it fell short by £2).[17] Twenty years later, on January 5, 1384, the cheese seller Giovanni di Paolo employed the services of a banker, Simone di Ser Michele, in order to make a loan of £75 s.6 d.8 to another Pratese.[18] An entry in Giovanni's account book at the end of the century provides a possible example of a giro. On March 2, 1397, Giovanni noted a number of sales to Ser Andrea for a total price of £9 s.18; a subsequent entry in the same account shows that on May 2 a banker, Fazino di Ser Stefano, credited Giovanni's bank account ("puose a mia ragione") with £6 s.10 and on the same day gave him £3 s.8 in cash ("mi diede di contanti").[19] Whether Ser Andrea ordered payment from an account with the banker, or whether he paid the banker cash to be credited to Giovanni's account, cannot be determined. Since we have no corresponding entry for either of the other parties, we can be sure only that the debtor Ser Andrea fulfilled his obligation through a banker as the intermediary.[20]

In the registers of the cheese seller Paolo di Ser Ambrogio, twenty-eight entries indicate the use of a banker for all of the services ordinarily associated with a current account.[21] Paolo made a cash deposit, payable on demand, with the banker Benedetto di Filippo for the large sum of £70 ("settante di grossi") and 13 florins ("sette gravi e sei nuovi"); he received credit from the same banker for a deposit of £11 by the innkeeper Cambio di Ferro; he paid a debt to the cheese seller Bosco d'Andrea through the banker Fazino di Ser Stefano; and he ordered Fazino to pay a debt of f.32 s.19 d.2 to the banker Ser Conte di Nerozzo.[22] All told, Paolo employed the services of eight bankers, and only in the final years of his ledger (1405–11) did one of these, Benedetto di Filippo, appear to have become his regular banker.[23]

The druggist Paolo di Bonaccorso di Tano actually had a current account with a banking firm, a relationship that illustrates local trades-men's increased involvement with bankers by the last decade of the fourteenth century.[24] This current account of a Pratese druggist can be compared with the nearly contemporary current account of the Pisan druggist Gherardo di Ser Meo. (The latter was reconstructed by Melis from the banker's, not the druggist's records).[25] Gherardo's ac-count with the bank of Donato and Parazone ran for nine months in 1373–74; Paolo's account ran for three years, from December 7, 1392, to February 9, 1396.[26] The Pratese druggist's transactions with the bank cover 5½ folios in his book, with a total of twenty-six debits and cred-its each.[27] Unfortunately, the pages are somewhat mutilated at the bottom, making it impossible to interpret some final entries and to re-construct a remaining balance.[28] The first entry on the opening page (fol. 2r) of the account shows a transaction with Paolo di Bertino Guerzani, "tavoliere"; the second mentions Biagio di Ser Jacopo, also "tavoliere." The final entry on the same page mentions a Giovanni along with Paolo ("a Pauolo e Giovanni"), and on the other five pages Giovanni di Ser Jacopo (often called Nanni) appears along with Paolo di Bertini and Biagioi di Ser Jacopo. In sum, the Pratese druggist had his current account with the banking firm of the sons of Ser Jacopo, members of an illustrious and ancient Pratese family, one of whose an-cestors had been consul in 1211; Paolo di Bertino Guerzani was either an employee or a partner in that firm. Fiumi listed five brothers as sons of Ser Jacopo in the last decades of the Trecento[29]—Stefano, Biagio, Leonardo, Piero, and Giovanni—all of whom, except Piero, appear in our documents as bankers *(tavolieri)*.[30] He neglected to mention an-other brother, however—Lodovico, who also worked in the firm.[31] The business continued into the next generation, for we find refer-ences to Fazino and Pacino di Ser Stefano, grandsons of Ser Jacopo, in the entries of other tradesmen.[32]

There is no way to determine with certainty whether Paolo was opening a new account or whether these entries continued a previous account already active with the bankers. In the latter case one would expect to find, on fol. 2r where the current account commences,[33] a reference to a posting from a former ledger. No such reference appears, but the first entry for the account on fol. 2r dated December 7, 1392, confirms that Paolo had been conducting business with this firm. It shows that on that day he had deposited 3 florins with the banker Paolo di Bertino Guerzani. He did not receive credit for the full amount, but noted that fol. 193 of the bank's book contained a debit for him of £1 s.6 ("fiorini di tre d'oro meno lira e s.sei"), resulting in a balance of f.2 £2 s.12 to be posted to the credit of the druggist.[34]

Although the druggist used his current account only rarely in the conduct of his daily business, the transactions he recorded are typical of those found in other current accounts of the time. The opening entry in his book, which records his deposit of 3 florins, also records a giro—the transferral of £4 from his account to the account of a creditor, Ridolfo di Niccolao—and notes that the giro is recorded on fol. 176 of the bank's register. From the first page onward, the druggist recorded cash transactions of deposits, withdrawals, and payments to third parties by the bank. He did not specify whether his requests to the bank to make third-party payments were verbal or written.

It is not clear whether during the first months of activity in his account the bank allowed the druggist the privilege of overdraft. The first folio of his record (2r) shows a cash withdrawal of s.12 on February 17, 1393, and a resulting overdraft of s.7, an insignificant amount; the next withdrawal of f.1 £5 s.18 is shown as producing a larger debit of £10 s.3. A third withdrawal of s.18 brings the debit to £11 s.1. Two deposits follow, one of £9 from receipts of the store and one of £1 s.17 from a source not identified. The closing entry on that page shows a debit of s.4 ("avere da me in questa ragione—s.4")—the exact amount due the bank after calculating the preceding deposits and withdrawals. However, the second page of transactions with the bank (fol. 8v), which shows only deposits, contradicts this balance. The first six deposits on this page, amounting to f.16 £41, are dated January 7, 1393, through February 1, 1393. Thus, all were made two or more weeks before the noted overdrafts commenced on the previous folio. The deposits would have amply covered those debits. It looks as if Paolo had failed to en-

TABLE 5
Paolo di Bonaccorso's Lapse into Overdraft

Date	Activity	Debits	Credits	Balance
2/10/1393	brought forward		£105 s.12	£105 s.12
2/15/1393	received cash		£3 s.15	£109 s.8
2/22/1393	received cash		£12	£121 s.8
2/22/1393	payment	£13		£108 s.8
2/28/1393	received cash		£33 s.4	£141 s.12
n.d.	payment	£171		(£29 s.8)
n.d.	payment	£1 s.10		(£30.18)
3/26/1393	payment	£34 s.4		(£65 s.2)
3/26/1393	received cash		£9	(£56 s.2)
n.d.	received cash		£12 s.12	(£43 s.10)
n.d.	received cash		£7 s.16	(£35 s.14)
n.d.	received cash		£33	(£2 s.14)

SOURCE: Ceppi 1415, fol. 14v (for an explanation of references to manuscript sources, see "Abbreviations" at the beginning of the notes section).
NOTE: The value of the florin was s.76.

ter his deposits in the usual chronological order and then decided that these deposits should be recorded on a separate page. The opening entry of the third folio (14v) refers to the previous folio (8v) and records a credit balance in the account of f.17 £41.[35]

Nevertheless, the bank did allow Paolo the privilege of overdrafts; and for much of the three-year life of the account it remained in debit. On the third page a credit balance of f.22 £60, dated February 28, 1393 (fol. 14v), was far from adequate to cover the following debit, a payment by the bank to Cristofano di Paolo of 45 florins. At the end of this page the druggist owed £2 s.14 to the bank, and he continued to overdraw his account until final settlement on the sixth and last page (fol. 118r). The first entry of that page, dated March 26, 1395, shows that the druggist owed the bank £20 s.9 ("per resto d'una loro ragione salda con Giovanni"), which he posted from fol. 97v. With five more deposits and no debits, he extinguished his debt and apparently closed the account sometime after February 9, 1396.[36]

The total of Paolo's transactions in his three-year current account was less than a third of the total for the Pisan druggist's current account, which in just nine months came to 461 florins.[37] Both accounts included numerous cash deposits and withdrawals as well as debit and credit transfers with third parties. Paolo's account shows no instance of

a transfer by his bank to another bank to settle an obligation to a third
party, as is found in the Pisan account. The principal contrast between
the two accounts, however, is in the use of overdrafts. Melis thought
that the Pisan druggist might have overdrawn his account a few times,
but could not assert this as a certainty.[38] The Pratese druggist, however, not only occasionally overdrew his account by large amounts, but
maintained a moderate debit for much of the time it was open. He
recorded no payment to the bank for his lengthy use of its money. Similarly, in the extant accounts of fifteenth-century Florentine banking
transactions, no record has been found of interest charges for overdrafts
in either bankers' or clients' books.[39]

Like many well-to-do businessmen and rentiers, local tradesmen
provided services now associated with financial institutions.[40] In addition to frequent lending and extension of credit they engaged in
money changing, accepted deposits, and facilitated transfers of obligations. Although only one entry in the documents of this study shows
money changing and a charge for it, the form of the entry suggests that
money changing may have been a common practice. The entry, which
appears in the waste book of the druggist Benedetto di Tacco, shows a
charge of d.8 for money changing *(canbio di moneta)* at the time of a
purchase of saffron for s.1 d.4; however, only the cost of the saffron is
recorded in the column on the right.[41] It would appear that the mention of the d.8 was somewhat accidental and that the small fee charged
for money changing ordinarily was just dropped in the cash box.[42]

A few tradesmen accepted deposits, some of which were substantial; but customers left them for so brief a time that a tradesman could
not meaningfully use them as operating capital. Two of Benedetto di
Tacco's seventeen depositors[43] entrusted the druggist with sums in excess of £100 but withdrew the total amounts within a few months.
Records of other deposits accepted by tradesmen have been found
from as early as 1338 (in the register of the cloth seller Giovanni di
Spinello) and as late as the first decade of the fifteenth century (in the
ledger of cheese seller Paolo di Ser Ambrogio).[44] Benedetto di Tacco's
records suggest one person's reasons for using a shopkeeper as a
"banker." During the course of each year Monna Pacina Trica made
small deposits of s.2–4 with Benedetto; then once a year he paid her

rent to Brother Alberto.[45] Perhaps she felt the druggist provided safe-keeping for her funds, or she felt she needed the enforcement of a lay-away plan. Depositors probably entrusted funds to a tradesman for short-term security and for the convenience of an occasional offset for purchases from the tradesman or payments by them to third parties.[46] There is no indication that the tradesmen paid interest on these deposits.

The tradesmen's payments to third parties and other services they performed in connection with customers' deposits were the same services bankers provided for holders of current accounts. The ledger of the cheese seller Giovanni di Paolo shows a transfer of 6 florins to the merchant banker Ser Conte di Nerozzo to pay an obligation of one of Giovanni's depositors.[47] In 1339 the cloth seller Giovanni di Spinello performed this kind of transfer to settle one of his own obligations. To repay his debt to a carder for work performed, he made two payments to third parties, one for s.6 d.6 in cash to Monna Giovanna, a creditor of the carder, and another for s.15 by giro from one of his own debtors to the carder.[48] Paolo di Ser Ambrogio's payment of an amount in excess of that which a priest had on deposit represented an overdraft on the priest's "current account" with the cheese seller.[49]

Did the small businessman really operate differently from the more prominent merchant banker? Or was it just a matter of degree—of financial services coupled with retail trade on the one hand, and the same services coupled with wholesale trade on the other? The essential ingredients of *credito di esercizio*, which Melis hailed as a linchpin in the development of deposit banking, were present in the local economy of Prato. When storekeepers occasionally sold in bulk to fellow entrepreneurs, they granted the same credit terms typically offered by the large merchant wholesalers.

Local tradesmen first began using bankers for a line of credit—thus fulfilling Melis's definition of *credito di esercizio*—when they recognized that the local merchant bankers, with their contacts outside the Pratese district, could provide the necessary credit for purchases at a distance. For a while, wholesale suppliers continued to be the main source of credit for local purchases. Before long, however, local suppliers must have realized that they, too, could obtain full payment through a banker and not have to wait for reimbursement over a long period; consequently credito di esercizio began to provide the money for exchanges on the local marketplace. Whether the line of credit was the first type of service for which the tradesmen turned to bankers cannot be determined. The evidence for their use of various banking services is recorded contemporaneously in the documents. By 1400, however, it is clear that the banker had entered the world of small businessmen—and that the businessmen themselves were performing certain banking functions.

Conclusion

A thirty-minute train ride will take a traveler from Florence to the small station within the fourteenth-century walls of the historic center of Prato, but few tourists bother to make the trip. Why go to Prato when in only a little more time you can visit the famous cities of Arezzo, Siena, or Lucca? Prato is not considered a tourist attraction but a working city,[1] the third largest in central Italy. It is the textile capital of the country and, like Milan and Turin, a mecca for those from the south seeking employment. Yet of all Italian cities perhaps Prato most harmoniously blends the old and the new. The cathedral square of Pistoia has preserved its medieval appearance with no modern intrusions and stands apart from the daily life of the modern world. In contrast, the Piazza del Duomo in Prato bustles with activity from early morning to late at night. On one side, the medieval cathedral in alternating bands of white and green marble rises above its mundane surroundings. On the other three sides are modern structures, including a hotel, a bus office, a bar, and a butcher shop.[2] Similar contrasts appear throughout the historic center, still almost completely surrounded by walls. Truncated towers from the twelfth and thirteenth centuries crop up on the most unlikely places beside modern buildings; small, dark alleys of medieval origin connect the present commercial avenues. Called the "Manchester of Italy," Prato is also known as the "City of the Madonna," and its numerous churches represent almost every style of ecclesiastical architecture from the twelfth century forward.[3]

This was the world of the tradesmen whose business records now reside in the former home of Francesco di Marco Datini. The cloth seller Giovanni di Spinello Viviani had his home a little northeast of the cathedral square in the section called Travaglio; Giovanni di Paolo located his delicatessen on the communal square still dominated by the Palazzo Pretorio; the druggist Benedetto di Tacco bought a home and a little land further south in Porta Santa Trinità. The location of the house that the doublet maker Marco di Sandro rented to a slipper maker in 1384 bears today the same name—"Tre Gore"—although the small canals have long since disappeared.[4] No trace remains of the houses and shops of the tradesmen of this study; but similar small residences and stores intermingle with the larger modern buildings.

Although it is difficult to reconstruct the physical environment of the tradesmen, we can catch a glimpse of the way they lived and can outline in some detail their ways of conducting business. With incomes far above the subsistence level at which the majority of the population lived, these tradesmen were comfortable by the standards of their times. Few of the luxuries enjoyed by Datini and others of his economic stature were within their means, however. Whatever excess funds they had available appear to have been invested in real estate: land and houses, in the city and the countryside. The extensive real estate purchases of the druggist Benedetto di Tacco reveal the continued growth of his net worth.

For many years economic historians have documented the widespread use of credit by the great international merchant bankers as an essential basis of their operations, but the scarcity of records of small operators confined to the local market has precluded any comparable study of their business practices. Indeed, some historians explain the lack of documentation for local businesses by assuming they must have functioned within a cash and barter dynamic that generated no written records. The numerous account books of the Pratese tradesmen, however, belie such an interpretation. All of these tradesmen extended credit to men and women on all rungs of the social ladder; and credit sales, far from being occasional, constituted a large portion of their business. Moreover, for all their dependence on credit they suffered few defaults or excessive losses: their collection rates averaged higher than

95 percent. Finally, they kept written track of all this activity with accounting skills comparable to those of their great contemporary Francesco di Marco Datini himself.

In order to offset the capital tied up in credit to customers, the tradesmen sought and obtained credit for their own purchases from suppliers. Although most suppliers were also local businessmen, some even beyond the Pratese district allowed deferred payment. Toward the end of the fourteenth century merchant bankers appeared as middlemen to secure supplies and extend credit for payment. It seems plausible that the extension of credit by suppliers and indirectly by merchant bankers contributed to the development of *credito di esercizio*.

Credit extension to customers was not the only financial service offered by the Pratese tradesmen. All of the ledgers of this study contain entries for loans both to the tradesmen's frequent customers and to people who wanted only to borrow. Both types of borrowers, like the people who bought on credit, came from all walks of life and usually sought small amounts. The collection rates for the loans mirrored those for credit for purchases, averaging higher than 95 percent. The frequency of moneylending by Pratese artisans and shopkeepers calls into question the claim that pawnbrokers were the exclusive source of loans for these tradesmen and their customers, and that most loans were sought for purposes of consumption.

Given the church and governmental prohibitions against usury, it is not surprising that interest charges were rarely recorded; only a few large loans include any reference to interest. The broker Matteo di Matteo Toffi did not hesitate to detail the interest charges on loans he arranged between other parties, but in connection with his own lending there is no mention of interest. The conclusion seems clear: only the person who benefited from usury needed to fear prosecution. Though no study has been made of the intellectual climate of usury and the enforcement of the prohibition against it in fourteenth-century Prato, the extensive literature on this subject at Florence provides information undoubtedly applicable to the situation at Prato after its subjection to Florence in 1351.

The sources of capital for the local businesses of Prato have been mentioned only in passing in this study. The subject deserves detailed

consideration, but unfortunately the records provide little information. The amounts of capital necessary to start the various businesses
studied here would have ranged widely, from large sums in the case of
a druggist or an innkeeper to zero in the use of the broker Matteo di
Matteo Toffi. Inheritances and dowries may have been sources.

Richard Goldthwaite, in his study of the world of construction
workers in Renaissance Florence, including both unskilled laborers and
skilled artisans, emphasized many of the themes that have been discussed in this book: the monetization of economic relations, the au-
tomatic and nearly universal use of moneys of account, the importance
of the written record, offsetting of debits and credits, and reliance on
credit and trust. All of these themes theretofore had been explored only
in the study of prominent entrepreneurs active in the forward sectors
of one of Europe's most advanced economies. The present study push-
es the temporal and geographical confines of Goldthwaite's work back
into the fourteenth century and beyond the capital city, and it expands
his chosen social parameters to take in many other kinds of economic
operators, especially in the retail-commercial and tertiary sectors. It
also differs from Goldthwaite's work in making use of the extensive
records of the local operators themselves to uncover the economic
foundation of their world. Perhaps further investigation of retail trade
in other areas of Italy will determine the extent of the practices found
in Prato. Did credit form an essential part of other local economies?
Were local tradesmen a significant source of small loans? To what extent did the tradesmen turn to bankers and brokers to facilitate their
operations? Did guilds play an important role in the conduct of daily
business? What was a tradesmen's standard of living, and what were the
possibilities for building a patrimony as the tradesmen did in Prato?

Although comprehensive and detailed records such as the account
books of Prato may not be available elsewhere, other sources can provide some answers to these questions. A few years ago Marco
Tangheroni suggested that possible sources for the investigation of retail trade might be guild statutes, entries in the *recordanze* of the well-
to-do who did business with tradesmen, tollgate records, and notarial
documents.[5] The practices documented at Prato can help to guide the
interpretation of the sometimes vague or isolated references derived

from such sources. They may also shed light on the work that some scholars already have done. For example, Thomas Blomquist, in analyzing the cartulary of a Lucchese notary, identified 141 credit sales of cloth during a seven-month period in 1246 as being wholesale sales to rural peddlers rather than retail sales to customers from the countryside, even though the value of the average sale was only £1 s.14 d.5.[6] He explained this interpretation by asking, "Would a draper, were he selling retail, have been likely to advance short-term credit, with all the risks involved, to individuals dwelling in some cases miles away from Lucca?" Knowledge of the extensive use of credit less than a hundred years later by the cloth seller Giovanni di Spinello in his numerous sales to customers living many miles from Prato would have suggested to Blomquist that some of these earlier credit sales at Lucca were probably retail.[7] Another scholar, Armando Sapori, might have formed a different view of the large retail operation of the fourteenth-century Florentine Del Bene firm had he been acquainted with the Pratese tradesmen's accounts. No records of the firm survive, and Sapori concluded, on the basis of the prohibition against credit for retail purchases in the guild statutes, that all of its sales must have been cash transactions.[8] In a later article Sapori cautioned against relying on guild statutes as representing the reality of the marketplace; undoubtedly, the knowledge of Giovanni di Spinello's extensive credit operation in the same business only a few years later in Prato would have suggested to Sapori that many of those sales could have been on credit.

Through the centuries local artisans and shopkeepers, though not protagonists in major economic developments, contributed an essential link in the chain along which a product moves from producer to consumer. The peasants of the countryside raised the food; the industrialists provided manufactured goods; and the international merchants secured the raw materials and products not found in local areas. Although international merchants sometimes sold directly to consumers, the local tradesmen in village, town, and city supplied most consumer needs at all levels of society. To neglect their role in the study of local economies is to obscure the picture of the way these economies actually functioned.

List of Account Books

⟋⟍he account books of the Pratese tradesmen are listed here in
⟍⟋ chronological order; all except no. 18 are in Archivio di Stato di
Prato. All of the books were kept in single entry, and most contain entries for some household expenses and real estate investments. For an
explanation of references to manuscript sources, see "Abbreviations"
at the beginning of the notes section.

1. Sinibaldo, moneylender (Ospedale 2466; L. Serianni, *Testi pratesi
della fine del Dugento e dei primi del Trecento* [Florence, 1977], 103–61).
June 19, 1285, to April 23, 1286. Serianni transcribed the text as an example of one of the earliest in the vernacular in Prato, and his comments concern its linguistic aspects. The unbound pages are from a
ledger recording loans and subsequent repayments.

2. Giovanni di Spinello Viviani, retail cloth seller (Ceppi 1407). January 1, 1337, to January 13, 1347; *mezzana* (9″ × 12″) with 100 folios
of accounts. The fact that Giovanni belonged to the well-known and
powerful Arte della Lana and engaged in some production of cloth
might suggest that he should not be included with the other petty entrepreneurs of this study. Yet his sales are of modest amounts of cheap
cloth and all on a local basis. Furthermore, the inventory of his possessions (detailed on a detached sheet found in the flyleaf) lists only a small
house, modest and poor furnishings, and a little land outside Prato. His
apparent mode of operation and way of life place him in the same category as the other tradesmen considered in this study rather than
among the members of the merchant-industrial elite.

3. Benedetto di Tacco, druggist (Ospedale 793-F1, 795-F1, 796-F1,
797-F1). October 20, 1344, to February 21, 1393; all except 795-F1 are
mezzane; 795-F1 is a vacchetta (4½″ × 12″), containing entries posted to the ledger (796-F1) and many other entries recorded only in this
supplementary book. On the opening page of the vacchetta Benedet-

to suggests a possible reason for its use: he will allow his apprentice to make entries in it but presumably not in the main ledger. The period covered is almost fifty years. Later entries have been added to some accounts by the apprentice at the direction of Benedetto's sister and heir. In spite of two lacunae covering eleven years, these books are the most important source for the present study. The first lacuna, from 1358 to 1365, which occurred between Benedetto's first and second extant registers, clearly was covered in a lost ledger, the evidence for which is in numerous postings from it to the second surviving ledger. The second lacuna, from 1379 to 1382, which occurred between this second ledger and the final one, must have been a period of relative inactivity in Benedetto's business. The period is too brief to have been covered by a lost register, given the length of the surviving ones; and in fact all of the postings transferred to the last ledger have corresponding entries in the second extant one. The three-year gap coincides with the rule of the more liberal guild regime at Florence after the revolt of the Ciompi, which ended with the return to oligarchic rule in January 1382. Was Benedetto sick, or could the revolution in Florence have in some way affected his business?

4. Bonagiunta Zucassi, retail cloth seller (Ospedale 794-F1). January 2, 1348, to July 20, 1348; vacchetta with only 15 folios for his own entries and 3 folios for the listing of his assets and liabilities at the request of his widow. Bonagiunta died in debt at the height of the Black Death in Tuscany. The rest of the book contains entries for the Hospital of the Misericordia, starting in 1374.

5. Domenico di Jacopo, tailor (Ospedale 799-F2, 803-F2). December 25, 1364, to March 25, 1409; mezzane with very few folios, used toward the end of his career. For a number of years Domenico rented half the store of the doublet maker Marco di Sandro (no. 8 in this list). The similarity in their businesses led to many product exchanges and frequent loans to one another.

6. Ferro di Cambio and descendants, innkeepers (Archivio del Patrimonio Ecclesiastico, 419-AV1112, 420-AV1113, 421-AV1114, 422-AV1115, 423-AV1116, 424-AV1117, 425-AV1118, 426-AV1119, 427-AV11110, 428-AV11111, 429-AV11112, 430-AV11113, 431-AV11114, 432-AV11115, 433-AV11116, 434-AV11117, 435-AV11118). 1368–

1484; mezzane. Ferro di Cambio, his son Cambio di Ferro, and his grandson Antonio di Cambio managed the Stella Inn for almost a century. The last three books contain the records of the inheritance of the grandson, including his gift to the Chapel of the Holy Belt of the Virgin Mary, in whose archive all these books were discovered.

7. Jacopo di Bartolomeo Mati, shearer of cloth (Ospedale 802-F2). May 16, 1377, to December 14, 1381; mezzana with 145 folios (only 68 used). Jacopo's frequent use of *fiorini a fiorino* (f.1 = s.29) and the large sums recorded for his transactions (including one over £2,000), suggest that Jacopo was operating on a financial level far above that of most of the other tradesmen studied.

8. Marco di Sandro, doublet maker (Ospedale 804-F4). June 26, 1377, to October 4, 1384; mezzane with 99 folios. Marco died before any of his five children had reached their majority. Two of his sons, Sandro and Giuliano (known as the Marcovaldi brothers), became prominent Pratese merchants in the first half of the following century.

9. Giovanni di Paolo, cheese seller (Ospedale 809-F3, 810-F4). March 31, 1380, to October 7, 1408; mezzane. Because Giovanni's registers and those of Prato's other cheese seller, Paolo di Ser Ambrogio (no. 15), cover many of the same years, their entries afford an opportunity to compare two similar businesses during the late fourteenth and early fifteenth centuries.

10. Partnership of Niccolò Guardi, Chimenti di Ghino, and Biagio di Giovanni, wallers *(muratori)* (Ospedale 928-F, 929-F31, 930-F31). August 7, 1384, to March 10, 1389; mezzane. These records, which detail the partners' work for the commune on the fourteenth-century walls of Prato (still standing, for the most part), give valuable data on building materials and salaries for masters and unskilled laborers.

11. Lorenzo Cosi and partners, and Piero di Lotto, butchers (Ospedale 961-F). December 1, 1388, to November 27, 1389 (Lorenzo and partners, 4 folios), and November 17, 1390, to March 2, 1394 (Piero, 19 folios); vacchetta. This small journal with a paper cover probably belonged to the Hospital of the Misericordia at Prato and includes only purchases of meat by the hospital from the two firms. At irregular intervals the sales are totaled and posted to ledgers, which have not survived. The frequent entries for Lorenzo Cosi in other extant registers

indicate that this firm was a prominent meat supplier in the late fourteenth century.

12. Partnership of the brothers Biagio and Giuliano di Giovanni Bertelli, manufacturers of paper and sellers at retail (Ospedale 811-F5). March 1, 1389, to April 28, 1396; mezzana with 26 folios. The rent of 43 florins a year that the brothers paid to the monastery of San Salvatore at Viano suggests a financial level similar to that of the shearer Jacopo di Bartolomeo Mati, higher than that of the other tradesmen.

13. Stefano di Cecco, retail grain seller (Ceppi 1322). October 11, 1389, to June 8, 1390; mezzana with 100 folios. Stefano sold flour and a variety of unprocessed cereal products. The book names people who worked with him: Jacopo (his brother), Benedetto (possibly another brother), and Mattea (perhaps his wife), all of whom made sales and collected debts. The butcher Lorenzo Cosi (no. 11), sometimes called a tavern keeper by Stefano, and the waller Chimenti di Ghino (no. 10) frequently bought from him.

14. Matteo di Matteo, druggist (Ospedale 815-F6). January 1, 1390, to October 16, 1400; *reale* with 86 folios. Matteo's book covers most of the same years as the books of another Pratese druggist, Paolo di Bonaccorso di Tano (no. 17). A comparison of Matteo's debit entries with Paolo's credit entries indicates markups for a number of their frequently sold commodities.

15. Paolo di Ser Ambrogio, cheese seller (Ospedale 812-F5, 814-F5, 921-F25). January 10, 1390, to June 1, 1414; mezzane. Ospedale 812 is a debit book with 111 folios from January 10, 1390, to May 31, 1412; Ospedale 814 is a credit book with 122 folios from August 16, 1402, to June 1, 1414; Ospedale 921 records Paolo's term of office from September 1, 1399, to September 1, 1400, as mayor, treasurer, and collector of sales tax for Porta Gualdimare. Paolo is one of only two tradesmen whose debit ledgers have survived, and a comparison of entries in his two account books indicates markups for various products. He employed the broker Matteo di Matteo Toffi (no. 18) to arrange a number of his sales and purchases.

16. Taddeo di Chelli, secondhand dealer (Ospedale 827-F9). September 10, 1390, to March 31, 1408; mezzana with 93 folios. Taddeo bought and sold merchandise of every description at prices rarely high-

er than a few lire; purchases and sales of white stockings far exceed entries for any other commodity. Judging from the carelessness of his record keeping, it is not surprising that both suppliers and customers often made their own entries in his account book.

17. Paolo di Bonaccorso di Tano, druggist (Ceppi 1414, 1415). March 19, 1392, to August 10, 1400; mezzane (Ceppi 1414 is a debit book with 213 folios from March 19, 1392, to August 10, 1400; Ceppi 1415 is a credit book with 283 folios from December 7, 1392, to April 5, 1400). The first readable page in the debit book is 38r, as the beginning of the book is badly mutilated with many pages missing. Unfortunately, it was not possible to compare entries in the two books to determine markups; the condition of the credit book was so poor that it was sent to Florence to be repaired and more than a year later had not been returned. Paolo died sometime between August 10, 1400 (his last entry), and March 4, 1401, when a final entry was made by the executor of his estate.

18. Matteo di Matteo Toffi, broker (Biblioteca Roncioniana Q-I-52; Ospedale 816-F2, 817-F6). July 2, 1408, to January 30, 1411; mezzane (Biblioteca Roncioniana Q-I-52 [6″ × 9″] has 95 folios from July 2, 1408, to July 21, 1410; Ospedale 816-F2 has 22 folios from August 1, 1410, to January 30, 1411; Ospedale 817-F6 has 72 folios, only 4 of them used, all dated July 21, 1410). The first book is a record of Matteo's brokerage business in products and real estate. The other two books show his transactions as an assessor for the commune and a private party. Because Matteo recorded many of his commissions for the brokerage operation, it is possible to estimate his annual income from that business.

N O T E S

Abbreviations

Most references to documents found in the Archivio di Stato di Prato are either to the inventory labeled "Ospedale" or to the inventory labeled "Ceppi."
The inventory names are used to indicate references (e.g., Ospedale 793-F1
for the first ledger of the druggist Benedetto di Tacco, Ceppi 1407 for the
ledger of the cloth seller Giovanni di Spinello Viviani). The innkeepers' account books, found in the Archivio di Stato di Prato, and the book of the broker Matteo Toffi, found in the Biblioteca Roncioniana in Prato, are referred to
by the names of their owners. References to other manuscript sources are giv-
en in full.

Introduction

   1. L. Serianni, *Testi pratesi della fine del Dugento e dei primi del Trecento* (Florence, 1977), 103–61.
   2. G. Pampaloni, "Prato nella republica fiorentina," in *Storia di Prato* (Prato, 1971), 2:70 n. 108. The author lists the theses completed at the University
of Florence: I. Iannucci, "Domenico di Iacopo da Prato, sarto, 1364–1409,"
1970–71; L. Cavaliere, "Masnieri di Benino da Prato, fabbro, 1454–1476,"
1971–72; L. Pasquetti, "L'albergo della Stella in Prato tra la fine del Trecento
e la metà del Quattrocento," 1971–72; R. Perri, "Andrea Bertelli, cartolaio e
merciaio in Prato, 1388–1429: Vita, attività e ambiente socio-economico di
un piccolo artigiano pratese," 1971–72; P. Sorri, "Lorenzo Talducci, calzolaio
in Prato, 1427–1466: Vita e attività e ambiente socio-economico di un piccolo artigiano pratese," 1974–75. Pampaloni did not include the thesis on the
druggist Benedetto di Tacco completed in 1970–71 by Sonia Rosati.
   3. D. Herlihy, *Medieval and Renaissance Pistoia: The Social History of an Italian Town, 1200–1430* (New Haven, Conn., 1967), 246–49, speaks of the impressive growth of legacies to hospitals and charitable institutions during the
fourteenth century. Prato and part of its district were under the Pistoiese epis-
copate at this time. In *Death and Property in Siena, 1205–1800* (Baltimore, 1988),

Samuel Cohn examines the changing patterns of legacies in another Tuscan town over a period of six hundred years.

4. These documents all have been collected at the Archivio di Stato at the restored mansion of the merchant banker Francesco di Marco Datini in Prato. The Ceppi collection there includes the documents of both the "old" and the "new" Ceppo, the latter founded by the substantial legacy of Datini in 1410. The books of the innkeepers can be found in the Archivio del Patrimonio Ecclesiastico at the Archivio di Stato; the ledger of the broker Matteo di Matteo Toffi is located at the Biblioteca Roncioniana in Prato. The state of preservation of most books is remarkably good. Unfortunately, the information in the inventory of the archives leaves much to be desired; many names, dates, and occupations prove erroneous. The two inventories of Ruggero Nuti—"Inventario dell'Archivio dei Ceppi di Prato," *Rivista storica degli archivi toscani* 6 (1934), 136–46, and *Inventario sommario del'Archivio di Stato di Prato,* ed. R. Nuti (Prato, 1939)—contain errors and do not disclose the true contents of these registers. Except for a few corrections, the more recent *Inventario sommario dell'Archivio di Stato di Prato,* ed. G. Pampaloni (Florence, 1958), tends to follow the present, faulty entries in the inventory at the archives.

5. Studies on this tragic event include I. Modesti, S. Brami, and S. Guizzalotti, "Tre narrazioni del sacco dato alla terra di Prato dagli spagnoli, 1512," *Archivio storico italiano* 1 (1842), 237–63, and C. Guasti, *Il sacco di Prato e il ritorno dei Medici in Firenze nel 1512; 2 vols. (Bologna, 1880).

6. See *Storia di Prato,* (Prato, 1981) for an overview of Pratese history from earliest times to the present. Also see G. Cherubini, ed., *Prato storia di una città,* 2 vols. (Prato, 1991), which covers the period from earliest times to 1494 and has updated and greatly expanded the information found in the earlier work. Older studies still worth consulting are R. Caggese, *Un comune libero alle porte di Firenze nel secolo XIII (Prato in Toscana)* (Florence, 1905); F. Carlesi, *Origini della città e del comune di Prato* (Prato, 1904); S. Nicastro, *Sulla storia di Prato dalle origini alla metà del secolo XIX* (Prato, 1916).

7. For a fuller treatment of Prato's expansion into the countryside and the sources for the progression to complete episcopal autonomy, see E. Fiumi, *Demografia, movimento urbanistico e classi sociali in Prato dall'età comunale ai tempi moderni* (Florence, 1968), 2–8, 21. See also E. Cristiani, "Il libero comune di Prato, secolo XII–XIV," in *Storia di Prato,* (Prato, 1981), 1:371, and Caggese, *Un comune libero,* 21–25, for information on and evidence for Prato's becoming a direct imperial fief.

8. E. Cristiani, "Il libero comune di Prato," 1:363–412, provides numerous examples of both independent actions and Florentine influence. R.

Caggese, *Un comune libero,* 4, referring to the city's two hundred years of free-dom, sums up the position of Prato: "Trattò da pari a pari con Firenze, con Siena, con Pisa," but adds, "i suoi vessilli sventolarono in battaglia, sempre e dovunque sventolaron quelli di Firenze."

9. R. Fantappiè, "Nascita e sviluppo di Prato," in *Prato storia di una città,* ed. G. Cherubini (Prato, 1991), 1★:94–97, 117–18, downgrades the importance of both Alberti and the emperors in controlling events in the Prato area. E. Fiumi, *Demografia,* 12–17, and S. Raveggi, "Protagonisti e antagonisti nel libero Comune," in *Prato storia di una città,* 1★★:614–17, take a different view and un-doubtedly would agree with the characterization of the Alberti and the em-perors as buffers. Raveggi (695 n. 13) refers to the comment of the jurist Gui-do da Suzzara asserting direct imperial control late in the thirteenth century. While reprimanding the Pratesi who hesitated to swear an oath of loyalty to the imperial legate in 1281, Guido stated that Prato could claim no autonomy because it had been bought by the emperor (from the Alberti) as one buys a horse or a field.

For a brief discussion of the fortress, see S. Bardazzi, "Il castello dell'Im-peratore," *Archivio storico pratese* 31 (1955), 26–35. For a longer account, see G. Giani, *Prato e la sua fortezza dal secolo XI fino ai giorni nostri* (Prato, 1908).

10. Cristiani, "Il libero comune di Prato, 1:401, 411.

11. See Raveggi, "Protagonisti e antagonisti," 1★★:625–27, and G. Sivieri, "Il comune di Prato dalla fine del Duecento alla metà del Trecento," *Archivio storico pratese* 48 (1972), 24. For a detailed account of the Angevin connection during the Trecento, see A. Martini, "La dedizione di Prato a Roberto d'An-gio," *Archivio storico pratese* 27 (1951), 3–44. Martini published the relevant doc-uments on 33–44 of this article. G. Brucker, *Florentine Politics and Society, 1343–1378* (Princeton, N.J., 1962), 145, points out that Joanna and her consort had deeded Prato to Acciaiuoli, who then sold it for the "ridiculously low price of 17,500 florins," yet Acciaiuoli still had difficulty in obtaining even this sum from the Florentine authorities.

12. E. Fiumi, "Fioritura e decadenza dell'economia fiorentina," *Archivio storico italiano* 115 (1957), 398 n. 45; Brucker, *Florentine Politics,* 104, 109.

13. Cf. M. Villani, *Cronica,* ed. F. G. Dragomanni (Florence, 1846), 1:73, where he writes, "presa la tenuta, incontanente levò le signorie, gli ordini e gli statuti de' Pratesi e recò la terra e il contado a contado di Firenze, e diede l'e-stimo e le gabelle a quello comune come a' suoi contadini."

14. J. Brown, *In the Shadow of Florence: Provincial Society in Renaissance Pe-scia* (New York, 1982), 16–20.

15. Caggese, *Un comune libero,* 248–50. The author ends his book at the

close of the thirteenth century with this judgment: "La missione dei piccoli Comuni [including Prato] era finita, e nessuna forza avrebbe potuto arrestarne la caduta."

16. Cristiani, "Il libero comune di Prato," 1:411.

17. Ibid., 409–10. In this passage, Cristiani mentions this decree with the quote, "super factis terre Prati."

18. Pampaloni, "Prato nella republica fiorentina," 2:22, calls Prato's small size and population its Achilles' heel.

19. Fiumi, *Demografia,* 83, presents demographical conclusions through 1339. His figures through 1339, as well as those for 1372, do not include religious nor does he attempt to estimate their numbers.

20. Although G. Pampaloni, "Popolazione e società nel centro e nei sobborghi," in *Prato storia di una città,* ed. G. Cherubini (Prato, 1991), 1*:364 n. 25; 366, agrees with Fiumi's number of households in 1339, he calculates a higher number of inhabitants.

21. Fiumi, *Demografia,* 85–87. The information used in note 23 below for 1339 is from 72–75.

22. If the population decline of the first part of the Trecento continued, the nine years from 1339 to 1348 must have lowered the population on the eve of the Black Death, a consideration that somewhat alters the conclusion below.

23. In Porta Fuia the number of households dropped from 349 to 232, or 33.5 percent; in Porta Capo di Ponte it dropped from 289 to 207, or 28.3 percent.

24. For example, Figline saw a decrease of 56.4 percent (from 117 to 51 households); Sorniana saw an increase of 183 percent (6 to 17); and San Giusto saw an increase of 22 percent (54 to 66).

25. See Fiumi, *Demografia,* 88–90, where Fiumi calls the estimo of 1372 "un vero e proprio censimento."

26. Ibid., 90. The average sizes of families in the city and in the contado approximated those of 1339, that is, 3.5 in the city and 4.7 in the contado.

27. Ibid., 111. On 7–8 Fiumi points out the significant fact that through the centuries the boundaries of the Pratese district have been altered only very slightly, making demographic comparisons in time far easier than for other localities. Although much of the information has been incorporated into *Demografia,* Fiumi provides additional information on this well-known census in "Stato di popolazione e distribuzione della ricchezza in Prato secondo il catasto de 1428–1429," *Archivio storica italiano* 123 (1965), 277–303. Employing many of the same sources as Fiumi, C. Klapisch, "Déclin démographique et

structure du ménage: L'exemple de Prato, fin XIVe–XVe," in *Famille et paren-té dans l'occident médiéval,* ed. G. Duby and J. LeGoff (Paris, 1977), 258, notes that the population of the city fell 72 percent from the beginning of the Tre-cento to the beginning of the Quattrocento. During the same hundred years, the population of the contado decreased only 35 percent. Recognizing the wealth of demographic information that is available on Prato, David Herlihy and Christiane Klapisch-Zuber used the rate of population decline in Prato to estimate the populations at Pisa, Arezzo, and Pistoia at the end of the thir-teenth century, in *Les Toscans et leurs familles: Une étude du catasto florentin de 1427* (Paris, 1978), 179–80.

28. Fiumi, *Demografia,* 90. In 1372, the midpoint of the period covered by the present work, the city had 1,721 households, or 6,045 inhabitants; the area outside the walls had 1,326 households, or 6,195 inhabitants.

29. Brown, *In the Shadow,* 27; Brown estimated that Pescia had 2,000 in-habitants in 1346 and 1,800 in 1427.

30. Herlihy, *Medieval and Renaissance Pistoia,* 76. Herlihy's figures are as fol-lows: for the city of Pistoia, 6,000 inhabitants in 1351 and 4,000 in 1401; for the countryside, 14,000 in 1383, 11,000 in 1392, and 10,000 in 1401.

31. R. Fantappiè, "Nascita d'una terra di nome Prato," in *Storia di Prato,* (Prato, 1981), 1:238.

32. Ibid., 235–55. In this chapter devoted to technological and industrial progress during the twelfth and thirteenth centuries, Fantappiè discusses the growth of fulling mills and other aspects of the textile industry.

33. For a survey of this mainstay of the Pratese economy, see E. Bruzzi, "Sulla storia dell'arte della lana in Toscana considerata nella sua genesi e nella sua legislazione," *Archivio storico pratese* 15 1937), 72–87, 126–40, 157–77; 16 (1938), 14–42.

34. Fiumi, *Demografia,* 93 n. 11; E. Bruzzi, "L'industria della carta in Pra-to," *Archivio storico pratese* 18 (1940), 109. G. Cherubini, "Ascesa e declino del centro medievale (dal Mille al 1494)," in *Prato storia di una città,* ed. G. Cheru-bini (Prato, 1991), 1★★:977, speaks of a paper mill as early as 1288 in the vil-lage of Colonica. Additional evidence is afforded by the extant account book (1389–96) of the paper manufacturing and retail firm of Biagio and Giuliano di Giovanni Bertelli; see appendix.

35. Fiumi, *Demografia,* 91.

36. Archivio del Patrimonio Ecclesiastico 49, fols. 4r–4v, and 53, fol. 4r. Seventeen guilds appear on both lists: judges and notaries, wool entrepreneurs, druggists, bankers, blacksmiths, woodworkers, button makers, tailors, bakers, cheese sellers, shoemakers, butchers, barbers, masters of stone, doublet mak-

ers, secondhand dealers, and innkeepers. Two guilds, the dyers and the sock makers, appear only on the 1396 list; two others, the shearers and the wine sellers, appear only on the 1401 list. In 1396 Paolo di Ser Ambrogio, whose two books are a source for this study, brought the candles for the guild of the cheese sellers.

37. It is only in modern times that such an abundance of records becomes available. The Datini archives, still in the process of being catalogued, include account books in excess of five hundred, more than two hundred thousand business and personal letters, and numerous bills of lading, insurance policies, and letters of exchange. The archives will provide an almost inexhaustible reservoir for future research. Although it is primarily a source for economic history, in recent years the correspondence has been used for political and social history as well. For example, G. Brucker, *The Civic World of Early Renaissance Florence* (Princeton, N.J.: 1977), 169–72, refers to twelve letters from the archives. For a popular biography of Datini, see I. Origo, *The Merchant of Prato* (New York, 1957), which is substantially correct in spite of F. Melis's harsh criticism in "Aspetti della vita economia medievale (studi nell'Archivio Datini di Prato)," *Prato storia e arte* 7 (1963), 8 n. 7. An older biography by Enrico Bensa is still worth consulting and has valuable appendices, including some excerpts from account books; see his *Francesco di Marco da Prato: Notizie e documenti sulla mercatura italiana del secolo XIV* (Milan, 1928). For a brief account in English, see R. Brun, "A Fourteenth-Century Merchant of Italy: Francesco Datini of Prato," *Journal of Economic and Business History* 2 (1930), 451–66. Cristiane Villain-Gandossi used materials in this archive for a study of the salt trade in southern France, which included a transcription of Datini's "Libro di ragione e conto di salle"; see C. Villain-Gandossi, ed., *Comtes du sel de Francesco di Marco Datini pour sa companie d'Avignon, 1376–1379* (Paris, 1969).

38. F. Melis, *Aspetti della vita economica medievale* (Siena, 1962), 455–627, refers to numerous other Pratese merchants and suppliers.

39. Although the inventory labels the ledger (see appendix) as belonging to Marco di Landro, it belonged to Marco di Sandro a doublet maker, who turns out to have been the father of the Marcovaldi brothers, Sandro and Giuliano. On fol. 6v, counting from the back (Ospedale 804-F4), Marco records that on July 18, 1378, he married Antonia, who brought a dowry of 340 florins. There follows a listing of the children born of this marriage, from October 1379 to February 1386; Sandro, Bartolomeo, Nicolao, Stefano, and Giuliano. From an extant ledger of the tailor Domenico di Jacopo (see appendix), it is possible to approximate the date of Marco's death, which occurred before any

of the five children had reached their majority. On August 1, 1390, we know that Marco was still alive because Domenico paid some taxes for him, in addition to debiting his account s.1 d.8 for buttons (Ospedale 803-F2, fol. 29r). After a line drawn across the same page, Domenico added, with a date of May 6, 1391, that he had made an agreement with Marco's brother Giovannino in settlement of five past accounts, which left a credit to Marco of £25. He ended by stating that Giovannino "è contento come tutore di fanciulli di Marco." Marco died sometime between these two dates.

See chap. 1 for further information about the rise of these sons of a local tradesman to the upper levels of Pratese society.

40. R. Nuti, "Mercanti e lanaioli pratesi: I Marcovaldi," *Archivio storico pratese* 16 (1938), 169–79, outlines the careers of the Marcovaldi brothers and describes the Pratese community at Ragusa. Employing the sources available at Dubrovnik (Ragusa), M. Popovic, "La penetrazione dei mercanti pratesi a Dubrovnik nella prima metà del secolo XV," *Archivio storico italiano* 112 (1959), 503–21, gives a fuller picture of this mercantile community of Pratesi.

41. R. Nuti, "Un mercante pratese in Ungheria nel secolo XV," *Archivio storico pratese* 12 (1934), 1–5.

42. G. Pampaloni, "L'economia cittadina," in *Storia di Prato* (Prato, 1981), 2:31–79, deals largely with the second half of the fifteenth century and is based almost entirely on the catasto of 1487. Unfortunately, M. Cassandro's "Commercio, manifatture e industria," in *Prato storia di una città,* ed. G. Cherubini (Prato, 1991), 1*:395–477, contains very little information not covered in previous works on Prato. At no time does he mention the numerous local tradesmen's account books or use material from them.

43. In a long footnote (57 n. 9) in F. Melis, *La banca pisana e le origini della banca moderna,* ed. M. Spallanzani (Florence, 1987), the author discusses the registers at Arezzo. He points out that documents from before 1384 are very rare but that the large number of documents available from that year forward in the Archivio della Fraternità dei Laici di Arezzo provide a rich reservoir for research.

44. G. Brucker, "The Ciompi Revolution," in *Florentine Studies: Politics and Society in Renaissance Florence,* ed. N. Rubinstein (London, 1968), 321.

45. R. de Roover, "The Development of Accounting Prior to Luca Pacioli According to the Account Books of Medieval Merchants," in *Business, Banking, and Economic Thought in Late Medieval and Early Modern Europe,* ed. J. Kirshner (Chicago, 1974), 165–68. The four French account books belonged to (1) an unknown draper operating at Lyon (1320–23); (2) Ugo Teralh, a notary and draper at Forcalquier in Provence (1330–32); (3) Jean Saval, a mer-

chant and draper in Carcassonne (1340–41); and (4) the Bonis Brothers, who sold cloth, spices, and pharmaceutical products and engaged in banking and moneylending (1345–68). De Roover also mentions a few books of tradesmen operating after 1410. At a recent meeting in Genoa in October 1990 ("Banchi pubblici, banchi privati e monti di pietà nell'Europa preindustriale"), Henry Dubois briefly discussed the moneylending activities of these tradesmen ("Banque et crédit en France aux deux derniers siècles du moyen âge," 6).

46. De Roover, "Development of Accounting Prior to Luca Pacioli," 172–76.

47. Ibid., 165–76. Chap. 5 of the present work cites the documents themselves in pointing out some similarities in credit practice. These French and German merchants cannot be classified simply as local tradesmen, however. In *Money, Banking, and Credit in Medieval Bruges* (Cambridge, Mass., 1984), de Roover's principal sources were books of fourteenth-century money changers.

48. L. Serianni, *Testi pratesi,* 103–61, for Sinibaldo; Ceppi 1407 for Giovanni; and Biblioteca Roncioniana Q-I-52 for Matteo.

49. Marco Tangheroni cites this lack of documentation as the reason for his inability to deal with local tradesmen. "Il sistema economico della Toscana nel Trecento," in *La Toscana nel secolo XIV: Caratteri di una civiltà regionale* (San Miniato, 1988; Centro di studi sulla civiltà del tardo medioevo), 49 n. 19.

50. R. Goldthwaite, *The Building of Renaissance Florence: An Economic and Social History* (Baltimore, 1980), gives an extensive account of the working conditions and standards of living of skilled and unskilled laborers in the construction industry. Goldthwaite provides a high level of detail, reporting even what one unskilled worker carried to work, which included 5 gold florins (294–95). It is regrettable that Goldthwaite was not aware of the survival of the three account books of the wallers at Prato from 1384 to 1389. These would have allowed him to extend his study of the Florentine region back into the fourteenth century and to include records of employees along with those of private, public, and religious employers.

51. For a survey of research in this field, see G. Cherubini, "Artigiani e salariati nelle città italiane del tardo medioevo," in *Aspetti della vita economica medievale* (Florence, 1985; Atti del convegno di studi nel X anniversario della morte di Federigo Melis, Firenze-Pisa-Prato, 10–14 marzo 1984). Cherubini includes bibliographies of studies on the construction industry, naval and military work sites, and the dispersion of workers, among other things. But in his commentaries he says little about artisans or shopkeepers, and he includes no bibliography of research on them.

52. M. Tangheroni, "La distribuzione al minuto nel medio evo," in *Mercati e consumi: Organizzazione e qualificazione del commercio in Italia dal XII al XX secolo* (Bologna, 1986; Il convegno nazionale di storia del commercio in Italia), 569–81.

53. R. Nuti, *La fiera di Prato attraverso i tempi* (Prato, 1939). Every Monday is still market day in the large parking lot a little north of the walled city.

54. Cristiani, "Il libero comune di Prato"; Pampaloni, "Prato nella republica fiorentina"; Cassandro, "Commercio, manifatture e industria"; Brown, *In the Shadow;* Herlihy, *Medieval and Renaissance Pistoia;* D. Herlihy, *Pisa in the Early Renaissance: A Study of Urban Growth* (New Haven, Conn., 1958).

55. A. Astorre, "Il 'libro delle senserie' di Girolamo di Agostino Maringhi, 1483–1485," *Archivio storico italiano* 146 (1988), 389–408; A. Astorre, "Appunti sull'esercizio della Speziale a Firenze nel Quattrocento," *Archivio storico italiano* 147 (1989), 31–62.

56. De Roover, "The Organization of Trade," in *The Cambridge Economic History of Europe,* (Cambridge, 1963), 3:103.

57. See A. B. Hibbert's overview of local economies in Western Europe, "The Economic Policies of Towns," in *Cambridge Economic History,* 3:157–230, and C. M. Cipolla's treatment of Italy and Spain, "The Economic Policies of Governments: The Italian and Iberian Peninsulas," in *Cambridge Economic History,* 3:397–419.

58. S. Thrupp, "The Gilds," in *Cambridge Economic History,* 3:230–80.

59. A. Doren, *Le Arti fiorentine,* vol. 1 (Florence, 1940), used guild statutes as his principal source. R. de Roover, "A Florentine Firm of Cloth Manufacturers," in *Business, Banking, and Economic Thought,* ed. J. Kirshner (Chicago, 1974), is based on the firm's account book. De Roover's article, first published in *Speculum* in 1941, is the example usually cited to show that reality is not always found in official documents such as guild statutes. But it was two years earlier, in 1939, that Sapori made the following comment: "Io credo di mantenere, ancora una volta, il mio di vista, secondo cui ricostruire la vita medievale sulla scorta delle leggi staturie non significa riprodurre la realtà di quella vita" ("Case e botteghe a Firenze nel Trecento," in *Studi di storia economica* [Florence, 1955], 1:329 n. 6).

Chapter One: Way of Life

1. For a survey of research on the medieval Italian diet with extensive bibliographical references, see M. Mazzi, "Note per una storia dell'alimentazione nell'Italia medievale," in *Studi di storia medievale e moderna per Ernesto Sestan,* ed.

M. Mazzi and S. Raveggi (Florence, 1980), 1:57–102. For the medieval diet in Prato see Enrico Fiumi, "Sulle condizioni alimentari di Prato nell'età comunale," *Archivio storico pratese* 42 (1972), 3–26.

2. Mazzi, "Note per una storia dell'alimentazione," 81. Goldthwaite, *Building,* 438–39, underscores the importance of grain in the diet of the time by translating the nominal wages of unskilled construction workers into the equivalent *staia* of wheat (1 staio = .686 bushels). G. Vigo, "Real Wages of the Working Class in Italy: Building Workers' Wages (Fourteenth to Eighteenth Century)," *Journal of European Economic History* 3 (1974), 381–82, speaks of the percentage of income spent by workers on bread or cereals for bread making as sometimes approaching 50 percent in preindustrial Europe. For the importance of wine see F. Melis, "Il consumo del vino a Firenze nei decenni attorno al 1400," *Arte e mercatura* 4 (1967), 6–33, and G. Pampaloni, "Vendemmie e produzione di vino nelle proprietà dell'ospedale della Misericordia di Prato nel Quattrocento," in *Studi in memoria di Federigo Melis* (Naples, 1978), 3:349–79. Giuliano Pinto, in his study of prices from 1395 to 1406, includes meat in addition to grain and wine as part of a daily ration for the workers at the Hospital of San Gallo ("Il personale, le balie e i salariati dell'Ospedale di San Gallo di Firenze negli anni 1395–1406: Note per la storia del salariato nelle città medievali," *Ricerche storiche* 4 [1974], 158).

3. Ospedale 795-F1, fol. 2v, gives one example of a shipment of 52 staia of grain by Benedetto di Tacco in 1370.

4. Ospedale 804-F4, no foliation at the end of the book.

5. These two prices appear in Ceppi 1414, fol. 103r, and Ospedale 804-F4, October 2, 1384 (no foliation), respectively. (For information on monetary units, see "Dates, Weights and Measures, and Money" at front of this volume. All prices are given in *lire di piccioli* unless otherwise stated.) It appears that white wine was less expensive than the red, but both varied in price. *Vino bianco* (white) is priced at s.4½ and s.8½ a barrel (Ceppi 1414, fols. 103r, 80r), *vino vermigli* (red) at s.18 and s.42½ (Ceppi 1414, fols. 143v, 163r). G. Pinto, "I livelli di vita dei salariati cittadini nel periodo successivo al tumulto dei Ciompi (1380–1430)," in *Il tumulto dei Ciompi* (Florence, 1981; Convegno internazionale de studi—Firenze, 16–19 settembre 1979), 190, gives the following average prices for the same period: 1381–83, s.39.2; 1384–93, s.71.2; 1394–1407, s.39.11. His lowest price of s.18 in 1414 is far above many prices recorded in the tradesmen's books.

6. Pinto, "I livelli," 170. Also, Mazzi, "Note per una storia dell'alimentazione," 93–94, states that all the authors agree that animal fats were used al-

most exclusively for flavoring; she further states that olive oil was rare because of its limited production even in the Mediterranean world.

7. Because there apparently were no restrictions on fishing in the Bisenzio, the tradesmen may have obtained the same trench and pike that Datini spoke of so often. See Origo, *Merchant of Prato,* 321–22.

8. Ibid., 322–25.

9. Pinto, "Il personale," 158–59.

10. See chap. 2 for the markups of cheese sellers and druggists. Pinto, "I livelli," 188, gives the wholesale price of grain from July through December, 1389, as s.38.6, and from January through June, 1390, as s.46.6—an average of s.42.6. This wholesale average, when compared with Stefano di Cecco's average retail price of s.52, produces a markup of 22 percent (Ceppi 1322). The average wholesale price of s.2 for dried meat *(carne secca)* (Pinto, "Il personale," 147), when compared with Giovanni di Paolo's average retail price of s.2 d.7 (Ospedale 810-F4), yields a markup of 29 percent.

11. A cost of £138 per year for bread, wine, and meat represents almost one half of the tradesmen's average estimated annual income of £300 (see chap. 2). Pinto's later study, "I livelli," 179, calculates s.3 as the daily ration for an adult in the period 1384–93. For a family of four this would amount to an expenditure of s.11 d.3 at retail prices, a figure that is well above half of the estimated average annual income.

12. C. M. de La Roncière, *Prix et salaires à Florence au XIVe siècle, 1280–1380* (Rome, 1982, 130–31, comes to the same conclusion about wine, although he then distinguishes various types and gives a wide range of prices through the years. Pinto's estimate of a daily ration of s.2 was based on an average price of d.10 per liter, or about s.28 per barrel ("Il personale," 158).

13. He paid the miller Meo s.4 d.6 for grinding 3 staia of wheat (Ceppi 1322, fol. 29r) and s.16 for 10 staia of rye (fol. 88r).

14. Stefano's average cost of 1 staio of wheat was s.52; his cost for 1 staio of rye was s.24.

15. Pinto, "Il personale," 158 (see table) speaks of the cost of extraction of flour from grain but makes no resulting adjustment in his cost of bread. He gives d.15 as the average cost of 1 kilogram of grain, then prices 650 grams of bread at d.10.

16. Although Vigo, like others who have constructed grain price series, used prices paid by public bodies or religious institutions, he pointed out that these prices may be exceptional because of their nature and continuity in time ("Real Wages," 385). A. V. Judges, "Scopi e metodi della storia dei prezzi," *Ri-*

vista storica italiana 63 (1951), 170, also questioned whether such evidence was
the best guide to understanding market movements: "Personalmente, sarei dis-
posto a sacrificare talune di quelle lunghe serie di prezzi . . . per qualche cosa
di più vario, anche se questo qualche cosa può far correre il rischio di confu-
sione ed errore." In the same article (164) Judges also stressed the importance
of using retail prices wherever possible.

17. In analyzing the data of the provision survey of Prato of December
1339, de La Roncière concluded that tradesmen of the middling class (his example was a mason) lacked sufficient grain provisions for the whole year and,
by winter, had to buy their supplies weekly or monthly in the marketplace at
increased prices (*Prix et salaires,* 430).

18. This rise of 43 percent is exceptional when compared with changes in
most other years. The year 1389–90 was a time of great scarcity of grain (Pinto, "I livelli," 166). Pinto, 188 (table), indicates, however, that for most years
from 1380 to 1410, the price of grain was higher from January through June
than from July through December. One staio is generally considered to be the
monthly ration of grain for an adult.

19. The price of broad beans *(fave),* which Stefano also sold, increased
more than 50 percent, from s.26 to s.40.

20. Pinto, "Il personale," 147–48. Pork had the lowest of the meat prices
Pinto recorded. He was referring to the entire animal sold at dead weight (148
n. 129); the meat from almost all of these animals, whether raised on the hospital's farms or purchased, was salted (148 n. 131). Pinto appears to have used
pork to figure the caloric value of the daily ration of meat but then used s.1
d.4 per pound, not s.1, as the cost of the meat (158, table). In another study
Pinto gave the following prices of pork per 100 pounds: 1360–65, s.81.7;
1370–75, s.133; 1400–1427, s.100 ("Forme di conduzione e rendita fondiaria
nel contado fiorentino [secoli XIV e XV]: Le terre dell'ospedale si San Gallo," in *Studi di storia medievale e moderna,* ed. M. Mazzi and S. Raveggi [Florence,
1980], 1:323).

21. The years 1380–84 would have been a period of prices similar to those
Pinto found at the end of the century rather than during the years 1384–93,
a time of higher prices ("I livelli," 179). In this later article Pinto discusses the
problem of arriving at a price per pound for an entire animal; and using data
from the records of the convent of the Carmine, he gives series of prices per
pound for dried meat, pork saddle, veal, and lard. His average price for pork
saddle *(arista)* in 1382–84 (he has no prices for 1380–81) is s.2 d.4, about 11
percent (d.3) below the price in table 2 for 1380–84. Mazzi, "Note di una storia," 75 n. 61, also points out that Fiumi's study of consumption ("Sulle con-

dizioni alimentari di Prato") erred in attributing today's higher weight to medieval cattle and calves.

22. Ospedale 810-F4, fols. 13v, 17v. Giovanni also recorded bulk sales of pork fat (17 pounds and 150 pounds in 1382) at discount prices of s.3 and s.2 d.8 (fols. 35v, 35r), lower than his usual prices of s.3 d.6 per pound for small quantities.

23. This information comes from the four books of the two cheese sellers (Ospedale 809-F3, 810-F4, 812-F5, 814-F5) and the two books of the druggist Paolo di Bonaccorso di Tano (Ceppi 1414, 1415).

24. The Pratese pound consisted of twelve ounces.

25. Loose sheet in flyleaf of Ceppi 1407; Ospedale 812-F5, fol. 66r.

26. Biblioteca Roncioniana Q-I-52, fols. 40r, 85v.

27. Origo, *Merchant of Prato,* 39, 264.

28. Ospedale 812-F5, fol. 49v.

29. The reference to digging and mowing *(vangare e segare)* is from Ospedale 796-F1, fol. 191v; the reference to pruning *(potare)* is from the same ledger, fol. 198r.

30. Ospedale 793-F1, fol. 98r; ibid., fol. 19v; Ceppi 1407, fols. 12r, 64r; Ospedale 804-F4, fol. 12r; Ospedale 793-F1, fol. 159v.

31. Ceppi 1415, fols. 66r, 75r.

32. Ospedale 793-F1, fol. 19v.

33. Ibid., fols. 5r, 8v.

34. Ceppi 1322, fol. 93v. Although not identified as such, Monna Mattea undoubtedly was Stefano's wife or a member of the family.

35. Ospedale 797-F1, fol. 4v (counting from the back).

36. According to Fiumi, *Demografia,* 97, the doublet maker Marco di Sandro's surname must have been Marcovaldi. Fiumi lists Marco's father, Sandro Giovannini, with an assessment of £100 in 1372. The catasto of 1428–29 also lists one of Marco's sons (ibid., 117). Neither in his own account book nor in the frequent references to him in one of the books of the tailor Domenico di Jacopo is the surname Marcovaldi ever used for the doublet maker.

37. Archivio di Stato, Florence, Estimo 215, fol. 561r.

38. Ibid., fol. 634v (for Taddeo Chelli, age 30), and fol. 695v (for Giovanni di Paolo, age 26). Although Taddeo by this age should perhaps have accumulated enough assets to rate an assessment (see below for the assessment of Domenico di Jacopo at the same age), his somewhat inept business procedures may have held him back.

39. Fiumi, *Demografia,* 88, discusses these two categories.

40. Archivio di Stato, Florence, Estimo 215, fols. 686v, 557v. Of the seven

categories of wealth listed by Fiumi, *Demografia*, 92, Domenico occupies the second from the bottom (5 to 50 lire), Benedetto the third from the bottom (50 to 100 lire).

41. Archivio di Stato, Florence, Estimo 215, fol. 591v.

42. Ospedale 794-F1, fols. 15r–18r.

43. Ceppi 1407, fol. 1r. The significance of this debtor list for the extension of credit is discussed in detail in chap. 5.

44. Ceppi 1407 (1337–47). This document also contains the names of witnesses and may be an inventory of Giovanni's legacy to the Ceppo, in whose building his account book was found.

45. Far different is the description of the house and furnishings (including seven books) of Ser Lorenzo d'Agnolo Ridolfi, whose inventory the broker Matteo di Matteo Toffi recorded on July 21, 1411 (Ospedale 817-F6, fols. 1r–3r). Ser Lorenzo had numerous rooms in his two-story house, and its furnishings were sold to Florentine secondhand dealers for £510 s.5.

46. Ospedale 796–F1, fol. 217r.

47. On the extensive real estate of Datini, see I. Imberciadori, "Proprietà terriera di Francesco Datini e parziaria mezzadrile nel '400," *Economia e storia* 3 (1958), 254–72.

48. Ospedale 827-F9, fol. 25r; Ospedale 811-F5, fol. 6v.

49. Two centuries later, druggists apparently continued to acquire properties in the country. L. Kotelnikova, "Artigiani-affittuari nelle città e nelle campagne toscane del XV–XVI secolo," in *Aspetti della vita economica medievale* (Florence, 1985; Atti del convegno di studi nel X anniversario della morte di Federigo Melis, Firenze-Pisa-Prato, 10–14 marzo 1984), 757, mentions a rich druggist's profitable purchases of country land, including vineyards and olive groves, from members of prominent Florentine families.

50. Ceppi 1414, loose sheet between fols. 66 and 67 (March, 1393).

51. See Ospedale 796-F1, fols. 213r, 215v, and 217, for the land he bought; fol. 218v, for the exchange of property during the period 1365–78; and 797-F1, fol. 94v, for the land purchase in 1386.

52. Ospedale 796-F1, fol. 217r.

53. Biblioteca Roncioniana Q-I-52, fol. 17r.

54. See Ospedale 796-F1, fol. 214v, for the purchase; 795-F1, fol. 6v (counting from the back), for the expenditure of £250.

55. Ospedale 796-F1, fols. 213r, 215r, 231v.

56. The financial resources necessary for such purchases contrast sharply with those of cheese sellers, or delicatessen owners, in the Po Valley in the late

Middle Ages. A. J. Pini's division of guilds into five social and economic categories places *formaggiai* and *pizzicagnoli* at the lowest level; for a summary of
Pini's categories, see Cherubini, "Artigiani e salariati," 724–25. Similarly, Pini's
ranking of stationers at the next-to-lowest level would be inappropriate for
the Pratese *cartolai* Biagio and Giuliano di Giovanni Bertelli, whose business
appears from the entries in their account book to have been one of the two
most economically successful of those studied. An occupational designation
can be deceptive about the true economic status of a person, and this was particularly true in late medieval times. For another example, see the contrast between the two secondhand dealers *(rigattieri)* in chap. 2 of the present work.
Goldthwaite, *Building,* 282–85, cites a number of consuls of the construction
guild in Florence (next-to-lowest in Pini's categories) as possessors of substantial wealth, some of whom belonged to the upper classes.

57. Ospedale 810-F3; see Giovanni's entries in the back of the account
book on the following dates: September 2, 1384; July 8, 1386 ("o vero Matalena mia donna"); and August 4, 1392; in Ospedale 809-F3, see his entries on
these dates: February 16, 1399; July 17, 1399; March 2, 1404 (for rental back to
seller); May 21, 1404; July 1, 1404 (for purchase of one half of house, then the
other half); and July 6, 1409 (for purchase of a cottage beside one of the houses
bought in 1404).

58. Ospedale 812-F5, fol. 66r.

59. In the tables at the beginning of vols. 1* and 1** of *Prato storia di una
città,* ed. G. Cherubini (Prato, 1991), a *soma* is defined as 68.376 liters for wine
or 50.143 liters for oil. Here, the term undoubtedly refers to an amount that
an average pack animal could carry.

60. It is not clear what is meant here by *misure.*

61. Ospedale 798-F2, 800-F2, and 813-F5 are some of the books that contain records of large loans.

62. Ospedale 812-F5, fol. 90r; Ospedale 799-F2, fols. 9r, 10r.

63. Ospedale 810-F3, fol. 809-F3, fol. 47v; and 810-F3, fol. 51r.

64. Ospedale 799-F2, fol. 74r.

65. Ospedale 796-F1, fol. 199v.

66. In addition to the many property acquisitions recorded in the tradesmen's own books, the broker Matteo di Matteo Toffi negotiated purchases for
three druggists (Biblioteca Roncioniana Q-I-52, fols. 17r, 40r, and 85v), two
shoemakers (14r, 61r), one blacksmith (7r), and a miller (10r).

67. J. Kirshner and A. Molho, "The Dowry Fund and the Marriage Market in Early Quattrocento Florence," *Journal of Modern History* 50 (1978), 414,

conclude that a fairly substantial number of tradesmen invested in the fund between 1425 and 1442 and that their investments would yield dowries amounting to 300 florins or less.

68. Ospedale 793-F1, last folio with date of November 22, 1345; Ospedale 804-F4, fol. 6v (counting from the back), dated July 18, 1378.

69. Ospedale 799-F2, fol. 6v. Twice in this entry Domenico mentions £50, but the amount entered to the right is only £30.

70. Ospedale 812-F5, fol. 94v.

71. Ospedale 810-F3, letter found between fols. 184 and 185. The dowries mentioned by the Florentine tailor Buoncorso del Mugellino di fu Bettino in the second half of the Trecento corresponded in size to those recorded by the Pratese tradesmen: he paid 125 florins for each of his two daughters and 150 florins for a granddaughter, and received 200 florins himself when he remarried. S. Cohn, *The Laboring Classes in Renaissance Florence* (New York, 1980), 66 n. 3.

72. See Ospedale 804-F4, fol. 6v (counting from the back) for the names and births of his five children.

73. In Ospedale 812-F5, fol. 48r, dated 1399, the cheese seller Paolo di Ser Ambrogio calls Giovannino a "farsettaio."

74. This information on the two brothers is found in Nuti, "Mercanti e lanaioli pratesi," 169–79.

75. M. Becker and G. Brucker, "The 'Arti Minori' in Florentine Politics, 1342–1378," *Mediaeval Studies* 18 (1956), 93–104, emphasized this diversity and pointed out (101) that the lower guildsmen selected for the high offices were the wealthy members of that group.

76. Biblioteca Roncioniana Q-I-52, fol. 82v.

77. Ospedale 802-F2, fol. 9r; Pampaloni, "Prato nella republica fiorentina," 2:55, 177.

78. Fiumi, *Demografia,* 97, 99. Of Fiumi's seven categories of wealth (92), Lazzaro occupies the second, counting from the bottom (5 to 50 lire), Giovanni the fifth (200 to 500 lire).

79. De La Roncière, *Prix et salaires,* 257–58.

80. Ibid., 372–77. The author's inclusion of notaries in his graphs has not been considered.

81. Ospedale 815-F6, fols. 10v, 12v.

82. C. Bec, "Sur la spiritualitè des marchands florentins (fin du Trecento-debut du Quattrocento)," in *Aspetti della vita economica medievale* (Florence, 1985; Atti del convegno di studi nel X anniversario della morte di Federigo Melis, Firenze-Piza-Prato, 10–14 marzo 1984), 676–93, discusses the religious

aspects of a businessman's life as exemplified by the more well-to-do Florentine merchants of the same time.

83. As early as 1254 and 1295, respectively, the Hospital of the Misericordia and the Ceppo came under the direction and supervision of the commune (Cherubini, "Ascesa e declino," 1★★:975). The new Ceppo, founded as part of the legacy of Datini in 1410, was to be a private charity and "in no way controlled by the Church or by any ecclesiastic"; see C. Guasti, *Lettere di un notaro a un mercante* (Florence, 1880), 2:289–90.

84. For more information on the inheritance of Antonio, see Archivio del Patrimonio Ecclesiastico 433, 434, 435. When Antonio was buried on June 16, 1450, the druggist Simone di Bartolomeo made the arrangements and received payment from the treasurer. Inside the front of 435 is a loose copy of Antonio's will in Latin, undated but referring to the folio on which the will can be found in a book belonging to the chapel.

85. Ospedale 795-F1, fols. 24r, 25v–26r.

86. Ospedale 812–F5, fols. 67r, 78v.

87. Biblioteca Roncioniana Q-I-52, fol. 7r.

88. Ospedale 811-F5.

89. Ospedale 797-F1, fol. 1r.

90. S. Thrupp, "Medieval Industry, 1000–1500," in *The Fontana Economic History of Europe,* ed. C. M. Cipolla (New York, 1976), 1:253.

91. Goldthwaite, *Building,* 348; Raveggi, "La condizioni di vita," 1★: 484–89.

92. All Sundays and religious holidays were verified in A. Cappeli, *Cronologia, cronografia e calendario perpetuo,* 3rd ed. (Milan, 1969).

93. Ospedale 1160-F3, fols. 30r, 31v.

94. Archivio del Patrimonio Ecclesiastico 427, no foliation. In 425, fols. 2r–14r, he recorded his service as a supervisor, but gave the date of his taking office as February 1, 1401, rather than 1407 as in 427.

95. See Ospedale 812-F5, fol. 52r, for Paolo's membership on the Eight of Prato, fol. 69v for the repayment of the loan.

96. Although the interdict imposed during the war with the Papacy must have had some adverse effects on Pratese commerce (see R. Trexler, *Economic, Political, and Religious Effects of the Papal Interdict on Florence, 1376–1378* [Frankfurt, 1964], and idem, "The Spiritual Power: Republican Florence under Interdict," in *Studies in Medieval and Reformation Thought,* vol. 9 [Leiden, 1974]), the Pratesi were exempt from the papal sanctions on Florentine merchants doing business abroad. In fact, according to Sapori, Datini took advantage of the Florentines exiled from Avignon to enrich himself at their expense when he

was left in charge of their merchandise. Most Pratesi, however, would disagree with Sapori's comment on Datini: "dimenticando la patria per il suo interesse." It was within thirty years of Florence's annexation of Prato that these events took place; to call Florence a Pratese's "fatherland" would perhaps have been as unacceptable then as today (see A. Sapori, "Economia e morale alla fine del Trecento: Francesco di Marco Datini e ser Lapo Mazzei," in *Studi di storia economica,* [Florence, 1955] 1:160–61).

97. Ospedale 799-F2, last folio:

In martedì dì 22 di giungno. Detto dì sopra si levò per lo popolo minuto e per cagione de'lavoranti de l'arte della lana di Firenze a romore e in questo dì arsono 13 case di grassi cittadini di Firenze cioè quegli del popol grasso. El detto dì rupono le stinche e uscirone fuori tutti i pregioni. 1378 in martedì a dì 20 di luglio si levò il secondo romore per la detta gente minuta e arsono 13 case overo palagi e istette la città di Firenze a romore e sotto l'arme insino a dì 22, il dì di Santa Maria Madalena, e in questo detto dì dispuosono i priori ch'erono in palagio e non compierono l'uficio che aveano a stare tutto luglio; e montarono nel detto palagio e regimento il popolo minuto cioè uno gonfalonieri per l'arte minuta de' lavoranti dell'arte della lana e istette solo in palagio de' priori e da sua parte andarono in questi dì tuti da sua parte tutti i bandi, e poi furono tutti i priori e furono fatti a mano e ressono e stettono ne' regimento tutto luglio ie agosto. E poi per lo terzo romore furono disposti e rimasono ne'regime[n]to l'arti di Firenze e certi popolari grassi fra quali fue fatto a mano e nel detto prioratico Giorgio delli Ischali e così tutto suo tenpo istette la città in tremore e in paura insino che seguiteremo di scrivere.

98. "Cronache e memorie sul tumulto dei Ciompi," in *Rerum Italicarum Scriptores,* ed. G. Scaramella, rev. ed., vol. 18, pt. 3 (Città di Castello, 1917–34), 41, 83, 118, 121, 131, 152, indicates that Giorgio became a prior at the beginning of September, he replaced the carder Giovanni di Domenico (41, 118). Also during the reign of the Ciompi, he was selected by the Eight of War to be prior but was not approved by the *popolo* (33).

99. To compare Domenico's brief description with some detailed studies of the Ciompi Revolt, see N. Rodolico, *La democrazia fiorentina nel suo tramonto, 1378–1382* (Bologna, 1905), and the more recent accounts of V. Rutenburg, *Popolo e movimenti popolari nell'Italia del '300 e '400* (Bologna, 1971), and Brucker, "Ciompi Revolution." Giorgio degli Scali was one of the patrician leaders of the liberal faction; he was executed in January 1382 on the return to oligarchic rule. See the index of Brucker, *Florentine Politics,* for many references

to Giorgio's political role; see idem, *Civic World*, 60, for an account of Giorgio's death. A. Molho and F. Sznura, eds., *Alle bocche della piazza diario di anonimo fiorentino* (Florence, 1986), 17–19, commences with an account of Giorgio's execution for conspiring to hand over the city to Bernabò Visconti.

100. Becker and Brucker, " 'Arti Minori' in Florentine Politics," 101.

Chapter Two: The Conduct of Business

1. Ceppi 1407, fol. 1r (counting from the back).
2. Ospedale 810-F3, fol. 51r.
3. G. Nigro, *Gli Uomini dell'Irco* (Florence, 1983), 82, discussed these two meat businesses. In his view the reason that one book contained the sales of both was that the book belonged to the hospital, which had the two tradesmen make their own entries in it.
4. See Ospedale 961-F, fol. 6v, for Peruzzi; see fol. 8v for Piero. Although only the small journal has survived, the name Lenzo Cosi (Lorenzo and Lenzo are used interchangeably) often appears in the other books.
5. Ospedale 811-F5, fol. 4r.
6. Ospedale 928-F, no foliation. See the entry recorded on June 10, 1385, for the payment in cash and the credit in the *corpo*.
7. See Ceppi 1322, fol. 78v, where Jacopo is identified as the brother of Stefano, and fol. 84r, where an entry in a different and more legible hand is identified as Jacopo's ("a me Jacopo"). There are a number of entries in this same hand.
8. Vimano's investment and payment of rent as found on the last page of Ceppi 1407; the partial payment of the entrance fee is recorded on fol. 4r.
9. The laborers from Rome appear in Ospedale 928-F, June 5, 1385, those from Todi, in 929-F, fol. 16v; those from Como, in 929-F, fol. 17r. There are references to six masters from Rome (930-F, fols. 20r, 20v, 23v, 26v, 28v, and 32v); two from Todi (930-F, fols. 9r, 9v); and three from Como (930-F, fols. 19v, 32v, 46v).
10. Ospedale 928-F, September 15, 1384; 929-F, fol. 27r.
11. The unskilled laborer most frequently cited in the work records over a number of years is Matteo di Giovanni, whose pay never exceeded s.6 per day—perhaps a young apprentice?
12. Goldthwaite, *Building*, gives the average rate for unskilled laborers in Florence in 1384–89 as s.10.6 (p. 436); for skilled laborers, as s.16.8 (p. 437). In addition to a possible difference in supply and demand in the two areas, the higher figure for skilled workers in Florence may reflect Goldthwaite's inclu-

sion in his averages of the daily rates for the more specialized masters, such as wood and stone craftsmen. See 321–22 for the author's discussion of the diversity of wages for skilled workers.

13. In the three books Ospedale 928-F, 929-F31, and 930-F31, the entries for the work on the city walls extend from August 7, 1384, to March 10, 1389.

14. For a later period in Florence, Goldthwaite (*Building,* 287–351) found a reduction in pay during the winter months for both skilled and unskilled laborers; the Florentine employers also provided bread and wine for their workers, usually when a significant part of the job was completed.

15. Ospedale 928-F, February 23, 1385, and June 21, 1385.

16. Ibid., September 7, 1384.

17. Ibid., August 29, 1384.

18. Ibid., September 11, 1384 (the day he received the loan), and November 22, 1384 (the day he repaid it).

19. Goldthwaite, *Building,* 309, 312.

20. The three partners and some other masons kept a record book *(bastardello)* of those in their crew; at random times the work record for each worker was entered in the ledger and the pay calculated.

21. See Ospedale 928-F, June 21, 1385, to November 23, 1985, for delay in pay.

22. Ibid. He worked on October 24, 1384, and was paid on November 30, 1385, at a rate of less than s.6 per day.

23. See Ospedale 930-F31, fol. 28v, for wage of s.12, fol. 33r for wage of s.11.

24. Ospedale 928-F, August 28, 1385.

25. Inside the cover of Ospedale 928-F.

26. L. Serianni, *Testi pratesi,* 112, and Ceppi 1415, fol. 100r, respectively.

27. Ospedale 810-F3. For the loans, see fols. 117r (not repaid), 136r, 152v; for the sales, see fols. 140v, 143v.

28. Ceppi 1322, fol. 93v.

29. Ceppi 1407, fol. 74r (Monna Luca); Ospedale 796-F1, fol. 5v (Monna Lagia); Ceppi 1416 (an account book of a cloth merchant, briefly scanned; Monna Lorenza, a *fornaia,* is mentioned on fol. 78r). The grain seller Stefano di Cecco frequently supplied the baker Monna Bertina with flour; Ceppi 1322, fol. 86v, shows a sale to her of flour worth £50.

30. Monna Lippa, a *fornaciaia,* sold firewood to the two partners who manufactured paper (Ospedale 811-F5, fol. 2v) and bricks to the wallers (Ospedale 930-F, fol. 56v); Monna Giovanna was also a kiln operator (Ospedale 812-F5, fol. 24r).

31. Biblioteca Roncioniana Q-I-52, fol. 37v.

32. Ospedale 814-F5, fol. 9r. One of the furrier's payments for white thread that she bought from the cheese seller Paolo di Ser Ambrogio was made "in her shop."

33. Ospedale 810-F1, fol. 142r.

34. Ceppi 1415, fol. 203v.

35. Ospedale 810-F1, fol. 158v.

36. Ospedale 793-F1, fol. 55r.

37. Ospedale 812-F5, fols. 21r, 24r.

38. In Biblioteca Roncioniana Q-I-52, fols. 19r (October 10, 1408) and 24v (November 6, 1408), she is identified as the wife of Bosco; on fol. 37v (January 31, 1409), as the widow of Bosco and operator of the store; and on fol. 71r (January 3, 1410), as the wife of Zanobi, new owner of the business. Perhaps the delicatessen constituted her dowry.

39. See Ceppi 1322, fol. 9r, for an example of the variety and large amounts of cereal products she sent to the grain dealer.

40. For two examples, see Ceppi 1407, fols. 27r, 44v.

41. Ospedale 810-F3, fol. 158v.

42. Ibid., fol. 62v.

43. D. Herlihy, "Le attività urbane" (paper presented at the annual seminar "La donna nell'economia, secc. XIII–XVIII," Istituto Internazionale di Storia Economica "F. Datini," Prato, April 1989).

44. Ospedale 799-F2, fol. 45v; Ospedale 799-F2, fol. 70v; Ospedale 803-F2, fol. 34r.

45. "XXI Settimana di Studi" (paper presented at the annual seminar "La Donna nell'economia, secc. XIII–XVIII," Istituto Internazionale di Storia Economica "F. Datini," Prato, April 1989).

46. Because this comment was not made in one of the official reports, it has not been published. No one questioned the percentage asserted or asked for supporting evidence. The comment, however, led me to check for possible verification in the account books at Prato.

47. Numerous times the druggist Paolo di Bonaccorso di Tano refers to them as paper sellers ("cartai"), for example, in Ceppi 1414, fols. 50r, 125r. Yet on 148r and 152v, he calls them druggists ("speziali").

48. In Ospedale 796-F1, fols. 108r, 108v, are twenty-three entries of payments for the funeral of Monna Spezzia. Fols. 122v and 123r show two more funerals that Benedetto arranged. Later in the century the druggist Matteo di Matteo also arranged a funeral (Ospedale 815-F6, fol. 49r).

49. Biblioteca Roncioniana Q-I-52.

50. Ibid., fols. 4r, 4v.

51. This information on Benedetto di Tacco comes from Ospedale 793-F1 and 796-F1.

52. Ospedale 812-F5, fols. 67v, 107r (purchases); 814-F5, fols. 12r, 13v, 22r, 23r, 61r, 79r (sales).

53. Ospedale 812-F5, fols. 69r, 80r, 103v (purchases); 814-F5, fols. 29v, 31r, 88r, 88v (sales).

54. Ospedale 812-F5, fol. 66r (purchases); 814-F5, fols. 23r, 25v, 26v (sales).

55. Ospedale 812-F5, fols. 64v, 65r, 82v, 106v (purchases); 814-F5, fols. 11r, 13v, 15r, 21v, 28v, 36r, 54v, 68v, 85r (sales).

56. Ospedale 812-F5, fol. 58v (purchase); 814-F5, fol. 8r (sale); 812-F5, fols. 23r, 27r, 27v, 32r (purchases); 809-F3, fols. 3r, 11r, 12r, 13r, 16v (sales).

57. Ceppi 1414, fols. 54r, 68v, 121v (purchases); Ospedale 815-F6, fols. 34v, 68r, 70v (sales).

58. Ceppi 1414, fols. 106r, 145r (purchases); Ospedale 815-F6, fols. 51v, 68v (sales).

59. Ceppi 1414, fols. 59r, 80v (purchases); Ospedale 815-F6, fols. 38r, 44r (sales).

60. Ceppi 1414, fols. 54r, 126v, 130r (purchases); Ospedale 815-F6, fols. 35v, 60r (sales).

61. Ospedale 814-F5, fol. 75r.

62. Ospedale 796-F1 (ledger), 795-F1 (supplementary book).

63. See chap. 6 for loans recorded by the broker Matteo di Matteo Toffi at 30 percent interest. A conservative figure of 25 percent is used for estimating this return from moneylending. S. Rosati, *Benedetto di Tacco da Prato Speziale, 1345–1392: Vita, attività, ambiente sociale ed economico* (tesi di laurea, Facolta di lettre e filosofia dell'Università di Firenze, 1970–71), 1:204–27, concluded that all of Benedetto's loans were made as favors to customers and that he charged no interest. This conclusion seems unlikely because in 1370 Benedetto lent more than f61, and a check of thirty people who received only loans shows that eleven of them made no purchases in 1370 or in the two years before or after 1370.

64. His average charge of s.1-1/2 per pound applied to the total poundage in 1370.

65. See Ospedale 793-F1, fol. 59v, for Master Alberto, fol. 65v for Master Salimene.

66. One funeral was noted on January 6, 1370 (Ospedale 796-F1, fol. 122v), the other on February 16, 1370 (fol. 126v). See Ospedale 815-F6, fol. 49r, for Matteo's charge of s.20.

67. Ospedale 795-F1, fol. 1v (counting from the back). Brown, *In the Shadow*, 132–38, gives an account of guard and militia service that Florentine officials required of citizens of Pescia from the second half of the fourteenth century through the sixteenth. Similar services undoubtedly were required of the Pratesi.

68. See Ospedale 796-F1, fols. 124v, 6r, 78r, for the village of Gherignano; 797-F1, fol. 93r, for the village of Mezzana; and 796-F1, fol. 49r, for collecting the *gabella* on wood.

69. Ospedale 796-F1, fol. 131v.

70. Ospedale 796-F1, fols. 215v–217r. In 1369 he raised the rent on the £10 house to £12, but in 1370 it was again £10.

71. Ospedale 797-F1, fol. 4v.

72. On September 21, 1370, Simone Nucucci bought some spices and saffron for s.1 d.8, yet Benedetto concluded the entry with "posti a libro s.2" (Ospedale 795-F1, fol. 14v). With the same date on fol. 132v of his ledger (Ospedale 796-F1), he recorded the subsequently collected s.2. For a more detailed example of Benedetto's tendency to add a little extra to a customer's account, see chap. 2.

73. Ospedale 812-F5, fols. 80v, 83r, 83v.

74. Ceppi 1407, fol. 4v (counting from the back).

75. Ospedale 803-F2, fol. 35v.

76. Ibid., fol. 33r.

77. An unskilled laborer working 260 days at s.10 per day earned £130; a skilled laborer, at s.13 per day, earned £169. See chap. 2 for wages of construction workers.

78. Serianni, *Testi pratesi,* 103–61. Sinibaldo often gave the value of the florin as s.36, and this figure is used in converting the loans he made in florins into lire.

79. Ospedale 802-F2, fol. 9r.

80. When the cheese seller Paolo di Ser Ambrogio bought 112 spigots in Pistoia, he recorded the expense for transportation and gate duty separately as s.5 d.6, or 6 percent of the cost of £4 s.13 d.6 (Ospedale 814-F5, fol. 72v).

81. Ospedale 793-F1, fol. 192v.

82. Ibid., fol. 189r.

83. See ibid., fol. 187v, for stages of £3 s.15, £6, and finally, £8.

84. Ibid.

85. See Ospedale 796-F1, fol. 214r, for the £11 s.2, and fol. 216v for the 4 florins. The latter entry, recorded in 1370, is the last in his books.

86. Ospedale 810-F3, fol. 5r (counting from the back); Ospedale 812-F5, fol. 37r.

87. Ospedale 804-F4, fols. 2r, 5r.

88. Sapori showed the importance of comparing rents for the same properties in order to establish a trend in rental expense. For rents of the Del Bene family in Florence from 1314 to 1367, see A. Sapori, "Case e botteghe," 1:307–52.

89. Ospedale 793-F1, fols. 189v–192v.

90. Ibid., fol. 188r.

91. Ibid., fol. 186v. This is the last rent Benedetto recorded in his books.

92. Ceppi 1407, fol. 4v (counting from the back). This is the only instance of a payment to a guild in the entries of all the shopkeepers and artisans. If the tradesmen were required to pay annual dues, reference to such payments would be expected in the extant debit ledgers of the cheese seller Paolo di Ser Ambrogio and the druggist Paolo di Bonaccorso di Tano. However, the ledger of Paolo di Ser Ambrogio shows only payments to him by the guild of the *pizzicagnoli* for purchases he made for it (Ospedale 814–F5, fols. 63r, 78r, 82r, 114r). The officials of the guild took years to pay him; on fol. 82r he states that he had to ask the *rettori* to pay him what was owed.

93. See Ospedale 803-f2, fol. 22v, for both loans.

94. Ospedale 796-F1, fol. 209r.

95. In Ospedale 928-F, fol. 2, under the date of August 7, 1384, he wrote that he would list all the expenses of the partners.

96. The average cost per barrel was £2½, except for six barrels Jacopo bought from the mother of the priest of Sant'Andrea at s.15 per barrel.

97. All of these expenses are recorded in Ospedale 928-F from August 7, 1384, to April 14, 1385. Biagio ordered his fine dinner on November 4, 1384.

98. The purchase took place on August 13, 1384, seven days after the first entry in Ospedale 928-F. The two books may be the other extant account books, 929-F31 and 930-F31.

99. These accounts of the wallers, running from 1384 to 1389, cast some doubt on the traditional date of 1384 for the termination of construction on the third circle of the walls of Prato. Nowhere is it made clear whether the wallers' contract with the commune was for repair work or new construction. However, one agreement with two haulers on July 23, 1385 (Ospedale 928-F), specified that they supply all the gravel necessary for the foundation of the walls.

100. Throughout the accounts, the suppliers of stones, gravel, and sand are

referred to as *veturali*. Whether they did only the hauling for vendors of the materials or whether the vendor and hauler were the same person is not specified. The numerous contractual agreements made for future delivery with earnest money paid by the wallers suggests the latter. See July 23, 1385 (Ospedale 928-f), for an example of such an agreement with two vendor haulers.

101. Ospedale 928-F, January 30, 1385.

102. Ospedale 810-F3, fols. 1r, 2v. Giovanni paid £176 for 44 1/2 sheep (perhaps including lambs, recorded as half-sheep).

103. Ibid., 76r, 76v.

104. Many of the purchases were large ones—for example, 57 pounds of wax bought for ff.6 s.63 d.3 in 1392 (Ceppi 1414, fol. 51v).

105. Ospedale 928-F. The record of these transactions with the hauler begins on August 25, 1384.

106. Ospedale 809-F3, fol. 45r.

107. Biblioteca Roncioniana Q-I-52, fol. 73v.

108. Ospedale 810-F3, fol. 16r. One of these purchases cost £20 s.15, the other £18 s.6.

109. Ospedale 796-F1, fol. 168v.

110. See Ospedale 796-F1, fol. 217v, for the grain; 796-F1, fol. 175v, for the house; 795-F1, fol. 4v (counting from the back), for the *mezzadria*.

111. Ospedale 795-F1, fol. 8v.

112. Ibid. The customer, Bindo Bonnucci, had overpaid by d.2.

Chapter Three: An Independent Broker and a Family of Innkeepers

1. A. E. Castellani, *Nuovi testi fiorentini del Dugento* (Florence, 1952), 2:708–803. On lines 90–91 and 763 are found two references in "Libro del dare e dell'avere di mercanti fiorentini in Provenza, tenuto da Matino Mannucci, 1299–1300."

2. Ospedale 809-F3, fols. 30r, 30v, 31r.

3. Ceppi 1407, fols. 77r, 80v.

4. R. Hatfield, *Botticelli's Uffizi "Adoration"* (Princeton, N.J., 1976), 14–17.

5. R. Goldthwaite, "Local Banking in Renaissance Florence," *Journal of European Economic History* 14 (1985), 11.

6. Astorre, "Il 'libro delle senserie,'" 389–408; idem, "Appunti sull'esercizio," 31–62.

7. R. Ciasca, *L'arte dei Medici e Speziali nella storia e nel commercio fiorentino dal secolo XII al XV* (Florence, 1927), 186–88, using guild statutes as his source, described how brokers who were inscribed in this guild functioned. The bro-

kers discussed in the preceding paragraph all belonged to the guild for whose members they handled transactions.

8. R. Piattoli and R. Nuti, eds., *Statuti dell'arte della lana di Prato (secoli XIV–XVIII)* (Florence, 1947), 25–26. See rubrics vii, viii, viiii, x, xi, and xii for provisions relating to the guild brokers.

9. Biblioteca Roncioniana Q-I-52. A number of references have already been made to this account book.

10. See Biblioteca Roncioniana Q-I-52, fols. 2v, 20v, 63v, for cloth purchases by Nanni di Bonaco of Pistoia; fol. 13r for those by Donato di Giovanni of Pescia; and fol. 89v for those by Francesco di Marco and Company of Florence. Perusal of the guild statutes through 1542 reveals no modification of the requirement that a guild sensale be present at all sales of cloth.

11. See Goldthwaite, "Local Banking," 11, for the commune's regulation of the brokers representing the Arte del Cambio at the end of the fifteenth century.

12. Biblioteca Roncioniana Q-I-52, fol. 49v.

13. Ibid., fol. 63r.

14. Ibid., fols. 19r, 24v, 37v, 40r, 44v, 47v, 49r, 50r, 52r, 71r.

15. Ibid., fol. 89v.

16. Ibid., fol. 82v.

17. See ibid., fol. 7v, for the house, and 8v, 17r, 54v (this folio refers to the son-in-law), and 58r for the land.

18. See ibid., fols. 32r–32v, for the Rucellai, 36v for the sale to the Pratese. At Canneto, a few miles north of Prato, descendants of the Rucellai family still own a villa. As is often the case among owners of villas with extensive gardens, they rent out rooms and small apartments to defray the increasing costs of upkeep.

19. Ibid., fol. 57v.

20. Ibid., fol. 15r.

21. See ibid., fols. 19r, 23v, 36r, 39r, 42r, 50r, 57v, 80r, 82r, 88v, for the broker's records; see Ospedale 812-F5, fols. 85v (two sales), 87r (two sales), 88v (two sales), 90r, 94r (two sales), and 814-F5, fol. 64v, for the cheese seller's records.

22. See Biblioteca Roncioniana Q-I-52, fol. 36r, for the broker's records; see Ospedale 814-F5, fol. 64v, for the cheese seller's records.

23. Ospedale 814-F5, fols. 64v, 87r, shows the payment of £25, s. 10 through a number of offsets. One payment of £7 s.8 is separated into £6 s.15 and s.13.

24. There is one entry in Matteo's book for the cheese seller Giovanni di

Paolo on April 4, 1410 (Biblioteca Roncioniana Q-I-52, fol. 77v). Giovanni is listed first in a sale of rope; but unfortunately, his extant accounts terminate in 1408 and whether he paid the commission cannot be ascertained. In Matteo's book Giovanni is called a basket maker *(corbellaio),* not a cheese seller; Giovanni's friend from Empoli also referred to him as a basket maker (see chap. 1).

25. Today, with perhaps a few exceptions, the seller pays the full commission whether the real estate broker represents the seller or the buyer.

26. Biblioteca Roncioniana Q-I-52, fol. 47r.

27. Ibid., fol. 38r.

28. Ospedale 812-F5, fol. 76r. Matteo is identified in these accounts as a resident of Porta Capo di Ponte. Entries in Matteo's ledger of purchases of land suggest that he probably owned land in the country at this earlier time.

29. Ospedale 817-F6, fols. 1r–3r.

30. Ospedale 816-F6.

31. Ibid., fol. 18r.

32. Ibid., fol. 13r.

33. Ospedale 816-F6.

34. Matteo di Matteo Toffi received £26 s.5 d.10; Ser Conte di Nerozzo received £20 s.14 d.10; and Nicolozzo di Ghetto received £21 s.18 d.6. If the total was £112 s.9 d.8, the fourth assessor, Betto di Ricardino, must have received the largest commission. Ser Conte di Nerozzo's principal occupation probably was merchant banker; he is designated as a *tavoliere* in 1401 and 1404 (Ospedale 812-F5, fols. 54v, 59r).

35. Ospedale 812-F5, fol. 98v.

36. Archivio del Patrimonio Ecclesiastico 433, fols. 7v–8r. A list of rents of the Chapel of the Holy Belt in 1376 includes one for Ferro di Cambio, who was renting a house on "via nuova" at the side of "quella di Bonciano"; he paid £6 and 2 capons per year for it.

37. Ibid., fols. 13r–15v.

38. Ibid. 421.

39. Ibid. 432, fols. 6v, 9v.

40. Ibid. 422, fol. 14v. Biagio del Sozzo guaranteed payment of f.1 £1 s.1 that Martino from Padua owed (March 2, 1392) and s.16 that Simone from Bologna owed (March 20, 1392).

41. For example, see ibid. 424, fols. 1r–2r. The first twelve entries include small loans as well as a few in florins.

42. Ibid. 419, fols. 10v–16v.

43. Ibid., fols. 16v–24v.

44. Ibid., fols. 40r–48v. This figure does not include a large bill of £81 s. 16 for the "signore di Pepionbino" (fols. 41r–41v).

45. Ibid., fols. 54v–61r.

46. Ibid., 422, fols. 41v, 61r. These employees may have been waiters or stable hands. Their wages approximate those of unskilled laborers in the construction industry.

Chapter Four: Bookkeeping

1. Origo, *Merchant of Prato,* 109.

2. See the introduction for extant account books of tradesmen and de Roover's use of those in France and Germany for his article on accounting. Melis's study of the Pisan bank, *La banca pisana,* 96–103, includes information on some small businessmen who dealt with the banking firm of Donato and Parazone at Pisa. Employing entries in the bank's register, Melis was able to reconstruct current accounts for Mone di Cennarino, a tavern owner (98–99), and Gherardo di Ser Meo, a druggist (100–101). Although the bank's register offers valuable data on deposits and withdrawals for these petty entrepreneurs, it reveals little with regard to their accounting procedures.

3. De Roover, "Development of Accounting Prior to Luca Pacioli," 131, divides the del Bene books into three categories: (1) the ledger, or *libro dei debitori e creditori;* (2) the register of purchases and sales, or *libro delle comprevendite;* and (3) the cashbook, or *libro d'entrata e uscita.* Most of the principal books of the Pratese tradesmen have characteristics of all three of these categories. The terms *ledger* and *register* both will be used in referring to them.

4. Charles M. de La Roncière similarly characterizes the records of the business activities and *recordanze* of Lippo di Fede del Sega, who was not an official money changer and engaged in a variety of financial activities. See *Un changeur florentin du Trecento: Lippo di Fede del Sega, 1285 env.–1363 env.* (Paris, 1973), 11–21. De La Roncière points out that, around 1275, prominent businessmen began to separate records of their professional affairs from those of family events and finances, into *libri del dare e dell'avere* and *recordanze,* respectively (12). Neither Lippo di Fede nor, many years later, the Pratese local tradesmen followed this format; instead, they used one book for both kinds of records.

5. Some examples are the substitutions of *b* for *p,* as in "abrile"; *i* for *e,* as in "spidale"; and *r* for *l,* as in "Filettore," the name of a nearby village. For these variations and others in the Pratese language of the period, see P. Fiorelli, "Il linguaggio dei pratesi," in *Storia di Prato,* (Prato, 1981) 3:297–329. A more de-

tailed account of the local "dialect" is found in Serianni, *Testi pratesi*.

In listing the sources available for study of "Pratese" prior to 1350, Serianni failed to note the existence of two sources: the account book of Giovanni di Spinello Viviani (Ceppi 1407 [1337–47]) and the early pages of the account book of Benedetto di Tacco (Ospedale 793-F1 [1344–58]). It seems that the extensive texts of these two sources might contribute more meaningful examples of everyday language usage than the numerous official sources cited. A third source (Ospedale 794-F1) should also be noted, although the text before 1350 is brief. This book is described in the inventory as belonging to "Ricordanze di Bonagiunta Zuccasi (1347–75)"; however, we find that Bonagiunta began his record on January 2, 1348 (fol. 1r), and ended it on May 24, 1348 (fol. 15v). Soon afterward he died, at the height of the Black Death in Tuscany. The next few folios (16r–19r) contain the business assets and liabilities of Bonagiunta's estate. The rest of the book, with a starting date of February 4, 1373, appears to have been used by the Hospital of the Miscericordia.

6. Ospedale 793-F1, fol. 39r, shows that the discrepancy in such cases was not always small. In May 1346, Lencio di Guccio let his account run up to £16 s.10 d.1 and then settled it for £16. This underpayment did not deter the storekeeper from continuing to do business with Lencio. An entry at the bottom of the same page shows Lencio purchasing three ounces of sugar on credit and receiving a loan of s.2.

7. Ospedale 796-F1. On fol. 150v Benedetto di Tacco entered s.7, posted from fol. 3v. This was almost double the correct amount of s.3 d.8.

8. Ospedale 928-F, 1385.

9. The father and the uncle of the druggist di Bonaccorso di Tano were druggists as well (Ospedale 799-F2, fols. 34v, 22v).

10. R. Goldthwaite and G. Mandich, *Studi sulla moneta fiorentina (secoli XIII–XVI)* (Florence, 1994), 60–61.

11. On fol. 17r of Ospedale 928-F, we find "per questa ragione per soldi quindici per dì—lire sedici soldi quindici"; on fol. 13v of Ospedale 812-F5, "debba dare s. ventiquattro d.sei." Arabic numerals were frequently used for dates.

12. At times, the druggist Paolo di Bonaccorso di Tano used arabic numerals for his entries to the right, for example, in the full-page account of Francesco di Nicolaio and Bartolomeo di Jacopo, *lanaiuoli*. The first four entries to the right are arabic: £44, £22, £45, and £15; the remaining entries are roman (Ceppi 1415, fol. 73r).

13. Ospedale 796-F1, between fols. 206v and 207r. In the same register, between fols. 159v and 160r and between fols. 162r and 163v, are two other

loose sheets, the first with 19 names and the second with 10. In Benedetto's earlier register (Ospedale 793-F1, between fols. 134v and 135r) is inserted another loose sheet with 64 names. This sheet is folded once, with the names on three panels only. Amounts appear beside each name, but there are no dates. Totals of £19 s.11, £54 s.2, and £23 s.11 are entered at the bottom of each side. Although no folio reference is given, it is possible to establish that the list begins with Ser Lapo, a priest from the village of Tobbiano, whose account bears the date of April 1, 1345 (fol. 8v). Last on the list is Jacopo di Vanni, with a date of July 1348 at the top of the page on which his account appears (97r); needless to say, at this time the Black Death was at its height in Tuscany. Of the 64 names, 34 are lined through, undoubtedly to indicate subsequent payment; the priest Lapo is neither crossed out on the list nor barred in his account in the register.

14. Ceppi 1407.

15. Prato was unique in having eight precincts *(porte);* other cities and towns of Tuscany usually had either three sections (e.g., Siena, Volterra, and Pisa) or four (e.g., Pistoia, San Gimignano, Arezzo, and Florence after 1343 [before that year Florence had six]). For the election of certain officials and for some administrative functions, the eight precincts of Prato were combined to form quarters.

16. Some common nicknames were *chiamato* and *vocato* (Francesco di Paolo's nicknames), *grande* (large), and *rosso* (red). A complete list of all the nicknames encountered would fill many pages. Ospedale 809-F3, fol. 185v, shows that nicknames were derived from behavioral as well as physical characteristics: Stefano d'Andrea is the "mal gharzone" of the monastery of San Fabiano. Some of the nicknames approximate the physical attributes *(segnali)* cited in Marco Spallanzani's discussion of purchasers of letters of credit; the purchasers' physical characteristics were recorded in order to identify them for the banker in the city where they had the money transferred. The tradesmen, however, did not record moles, warts, scars, or age in their identification of customers. See M. Spallanzani, "Alcune lettere di credito con 'segnali' dell'inizio del Cinquecento," in *Studi in memoria di Mario Abrate* (Turin, 1986), 757–64. The only racial identifications are "Daniello giudeo," "Gaio Dabran giudeo," and "Agnolo Dalia giudeo" (Ospedale 814-F5, fols. 40v, 42r, 90r).

17. See Ospedale 961-F, fols. 18r, 18v, 19r, 19v, for totals posted to the *quaderno longo;* and fols. 20r, 20v, 21r, 21v for totals posted to the "quaderno segnato b (B)." Ospedale 961-F is the one book that has a paper cover. Its survival is surprising because all the pertinent information was posted to a ledger.

18. Ospedale 795-F1, fol. 3r, and 796-F1, fol. 109v, respectively.

19. Benedetto also employed a supplementary book at the beginning and end of his career. In his first register (Ospedale 793-F1) he entered amounts posted from his *quadernuccio* (fols. 69v, 99v [this amount was posted twice], 106v). His last register (Ospedale 797-F1, fol. 105v) contains a reference to his *libriciuolo*.

20. Ospedale 795-F1, fol. 23v.

21. See Ospedale 797-F1, fol. 120r, for *tavola;* fol. 157r for *tavola gesata.*

22. Archivio del Patrimonio Ecclesiastico 422 and 426 contain numerous examples of these references.

23. For example, see Ospedale 793-F1, fol. 8v, and 797-F1, fol. 61r, for wax; 796-F1, fol. 2r, for candles; 796-F1, fol. 6r, for saffron; and 793-F1, fol. 38v, for rental payments.

24. Ospedale 796-F1, 210v. There are entries in Benedetto's last two registers that show payments he received for performing guard duty.

25. Ospedale 928-F. See fol. 20v for a reference to a hauler, 20r for the posting of a loan to a laborer, 16v for a reference to the waste book of the partner Chimenti, and 27r for a reference to the *libro suo* of the partner Guardi.

Chapter Five: A World of Credit and Trust

1. The works of Sapori have provided invaluable background for this study. See the collection of many of his important contributions in *Studi di Storia Economica* (Florence, 1955–67).

2. See Melis, *La banca pisana,* a collection of some of his important works.

3. This paper has been reprinted in Melis, *La banca pisana,* 307–24.

4. Ibid., 311. Also see Marco Tangheroni, "La distribuzione al minuto nel medio evo," 574. Tangheroni speaks of Pisan tailors receiving credit to purchase cloth from suppliers but having to pay off the debt before making a sale of the finished product. He does not, however, cite his source for this statement; in fact, he includes no references in his article. He undoubtedly obtained his information from the statutes of the tailors or from C. Violante, *Economia, società, istituzioni a Pisa nel Medioevo: Saggi e ricerche* (Bari, 1980), 257. Violante mentions this restriction on sales to customers before repayment of the debt to a supplier, as well as a time limit of one month for extension of credit by a merchant.

5. J. Bernard, "Trade and Finance in the Middle Ages," in *Fontana Economic History of Europe,* ed. C. M. Cipolla (New York, 1976), 1:302.

6. Ospedale 928-F, no foliation.

7. Ceppi 1407, fols. 1r–28r.

8. Ospedale 797-F1, fols. 1r–54v.

9. In the books of most tradesmen some accounts have a second entry, following the debit entry for purchase, indicating full payment, sometimes with the phrase "the said day" *(dì detto).*

10. At this time the district of Prato included forty-eight villages. See A. Cecconi, "Le 48 ville dell'antico distretto pratese alla fine del secolo XIII," *Archivio storico pratese* 3 (1920), 15–20; idem, "Toponomastica dell'antico distretto pratese," *Archivio storico pratese* 4 (1921), 152–59; and idem, "Origini delle 48 ville dell'antico distretto pratese," *Archivio storico pratese* 6 (1926), 15–26. Fiumi, *Demografia,* 109 n. 32, points out that between 1419 and 1420 the number of villages was reduced to 42. Although no list of the villages represented by customers was made, most if not all of the 48 villages are mentioned in the entries of the account books.

11. Ospedale 796-F1, fol. 208v.

12. Ibid., fol. 197r.

13. Ospedale 795-F1, fol. 3v. Fiumi, *Demografia,* 95, employing data from the estimo of 1372, lists the Saccagnini family as the wealthiest in Prato, with an assessment of £4,000. Giovanni himself had three family members and an assessment of £600.

14. Ospedale 796-F1, fol. 43v; 797-F1, fol. 1r.

15. Ospedale 827-F9, fol. 25r.

16. Ospedale 814-F5, fol. 30r.

17. Ibid., fol. 48v.

18. Ibid., fol. 60v.

19. Sapori, "Economica e morale alla fine del Trecento," 1:155–79. It was this article, followed by a similar portrayal of Datini in Origo, *Merchant of Prato,* that generated an acrimonious and inconsequential debate with Federigo Melis. For Melis's defense of Datini, see "Aspetti della vita economica medievale," *Prato storia e arte* 7 (1963), 1–13, in which he spends far more ink justifying his high opinion of Datini and harshly criticizing Sapori and Origo than in summarizing his recently published *Aspetti della vita economica medievale,* the alleged purpose of the article.

20. Ceppi 1407. See fols. 4r, 7r, 12r, 14v, 63r, 69r, 75r, 80r for laborers, and 64r, 64v, 70v, 78v, 81v for textile workers.

21. Ospedale 809-F3, fol. 16v.

22. Ospedale 797-F1, fols. 1r–54v.

23. These examples of occupations come from the earliest account book of Ceppi 1407, fols. 64v, 75,, and 81v, respectively. It would be possible to add

numerous other occupations by references to the later registers. See chap. 2 for other occupations of women.

24. See F. Edler de Roover, *Glossary of Mediaeval Terms of Business: Italian Series, 1200–1600* (Cambridge, Mass., 1934), 308.

25. See Ospedale 793-F1, fol. 78r, for a coat; Ceppi 1407, fol. 65r, for a hoe; Ospedale 793-F1, fol. 5r, for a pike.

26. Ceppi 1407, fol. 65r.

27. Ospedale 793-F1, fol. 78r.

28. Ospedale 793-F1, fol. 5r.

29. Ospedale 796-F1, fol. 145v.

30. Ceppi 1407, fols. 13v, 15r.

31. Serianni, *Testi pratesi,* 103–61.

32. Ibid. He used Bonaventura Copie, Ghino f. Arivieri, Pericetto, and Meo f. Ser Bonaventura 49, 22, 19, and 17 times, respectively.

33. Ibid., 155. That notary was Cacialoste f. del Ventura Angiorini.

34. Ospedale 804-F4, fol. 15v.

35. Ceppi 1407, fols. 54v, 55r.

36. Ospedale 799-F2, fol. 37r.

37. Ospedale 793-F1, fol. 5r; 804-F4, fol. 15v; Ceppi 1407, fol. 62v.

38. Giovanni di Spinello Viviani used the adjective *presente* to denote witnesses (Ceppi 1407, fols. 62v, 66v, 75v).

39. Ospedale 812-F5, fol. 12v.

40. Ospedale 809-F3, fol. 21r.

41. See ibid., fol. 45r, where the account is continued.

42. Ceppi 1407, fol. 66v.

43. Ibid., fols. 1r–2r.

44. Ibid., fols. 1r–61v.

45. Ibid., fols. 31r, 38v, 47v, 56v.

46. Ibid., fol. 31r ("Vimano ci dee dare li quali ci promise per Rosono Pacinini sono posti per arieto a sua ragione dove ci dee dare lo detto Rosono fue questo libro arieto a ff. 3–38").

47. Ceppi, 1407, opening folio (no foliation).

48. For an example of a debt older than two years for which Giovanni sought Vimano's help, see the account of Piero di Bocchi (ibid., fol. 48r), which includes a prior debt of s.24 posted from fol. 10 with a date of January 1338. For some other old debts, Giovanni also sought the assistance of his "collection agency": Vimano made payments for two customers noted on fol. 60v and for Pasquino Ferrovecchio (the last name on the list), noted on fol. 61v.

49. See ibid., fol. 5v, for the opening account, fol. 48r for the continuation.

50. Ibid., fols. 54v–55r.

51. Ibid., fol. 75v.

52. See Ospedale 793-F1, fols. 1v–46v, October 20, 1344, to October 18, 1346, for Benedetto's number and volume of sales. See Ceppi 1407, fols. 1r–28r, for Giovanni's number and volume of sales.

53. Benedetto granted a total of £103 s.4 d.2 in credit in 1344–46. Of this, only £2 s.19 d.8 was not paid during this time period. The later years of this register (Ospedale 793-F1) show a collection rate above 95 percent.

54. Ospedale 796-F1, fols. 2r–63v; 797-F1, fols. 1r–63v.

55. Ospedale 814-F5, fols. 15v–39v.

56. Archivio del Patrimonio Ecclesiastico 425, fols. 7r, 8r.

57. Ospedale 827-F9, fols. 35r, 45v.

58. Ceppi 1407, fols. 1r–14v (counting from the back).

59. Ibid., fols. 1v and 2r, respectively (counting from the back).

60. See ibid. (counting from the back), fol. 2r, for offset of a purchase, fol. 12r for payment to a third party.

61. Ibid., fol. 12r (counting from the back).

62. Ospedale 812-F5.

63. Ibid., fol. 2r.

64. Ibid., fol. 17v. The last entry without a date shows that the balance of £114 was paid by Paolo's father, Ser Ambrogio.

65. Ospedale 812-F5, fol. 40r. He bought £41 s.13 d.8 of cheese on June 27, 1398, and made his final remittance on July 10.

66. Ospedale 812-F5, fol. 41r. This supplier waited from August 21, 1398, to May 15, 1404.

67. Ospedale 812-F5, fol. 43r. Paolo recorded a credit of £5 in September 1398 and a debit for Rosso's purchase of £5 on April 8, 1399.

68. De Roover, "Development of Accounting Prior to Luca Pacioli," 125. Also see T. P. McLaughlin, "The Teachings of the Canonists on Usury (XII, XIII, and XIV Centuries)," *Mediaeval Studies* 2 (1940), 11. McLaughlin outlines the provisions but does not discuss their effects.

69. Castellani, *Nuovi testi fiorentini del Dugento,* 1:674–96.

70. Ceppi 1407, fol. 1r (counting from the back).

71. Ospedale 810-F3, fols. 78r, 78v.

72. Ospedale 809-F3, fol. 164r.

73. See Ospedale 814-F5, fol. 60v, for a payment of a debt of Datini's made four years after his death.

74. Ospedale 812-F5, fol. 2v. The evaluation was recorded on May 6, 1390. On June 1, 1396, the innkeeper Cambio di Ferro recorded the exchange rate of £4 s.18 for forty-five *bolognini* (Archivio del Patrimonio Ecclesiastico 423, fol. 2r). Both records cite a rate of slightly more than s.2 for one *bolognino.*

75. Ospedale 812-F5, fol. 22v.

76. See Ospedale 810-F3, fol. 47v, January 2, 1383, for the grossi; see fol. 42r for the quattrini. On September 20, 1392, Master Andrea of the *gramatica* made a payment of 4 grossi for a coat for his wife, and the tailor Domenico di Jacopo valued them at s.22, or s.5$^{1}/_{2}$ each—the same exchange rate as in 1383 (Ospedale 803-F2, fol. 34v).

77. See G. Giani, *Ebbe Prato una zecca? esame storico critico della controversa questione* (Prato, 1915), and M. Bernocchi, *Il gigliato pratese* (Prato, 1970). L. Travaini speaks of a mint active in Prato in 1336–43 ("L'organizzazione delle zecche toscane nel XIV secolo," in *La Toscana nel secolo XIV: Caratteri di una civiltà regionale* [San Miniato, 1988; Centro di studi sulla civiltà del tardo medioevo], 242).

78. Biblioteca Roncioniana Q-I-52, fols. 46v, 72r. Of the numerous entries for land sales in the account books studied, these are the only ones with such a specification.

79. See Ospedale 796-F1, fols. 122r, 184v, 122v, 119v, 163r, 42r, for transactions of 2, 3, 4, 5, 6, and 11 florins; see Ospedale 797-F1, fol. 16v, for a transaction of 17 florins.

80. The moneylender Sinibaldo also recorded values for the florin in 1285–86. See Serianni, *Testi pratesi,* 103 (for a value of s.36 d.2), 111 (for a value of s.35 d.9), 116 (for a value of s.36).

81. In Ospedale 796-F1, fol. 119v, June 6, 1370, see 2 florins "valono £3 s.6 l'uno"; to the right, see note of £6 s.12 for the price of the two. Ospedale 812-F5, fol. 35v, shows evaluations of s.80 per florin first, then an evaluation of £8 for 2 florins on November 8, 1397.

82. Ospedale 797-F1, fol. 159v (counting from the back): "anne dato dì detto" (December 12, 1390), "uno fiorf. d'oro—£3 s.18."

83. See Ospedale 827-F9, fol. 37r, January 24, 1394, "fiorini due d'oro" and "ff.2" to the right. Also see fol. 175r, July 8, 1390, where the type of florin is specified: "ff uno d'oro e fue di suggiello—ff1."

84. Goldthwaite, *Building,* 304–5.

85. C. de La Roncière, *Florence: Centre économique régional au XIVe siècle* (Aix-en-Provence, 1976), 310–13, notes the payment of florins to masons in the mid-fourteenth century at Florence.

86. C. M. Cipolla, *The Monetary Policy of Fourteenth-Century Florence* (Berkeley, 1982), 22–29.

87. See Ospedale 799-F2, fol. 6r, for Niccolò di Cambioni; Ospedale 812-F5, fol. 45r, for Datini.

88. Ospedale 827-F9, fol. 37r.

89. See Ospedale 929-F31, fol. 12r, for Bartolomeo; fol. 14r for Duccio. Another Bartolomeo also received payment in gold, for shoeing donkeys (928-F, fol. 11r).

90. P. Meyer and G. Guigue, "Fragments du grand livre d'un drapier de Lyon, 1320–1323," *Romania* 35 (1906), 428–44.

91. P. Meyer, "Le livre-journal de Maître Ugo Teralh, notaire et drapier à Forcalquier, 1330–1332," *Notices et extraits des manuscrits de la Bibliothèque Nationale* 36 (1899), 129–70.

92. C. Portal, "Le livre-journal de Jean Saval, marchand-drapier à Carcassonne, 1340–1341," *Bulletin historique et philologique du comitè des travaux historiques et scientifiques* (Paris, 1901–2), 423–49.

93. E. Forestié, ed., *Les livres de comptes des Frères Bonis: Marchands montalbanais du XIVe siècle,* 2 vols. (Paris, 1890–94).

94. Ibid., 2:419.

95. A. Chroust and H. Proesler, eds., *Das Handlungsbuch der Holzschuler in Nürnberg von 1304–1307* (Erlangen, 1934). The entries are all in Latin.

96. H. Nirrnheim, *Das Handlungsbuch Vickos von Geldersen* (Hamburg, 1895; reprinted, Osaka, Japan, 1977).

Chapter Six: Loans

1. Ospedale 1212-F11. For example, on the first page of his book he recorded a loan of 10 florins to Jacopo di Cecco on October 1, 1346, at a 22 percent rate of interest.

2. Serianni, *Testi pratesi.* Sinibaldo frequently quoted an exchange rate of s.36 for the florin. His loans ranged from £1 to £188 s.18.

3. Pampaloni, "Prato nella republica fiorentina," 2:37.

4. Fiumi, *Demografia,* 93 n.11.

5. Pampaloni, "Prato nella republica fiorentina," 2:37 nn. 17, 18; Fiumi, *Demografia,* 136–37. Judith Brown and Anthony Molho cite the activities of Jewish moneylenders in other areas of the Florentine region (Pescia and Arezzo, respectively) at the end of the fourteenth and beginning of the fifteenth centuries. See J. Brown, "Renaissance Pescia: An Economic and Social History of a Rural Commune in Tuscany" (Ph.D. diss., Johns Hopkins University,

1977), 220–21; and A. Molho, "A Note on Jewish Moneylenders in Tuscany in the Late Trecento and Early Quattrocento," in *Renaissance Studies in Honor of Hans Baron,* ed. A. Molho and J. Tedeschi (Dekalb, Ill., 1971), 99–119.

6. The terms *tavoliere* and *banchiere* often were used to designate the same individual. In Matteo di Matteo Toffi's ledger (Biblioteca Roncioniana Q-I-52, fols. 33v, 53r) Benedetto di Filippo is called a *banchiere;* in Paolo di Ser Ambrogio's (Ospedale 812-F5, fol. 90r) he is a *tavolieri.* Although no evidence has been found that local bankers in Prato operated as pawnbrokers, in Florence in the second half of the fifteenth century they operated as high-level pawnbrokers, often taking jewelry as pawns. See Goldthwaite, "Local Bankers," 28–29, for a discussion of loans granted by Bindaccio de' Cerchi and secured by jewelry or promissory notes.

7. See chap. 7. Benedetto's surname, Amadori, does not appear in these references, but such an omission was not uncommon, particularly when the individual was well known.

8. Pampaloni, "Prato nella republica fiorentina," 2:36–37.

9. Fiumi, *Demografia,* 136–37.

10. Ospedale 804-F4, fols. 9r, 10v.

11. Ceppi 1322, fol. 51r.

12. Archivio del Patrimonio Ecclesiastico 420, fols. 18v, 19r, 22r, 24r.

13. Ibid., fol. 24r; ibid. 419, fols. 30v, 65v.

14. Ospedale 812-F5, fol. 76v. Checco is also mentioned by the innkeeper Cambio di Ferro (Archivio del Patrimonio Ecclesiastico 426, fol. 2r).

15. Ospedale 795-F1, fol. 28r. The posted entry on fol. 165r of the main register (Ospedale 796-F1), gives the customer's name (Giunta) and splits the loan into two parts, £2 and s.4. Perhaps the s.4 represents the interest that Giunta had to pay the moneylender.

16. Ospedale 810-F3, fol. 185r.

17. Ospedale 809-F3, fol. 35v. The florin equaled £3 s.19$\frac{1}{2}$, or s.79 d.6. Agnolo is also mentioned by the innkeeper Cambio di Ferro (Archivio del Patrimonio Ecclesiastico 424, fol. 3v).

18. Matalena, the wife of the cheese seller Giovanni di Paolo, made loans (Ospedale 810-F3, fols. 117r, 136v, 152v).

19. See Ceppi 1322, fols. 15r, 16r, for examples of loans to people other than customers.

20. See Ospedale 793-F1, fols. 98v, 106v, for examples of multiple loans to the same person.

21. Ospedale 796-F1, 795-F1.

22. Ospedale 796-F1, fols. 148v–175r (102 of 231 accounts had loans).

23. Ospedale 797-F1, fols. 120v–147r.

24. See Ospedale 814-F5, fol. 3v, for two loans to Simone di Giovanni with a maturity of two years. For a loan repaid in a few days, see Ospedale 796-F1, fol. 28v. On this folio, Brother Matteo was debited s.2, which Benedetto di Tacco had paid to a Giovanni for him on May 2; on May 6 Matteo repaid it. For a loan repaid the next day, see Ospedale 797-F1, fol. 20v. For a loan repaid the same day, see Ospedale 796-F1, fol. 8r, which shows the tavern keeper Paolo d'Agostino borrowing £1 s.7 and returning it later in the day.

25. See Ospedale 803-F2, fol. 12v, for two loans of d.8 by the tailor Domenico di Jacopo. See Ospedale 804-F3, fol. 54v, for the loan of £450, which the doublet maker Marco di Sandro granted jointly to two customers.

26. Ospedale 793-F1 (average of s.15), 795-F1 (average of s.17), 796-F1 (average of s.16), 797-F1 (average of s.18).

27. Ospedale 810-F3, fols. 9r–18r; Ospedale 803-F2.

28. He recorded no loans in the last few months of 1344, covered by the beginning of his first ledger; during 1356–58 he confined his business to the making and selling of candles (see chap. 2).

29. Ospedale 793-F1, fol. 171r.

30. Ceppi 1415, fol. 95v; Ospedale 803-F2, fols. 2r, 3r.

31. Ospedale 797-F1, fol. 64r; 799-F2, fol. 7v; 809-F3, fol. 16v; 797-F1, fol. 116r; 795-F1, fol. 3v. Fiumi, *Demografia,* 95, ranks the Saccagnini family as the wealthiest in Prato in 1372.

32. Ospedale 797-F1, fol. 156r.

33. See S. Sahar, "The Regulation and Presentation of Women in Economic Life (Thirteenth to Eighteenth Centuries)" (paper presented at the annual seminar "La donna nell'economia, secc. XIII–XVIII," Istituto Internazionale di Storia Economica "F. Datini," Prato, April 1989), 11.

34. Ospedale 810-F3, fols. 9r and 21r, respectively.

35. Ospedale 803-F2, fol. 8v.

36. Ospedale 796-F1, fols. 40r, 153v, 159v; 795-F1, fol. 38v. Even earlier, in 1348, two married women are listed as borrowers on the same page of Benedetto di Tacco's register (his first register, Ospedale 793-F1, fol. 97v).

37. Ospedale 814-F5, fol. 103r.

38. Ospedale 796-F1, fol. 151r.

39. See Ospedale 795-F1, fol. 38r, for the knife; 797-F1, fol. 140v, for the red coat; 793-F1, fol. 116v, for the belt.

40. For example, see the notations "acci per sengnale uno travaliuolo" (he has [given] us a napkin as a marker), Ospedale 793-F1, fol. 75v; and "acci lasciato uno libricciuolo" (he has left to us a notebook), 796-F1, fol. 145.

41. Ospedale 797-F1, fol. 11r.

42. Ibid., fol. 107v.

43. See Ospedale 793-F1, fol. 118r ("acci pengno uno fiorino" for a loan of s.10 in 1349); 796-F1, fol. 8v (4 florins for a loan of £2 s.10 in 1365); 797-F1, fol. 85v (1 florin for a loan of £2 s.10 in 1385).

44. Ospedale 797-F1, fol. 64r.

45. Further evidence to support this interpretation is his contrasting practice of accepting a florin that is clearly labeled a deposit, then allowing the depositor to make fractional withdrawals. For example, in 1386 a customer deposited *(ci puose un diposito)* 1 florin, which Benedetto evaluated at £3 s.14 d.10. The customer subsequently made four withdrawals totaling this amount (Ospedale 797-F1, fol. 95r).

46. See Ospedale 797-F1, fol. 60v. The loans recorded here total £2 s.3 d.6; he paid this amount four months later, and *anne riauto lo fiof. d'oro.*

47. Ospedale 796-F1, fol. 4r.

48. Ospedale 795-F1, fol. 52v. The florin would have been worth £3 s.13 d.4.

49. Ospedale 804-F4, fol. 90r.

50. Ospedale 796-F1, fol. 199v.

51. See Ospedale 809-F3, fol. 49r, for a loan of 8 florins with the repayment conditions spelled out. Other examples are found in Ospedale 796-F1, fol. 217v, and 799-F2, fol. 37v.

52. Ospedale 803-F2, fol. 50r.

53. See Ospedale 799-F2, fol. 27v, for the 7 florins, fol. 28r for the 10 florins. The doublet maker Marco di Sandro had two borrowers write in his book for loans of 4 and 6 florins (Ospedale 804-F4, fol. 3r [counting from the back]). For similar examples from the books of the two cheese sellers, see Ospedale 809-F3, fol. 34v (£11) and 812-F5, fol. 19r (£39).

54. The slip of paper was found between fols. 94v and 95r of Ospedale 812-F5.

55. Ibid., fol. 95r. Why Paolo singled out the well-known and respected Hospital of the Misericordia in this case is not clear. Perhaps he had had a bad experience with the particular rector or accountant in office at the time.

56. Ospedale 799-F2, fol. 45v.

57. Some important studies on taxes in Tuscany are C. de la Roncière, "Indirect Taxes or 'Gabelles' at Florence in the Fifteenth Century," in *Florentine Studies,* ed. N. Rubinstein, (London, 1968); E. Fiumi, "L'imposta diretta nei comuni medioevali della Toscana," in *Studi in onore di Armando Sapori* (Milan, 1957); and D. Herlihy, "Direct and Indirect Taxation in Tuscan Urban Finance,

1200–1400," in *Finances et comptabilité urbaines du XIIIe au XVIe siècle* (Brussels, 1964).

58. R. Mueller, "Les preteurs juifs à Venise au Moyen Age," *Annales E.S.C.* 30 (1975), 1277–303; Molho, "Note on Jewish Moneylenders in Tuscany." The loans discussed by Mueller and Molho were far larger than those made by the shopkeepers at Prato.

59. See Ospedale 796-F1, fol. 69v, for an example of a man who borrowed to pay the salt tax in 1367; see 797-F1, fol. 116v, for a woman who borrowed for the same reason in 1387.

60. See Ospedale 796-F1, fol. 117v, for an example of borrowing for the estimo in 1369; see 797-F1, fol. 113v, for a similar example in 1387. See Ospedale 797-F1, fol. 98r, for a baker who borrowed £3 s.2 d.6 to pay the gabella.

61. Ospedale 797-F1, fol. 30v.

62. Ospedale 799-F2, fol. 21v. Domenico wanted no misunderstanding concerning this transaction; he named the seller, the price per staioro, and the notary who had drawn up the contract. The earlier description of the dinner party indicates a close relationship between Domenico and Filippo.

63. Ospedale 794-F1, fol. 2v.

64. See Ospedale 795-F1, fol. 43v, and the posting in 796-F1, fol. 194v, for the millet; 797-F1, fol. 111r, for the pig; and 797-F1, fol. 96r, for the wine.

65. Similarly, as indicated in chap. 5, the vast majority of recipients of credit for purchases were not required to furnish security or verification.

66. Ospedale 809-F3, fol. 35v. The innkeeper Cambio di Ferro also lent Agnolo money (f.2 £4) without security (Archivio del Patrimonio Ecclesiastico 423, fol. 75v).

67. Ospedale 814-F3. Fifty-two of Giovanni's 190 loans were for a florin or more; the total value of these large loans was £615 s.8, all of which he collected in full.

68. Ospedale 804-F4.

69. Ospedale 803-F2.

70. Ospedale 793-F1, 795-F1, 796-F1, 797-F1.

71. See Ospedale 795-F1 for the journal, 796-F1 for the ledger.

72. Ospedale 814-F5, fols. 18v, 28v, 70r.

73. Ibid., fol. 31v.

74. De Roover, "Development of Accounting Prior to Luca Pacioli," 125.

75. Ospedale 799-F2, fol. 74r. See fols. 39v and 73v for other loans in which the borrowers received 30 and 20 florins, and acknowledged receipt of 60 and 30 florins, respectively.

76. Castellani, *Nuovi testi fiorentini del Dugento,* 1:304.

77. D. Herlihy, "Santa Maria Impruneta: A Rural Commune in the Late Middle Ages," in *Florentine Studies,* ed. N. Rubinstein (London, 1968), 262.

78. Goldthwaite, "Local Banking," 36 n. 45.

79. Ibid., 35.

80. Ospedale 799-F2, fol. 74r. The florin in 1385 was valued at s.72, a staio of grain at s.30 (R. Goldthwaite, "I prezzi del grano a Firenze nei secoli XIV–XVI," *Quaderni storici* 28 [1975] 33). If questioned, would he have produced the receipt and hoped not to be asked to open the register?

81. Ospedale 803-F2, fol. 22v. Edler de Roover, *Glossary of Mediaeval Terms of Business,* 225, gives one of the meanings of *pro* as "interest," along with an illustration of that meaning.

82. Ospedale 803-F2, fol. 22v.

83. See Biblioteca Roncioniana Q-I-52, fol. 6v, for the reference to the lack of a commission. For examples of terms of agreement, see fol. 34r (maturity date of a year), 73r (demand loan at a rate of s.2 per florin per month, with a guarantor), and 85r (pledge of two bales of flax for a loan of £32).

84. For the ten loans, see ibid., fols. 2v (a loan of f.12), 5r (f.12), 6v (f.15 with 25% interest), 34r (f.13), 73r (f.14), 75r (£40), 83r (f.9), 85r (£32), 87v (f.15), 88r (f.25). When he refers to interest, he uses the term *providigione.*

85. Ibid., fol. 47. Matteo made four loans, totaling 24 florins, to Luparello di Verzone, a frequent customer of his. The purpose of one loan was to enable Luparello to pay the treasurer of the Commune of Prato.

Chapter Seven: Banking and the Local Economy

1. For example, R. de Roover, *L'évolution de la lettre de change, XIVe–XVIIIe siècle* (Paris, 1953), provides a detailed study of this important credit instrument from the fourteenth through the eighteenth centuries. His "New Interpretations of the History of Banking," in *Business, Banking, and Economic Thought,* ed. J. Kirshner (Chicago, 1974), 200–238, still provides a valuable survey of the history of banking from 1300 to 1800, although it was first published in 1954. De Roover's guide to bibliographies at the end of this article indicates sources for the vast literature on this subject. A. B. Usher, *The Early History of Deposit Banking in Mediterranean Europe* (Cambridge, Mass., 1943), focuses on a later period in Barcelona. The early sections of R. de Roover, *The Rise and Decline of the Medici Bank* (Cambridge, Mass., 1963) also provide information on the origins of banking. For an assessment of Melis's contributions, see L. de Rosa, introduction to *La banca pisana,* by F. Melis, ix–xxxv.

2. Melis, *La banca pisana*, 311–12. Although more about Melis's views on the origins of banking can be found in many of his writings, the essence of his interpretation is summarized in his "La grande conquista," 307–24. This article is the basis for the following review of Melis's conclusions.

3. De Roover, *Money, Banking, and Credit* (Cambridge, Mass., 1984) locates the origins of banking in the evolving practices of money changers.

4. Melis, *La banca pisana*, 315.

5. Ibid., 315–16.

6. Ceppi 1407, Ospedale 793-F1.

7. Ceppi 1407, fols. 1v, 11v.

8. Ibid., fol. 12r (counting from the back).

9. Ospedale 810-F3, fol. 4v.

10. Ospedale 812-F5, fol. 2v.

11. Ospedale 811-F5, fol. 17v.

12. Ospedale 812-F5, fol. 4v.

13. Ibid., fol. 12v.

14. In January and February 1393, Paolo employed a third brother, Biagio, for two purchases of cheese; he paid off the account the following August (ibid., fol. 17r).

15. Ibid., fol. 14v.

16. Ceppi 1415, fols. 14v, 59v, 97v, 118r. This current account is discussed in some detail in chap. 5.

17. Ospedale 799-F2, fol. 7v. Ser Jacopo was the father or grandfather of the aforementioned bankers who carried his name. This family of bankers often provided services for the tradesmen of Prato.

18. Ospedale 810-F3, fol. 67r. The loan was repaid by the end of the month.

19. Ospedale 809-F3, fol. 27v.

20. Other tradesmen whose dealings with bankers appear in the account books are the druggist Matteo di Matteo (Ospedale 815-F6, fols. 4r, 19v, 34r, 42v, 57r, 58r, 66r, 75r), the secondhand dealer Taddeo di Chelli (Ospedale 827-F9, fol. 38r), and the tailor Domenico di Jacopo (Ospedale 803-F2, fols. 2r, 13r, 20r).

21. Ospedale 812-F5, fols. 7v, 8r (two entries), 19r, 25r, 27r, 31v, 32v, 54v, 59r, 59v, 63v, 67v, 69r, 69v, 70r, 73v, 78v, 99v, 100r, 103r, 103v, 107r; Ospedale 814-F5, fols 19v, 32r, 38r, 86r, 94v.

22. Ospedale 814-F5, fol. 38r; ibid., fol. 94v; Ospedale 812-F5, fol. 27r; ibid., fol. 32v.

23. See ibid., fols. 63v, 69r, 70r, 73v, 99v, 103r, 103v, 107r, for references to Benedetto di Filiippo. Whether these entries represent a current account with Benedetto is doubtful; if they do, activity in the account was limited to about one transaction a year.

24. Fiumi, *Demografia,* 487, mentions Paolo's father, Bonaccorso, and his uncle Marco as members of the Tani family, although he is not sure they have the surname Tani. In the estimo of 1372 Bonaccorso and Marco have large assessments and are listed as *speziali.* Bonaccorso had nine children, one of whom was our druggist, Paolo. Fiumi further suggests that the family of Bonaccorso migrated to Florence. If this is true, the son Paolo returned to Prato and entered the occupation that his father had practiced.

25. For the reconstructed account of Gherardo di Ser Meo, see Melis, *La banca pisana,* 100–101; also see his brief discussion of it on 102–3. The reader may wonder why I have not given a summary of Paolo's entire account, as Melis did for the Pisan druggist. Unfortunately, in Paolo's ledger the deterioration of the folios at the bottom prevents a similar reconstruction.

26. Ceppi 1415, fols. 2r and 118r, respectively. There is one additional entry after February 9, but it has no date.

27. Ibid., fols. 2r, 8v, 14v, 59v, 97v, 118r (half a page). In Paolo's credit register (Ceppi 1414) there are a few additional entries for this current account, where the totals of debits and credits equal one another. On fol. 61v are two debits for the druggist (s.4 d.4 and s.15 d.15) and one credit (£1 s.10). On fol. 62v are two debits (£1 and s.10) and a credit (£1 s.10). These transactions took place in January and February of 1393, soon after the opening of the current account. Paolo does not indicate why these entries were not included in his debit register (Ceppi 1415) with all the others.

28. After my brief perusal of the ledger, it was sent to Florence for repair in order to prevent further erosion of the pages. A year later it still had not been returned to Prato.

29. In Ceppi 1415, fol. 105r, Ser Jacopo is further identified as "Ser Jacopo di Neri." Moreover, in Ospedale 815-F6, fols. 19v, 50v, we find "di Ser Jacopo di Neri" added to the names of Stefano, Biagio, and Nanni.

30. For more information on this family—cognomen Pipini—including Giovanni (Nanni) and Biagio, see Fiumi, *Demografia,* 452–53. For Leonardo, see Ospedale 815-F6, fol. 7r; for Stefano see Ospedale 810-F3, fol. 171v.

31. Ospedale 812-F5, fol. 4v.

32. See Ospedale 812-F5, fols. 27r (two references), 31v, 32v, for Fazino; Ospedale 815-F6, fol. 75r, for Pacino.

33. Paolo used fol. 1r (Ceppi 1415) for the customery invocation to God, etc; and fol. 1v is blank.

34. On fol. 2r the value of the florin was s.78, on subsequent folios it was s.76.

35. The last entry of fol. 8v shows a credit of "f.17 £x" with a tear right after the *x*. It is impossible to determine what the remaining numerals were or whether the debit of s.4 from the first page (2r) was subtracted before the posting to the third page (fol. 14v).

36. The sixth entry bears this date of February 9; a final, undated cash deposit of £1 closes the account.

37. Melis, *La banca pisana,* 100–101.

38. Ibid., 103. To judge with certainty, Melis would have needed the income-outgo journal to determine dates for pertinent debits and credits.

39. Goldthwaite, "Local Banking," 31–37, concludes that bankers and their clients were still wary of including any reference to interest in their accounts.

40. In "Local Banking," Goldthwaite points out the wide availability of "banking" services from businesses other than banking firms; see 44–45 for examples of businesses that accepted deposits and facilitated transfer and exchange.

41. Ospedale 795-F1, fol. 13v.

42. This may be an entry by the apprentice, who was allowed to write in the waste book (see Benedetto's note to this effect on the opening page of Ospedale 795-F1). Perhaps the apprentice wanted to make a complete record for his employer of all cash received.

43. See Benedetto's records of twelve deposits in Ospedale 796-F1, fols. 6v, 12r, 16r, 33v, 35v, 44r (over £100), 49v, 59r, 64r (over £100), 68v, 73v, 180r; two deposits in Ospedale 797-F1, fol. 95r; and three deposits in Ospedale 795-F1, fols. 6r, 6v, 38v.

44. For the former see Ceppi 1407, fol. 2r (counting from the back); see fols. 5v–7r for seven other deposits held by Giovanni. See Ospedale 812-F5, fols. 73v, 75r, 105r, for three deposits held by Paolo di Ser Ambrogio. One deposit held by Paolo for Monna Francesca, a servant of Paolo's father, may have been just an accommodation for a member of the household (fol. 73v). If the financial status of this particular servant in any way reflects the wage scale for others in Ser Ambrogio's employ, service in his household must have been eagerly sought: in the first six months of 1406 she made two deposits, one of 7 florins and one of £15 s.17 d.6. These apparently were surplus funds, for she did not withdraw them until 1409.

45. Ospedale 812-F5, fols. 16r, 33v, 35v, 68v.

46. Both forms of convenience are represented in the account of Piero di Rodolfo, which was used for a purchase of s.3 d.9 and two payments to the commune of £5 and s.3 (Ospedale 796-F1, fol. 59r).

47. Ospedale 809-F3, fol. 47r.

48. Ceppi 1407, fol. 2v (counting from the back).

49. Ospedale 812-F5, fol. 105r. The priest had deposited £4 s.2 d.9. After paying a creditor of the priest in excess of the amount on deposit, Paolo had to obtain from him the s.1 d.4 owed.

Conclusion

1. In July 1990, when the communes Poggio a Caiano and Carmignano held a referendum on sentiment for joining an anticipated Pratese province or remaining in the Florentine province, the local newspaper spoke of the choice as one between "noble and fun-loving" Florence and "working" Prato.

2. Throughout the year tradesmen set up their stalls, selling not tourist souvenirs as at the cathedral in Pisa, but commodities for everyday use.

3. In the middle of the nineteenth century E. Repetti spoke of Prato as representing for Tuscany what Manchester represented for England (*Dizionario Corografico della Toscana* [1855; reprint, Florence, 1977], 1083). This work is still valuable as a source of information on Prato itself and on many of the villages of the Pratese district. Comitato Mariano della diocesi, ed., *Prato: Città della Madonna* (Città di Castello, 1988), describes Prato's numerous churches and shrines devoted to the Virgin Mary. The holy belt of the Virgin, a relic displayed five times a year by the bishop and, in particular, on September 8, when representatives from all over Italy are present, emphasizes the importance of the cult of Mary for the Pratesi.

4. Ospedale 804-F4, 5v (counting from the back). The rent paid by the slipper maker, Stefano di Bartolomeo, was 2 florins.

5. Tangheroni, "La distribuzione al minuto nel medio evo," 576–79.

6. T. Blomquist, "The Drapers of Lucca and the Marketing of Cloth in the Mid-Thirteenth Century," in *Economy, Society, and Government in Medieval Italy: Essays in Memory of Robert L. Reynolds,* ed. D. Herlihy, R. Lopez, and V. Slessarev (Kent, Ohio, 1969), 67–72.

7. Because this average value was approximately equivalent to that of a florin at the time, the larger sales may well have been to rural peddlers. The smaller sales are more likely to have been to individuals on credit.

8. A. Sapori, *Una compagnia di Calimala ai primi del Trecento* (Florence, 1932),

49–50. Sapori cites the extant entries for retail sales of cloth for third parties, entries that show only cash transactions, as further evidence that all retail sales were for cash. Requiring cash was an understandable practice by a firm selling for other businesses, but it does not necessarily follow that the firm denied credit to its own retail customers.

BIBLIOGRAPHY

Manuscript Sources

Archivio di Stato di Firenze:
   Estimo 215

Archivio di Stato di Prato:
   Archivio del Patrimonio Ecclesiastico
   Ceppi
   Ospedale

Biblioteca Roncioniana (Prato):
   Q-I-52

Published Original and Secondary Sources

Astorre, A. "Il 'libro delle senserie' di Girolamo di Agostino Maringhi, 1483–1485." *Archivio storico italiano* 146 (1988), 389–408.

———. "Appunti sull'esercizio dello Speziale a Firenze nel Quattrocento." *Archivio storico italiano* 147 (1989), 31–62.

Badiani, Gabriele. *L'arte pratese: Storia arte e turismo.* Florence, 1989.

Baliani, Angiolo. "I restauri della Fortezza." *Archivio storico pratese* 16 (1938), 97–110.

———. "Il palazzo Datini." *Archivio storico pratese* 19 (1941), 49–53.

Bardazzi, Silvestro. "Struttura della città medioevale." *Archivio storico pratese* 30 (1954), 21–28.

———. "Il castello dell'Imperatore." *Archivio storico pratese* 31 (1955), 26–35.

Bec, Christian. *Les marchands écrivains à Florence, 1375–1434.* Paris, 1967.

———. "Sur la spiritualité des marchands florentins (fin du Trecento—debut du Quattrocento)." In *Aspetti della vita economica medievale* (Atti del convegno di studi nel X anniversario della morte di Federigo Melis, Firenze-Pisa-Prato, 10–14 marzo 1984). Florence, 1985.

Becker, Marvin M. "Three Cases Concerning the Restitution of Usury in Florence." *Journal of Economic History* 17 (1957), 447–50.

————. "Problemi della finanza publica fiorentina della seconda metà del Trecento e dei primi del Quattrocento." *Archivio storico italiano* 123 (1965), 433–66.

————. "Economic Change and the Emerging Florentine Territorial State." *Studies in the Renaissance* 13 (1966), 7–39.

————. "An Essay on the 'Novi Cives' and Florentine Politics." *Mediaeval Studies* 17 (1966), 35–82.

————. *Florence in Transition.* 2 vols. Baltimore, 1968.

Becker, Marvin M., and Gene A. Brucker. "Una lettera in difesa della dittatura nella Firenze del Trecento." *Archivio storico italiano* 113 (1955), 251–57.

————. "The 'Arti Minori' in Florentine Politics, 1342–1378." *Mediaeval Studies* 18 (1956), 93–104.

Bellosi, Luciano, Allessandro Angelini, and Giovanna Ragionieri. "Le arti figurative." In *Prato storia di una città,* edited by Giovanni Cherubini. Vol. 1★★. Prato, 1991.

Bensa, Enrico. *Francesco di Marco da Prato: Notizie e documenti sulla mercatura italiana del secolo XIV.* Milan, 1928.

Bernard, Jacques. "Trade and Finance in the Middle Ages." In *The Middle Ages.* Vol. 1 of *The Fontana Economic History of Europe,* edited by Carlo M. Cipolla. New York, 1976.

Bernocchi, Mario. *Il gigliato pratese.* Prato, 1970.

————. *Le monete della republica fiorentina.* 4 vols. Florence, 1974–78.

————. *Il sistema monetario fiorentino e le leggi del governo populare del 1378–1382.* Bologna, 1979.

Blomquist, Thomas W. "The Drapers of Lucca and the Marketing of Cloth in the Mid-Thirteenth Century." In *Economy, Society, and Government in Medieval Italy: Essays in Memory of Robert L. Reynolds,* edited by David Herlihy, Robert Lopez, and Vsevolod Slessarev. Kent, Ohio, 1969.

Bowsky, William M. "Direct Taxation in a Medieval Commune: The 'Dazio' in Siena, 1287–1355." In *Economy, Society, and Government in Medieval Italy: Essays in Memory of Robert L. Reynolds,* edited by David Herlihy, Robert Lopez, and Vsevolod Slessarev. Kent, Ohio, 1969.

Brown, Judith C. "Renaissance Pescia: An Economic and Social History of a Rural Commune in Tuscany." Ph.D. diss., Johns Hopkins University, 1977.

————. *In the Shadow of Florence: Provincial Society in Renaissance Pescia.* New York, 1982.

Brucker, Gene A. *Florentine Politics and Society, 1343–1378.* Princeton, N.J., 1962.

————. "The Ciompi Revolution." In *Florentine Studies: Politics and Society in Renaissance Florence,* edited by Nicolai Rubinstein. London, 1968.

————. "The Florentine Popolo Minuto and Its Political Role, 1340–1450." In *Violence and Civil Disorder in Italian Cities, 1200–1500,* edited by Lauro Martines. Berkeley, 1972.

————. *The Civic World of Early Renaissance Florence.* Princeton, N.J., 1977.

Brun, Robert, "A Fourteenth-Century Merchant of Italy: Francesco Datini of Prato." *Journal of Economic and Business History* 2 (1930), 451–66.

Bruzzi, Enrico. "Sulla storia dell'arte della lana in Toscana considerata nella sua genesi e nella sua legislazione." *Archivio storico pratese* 15 (1937), 72–87, 126–40, 157–77; and 16 (1938), 14–42.

————. "L'industria della carta in Prato." *Archivio storico pratese* 18 (1940), 106–14.

————. "L'organizzazione del lavoro nell'antica arte della lana pratese." *Archivio storico pratese* 19 (1941), 57–62.

Caggese, Romulo. *Un comune libero alle porte di Firenze nel secolo XIII: Prato in Toscana.* Florence, 1905.

Cappelli, A. *Cronologia, cronografia e calendari perpetua.* 3rd ed. Milan, 1969.

Cardini, Franco. "La cultura." In *Prato storia di una città,* edited by Giovanni Cherubini. Vol. 1★★. Prato, 1991.

Carlesi, Ferdinando. *Origini della città e del comune di Prato.* Prato, 1904.

Cassandro, Michele. "Commercio, manifatture e industria." In *Prato storia di una città,* edited by Giovanni Cherubini. Vol. 1★. Prato, 1991.

Castellani, Arrigo E. *Nuovi testi fiorentini del Dugento.* 2 vols. Florence, 1952.

Cecconi, Anatolia. "Le 48 ville dell'antico distretto pratese alla fine del secolo XIII." *Archivio storico pratese* 3 (1920), 15–20.

————. "Toponomastica dell'antico distretto pratese." *Archivio storio pratese* 4 (1921), 152–59.

————. "Origini delle 48 ville dell'antico distretto pratese." *Archivio storico pratese* 6 (1926), 15–26.

Cherubini, Giovanni. "Artigiani e salariati nelle città italiane del tardo medioevo." In *Aspetti della vita economica medievale* (Atti del convegno di studi nel X anniversario della morte di Federigo Melis, Firenze-Pisa-Prato, 10–14 marzo 1984). Florence, 1985.

————. "Ascesa e declino del centro medievale (dal Mille al 1494)." In *Prato storia di una città,* edited by Giovanni Cherubini. Vol. 1★★. Prato, 1991.

————, ed. *Prato storia di una città.* 2 vols. Prato, 1991.

Chiappelli, R., ed. *The Dawn of Modern Banking.* New Haven, Conn., 1979.

Chroust, Anton, and Hans Proesler, eds., *Das Handlungsbuch der Holzschuher in Nürnberg von 1304–1307.* Erlangen, 1934.

Ciasca, Raffaele. *L'arte dei Medici e Speziali nella storia e nel commercio fiorentino dal secolo XII al XV.* Florence, 1927.

Cipolla, Carlo M. *Studi di storia della moneta: I movimenti dei cambi in Italia dal secolo XIII al XV.* Pavia, 1948.

———. *Money, Prices, and Civilization in the Mediterranean World.* Princeton, N.J., 1956.

———. *Le avventure della lire.* Milan, 1958.

———. "The Economic Policies of Governments: The Italian and Iberian Peninsulas." In *The Cambridge Economic History of Europe.* Vol. 3, *Economic Organization and Policies in the Middle Ages.* Cambridge, 1963.

———. *Before the Industrial Revolution: European Society and Economy, 1000–1700.* New York, 1980.

———. *The Monetary Policy of Fourteenth-Century Florence.* Berkeley, 1982.

Cohn, Samuel K. *The Laboring Classes in Renaissance Florence.* New York, 1980.

———. *Death and Property in Siena, 1205–1800.* Baltimore, 1988.

Comitato Mariano della diocesi, ed. *Prato: Città della Madonna.* Città di Castello, 1988.

Cristiani, Emilio. "Il libero comune di Prato, secolo XII–XIV." In *Storia di Prato.* Vol. 1. Prato, 1981.

"Cronache e memorie sul tumulto dei Ciompi." In *Rerum Italicarum Scriptores,* edited by Gino Scaramella. Rev. ed., vol. 18, pt. 3. Città di Castello, 1917–34.

De La Roncière, Charles M. "Indirect Taxes of 'Gabelles' at Florence in the Fifteenth Century." In *Florentine Studies: Politics and Society in Renaissance Florence,* edited by Nicolai Rubinstein. London, 1968.

———. *Un changeur florentin du Trecento: Lippo di Fede di Sega, 1285 env.–1363 env.* Paris, 1973.

———. *Florence: Centre économique régional au XIVe siècle.* Aix-en-Provence, 1976.

———. "La condition des salaires à Florence au XIVe siècle." In *Il tumulto dei Ciompi* (Convegno internazionale di studi—Firenze, 16–19 settembre 1979). Florence, 1981.

———. *Prix et salaires à Florence au XIVe siècle, 1280–1380.* Rome, 1982.

De Roover, Raymond. "Aux origines d'une technique intellectuelle: La formation et l'expansion de la comptabilité a partie double." *Annales E.S.C.* 9 (1937), 171–93, 270–98.

———. "The Commercial Revolution of the Thirteenth Century." In *Enter-*

prise and Secular Change, edited by Frederic C. Lane and Jelle C. Riemersma. Homewood, Ill., 1953.

―――. *L'évolution de la lettre de change, XIVe–XVIIIe siècle.* Paris, 1953.

―――. "The Concept of the Just Price: Theory and Economic Policy." *Journal of Economic History* 18 (1958), 418–34.

―――. "The Organization of Trade." In *The Cambridge Economic History of Europe.* Vol. 3, *Economic Organization and Policies in the Middle Ages.* Cambridge, 1963.

―――. *The Rise and Decline of the Medici Bank.* Cambridge, Mass., 1963.

―――. "Labour Conditions in Florence around 1400: Theory, Policy, and Reality." In *Florentine Studies: Politics and Society in Renaissance Florence,* edited by Nicolai Rubinstein. London, 1968.

―――. "The Antecedents of the Medici Bank: The Banking House of Messer Vieri di Cambio de' Medici." In *Business, Banking, and Economic Thought in Late Medieval and Early Modern Europe,* edited by Julius Kirshner. Chicago, 1974.

―――. *Business, Banking, and Economic Thought in Late Medieval and Early Modern Europe,* edited by Julius Kirshner. Chicago, 1974.

―――. "The Development of Accounting Prior to Luca Pacioli According to the Account Books of Medieval Merchants." In *Business, Banking, and Economic Thought in Late Medieval and Early Modern Europe,* edited by Julius Kirshner. Chicago, 1974.

―――. "A Florentine Firm of Cloth Manufacturers." In *Business, Banking, and Economic Thought in Late Medieval and Early Modern Europe,* edited by Julius Kirshner. Chicago, 1974.

―――. "New Interpretations of the History of Banking." In *Business, Banking, and Economic Thought in Late Medieval and Early Modern Europe,* edited by Julius Kirshner. Chicago, 1974.

―――. "The Story of the Alberti Company of Florence, 1302–1348, As Revealed in Its Account Books." In *Business, Banking, and Economic Thought in Late Medieval and Early Modern Europe,* edited by Julius Kirshner. Chicago, 1974.

―――. *Money, Banking, and Credit in Medieval Bruges.* Cambridge, Mass., 1984.

Doren, A. *Le Arti fiorentine.* Vol. 1. Florence, 1940.

Dubois, Henry. "Banque et crédit en France aux deux derniers siècles du moyen âge." Paper presented at conference entitled "Banchi pubblici, banchi privati e monti di pietà nell'Europa preindustriale." Genoa, October 1990.

Edler de Roover, Florence. *Glossary of Mediaeval Terms of Business: Italian Series, 1200–1600*. Cambridge, Mass., 1934.

Fantappiè, Renzo. "Nascita d'una terra di nome Prato." In *Storia di Prato*. Vol. 1. Prato, 1981.

———. "Nascita e sviluppo di Prato." In *Prato storia di una città*, edited by Giovanni Cherubini. Vol. 1*. Prato, 1991.

Fiumi, Enrico. "Il computo della popolazione di Volterra nel medioevo secondo il 'sal delle bocche.'" *Archivio storico italiano* 107 (1949), 5–16.

———. "La demografia fiorentina nelle pagine di Giovannia Villani." *Archivio storico italiano* 108 (1950), 78–158.

———. "Economia e vita privata dei fiorentini nelle rilevazione statistiche di Giovanni Villani." *Archivio storico italiano* 91 (1953), 207–41.

———. "Sui rapporti economici fra città e contado." *Archivio storico italiano* 94 (1956), 18–68.

———. "Fioritura e decadenza dell'economia fiorentina." *Archivio storico italiano* 115 (1957), 385–439.

———. "L'imposta diretta nei comuni medioevali della Toscana." In *Studi in onore di Armando Sapori*. Milan, 1957.

———. "L'attività usuraria dei mercanti sangimignanesi nell'età comunale." *Archivio storico italiano* 119 (1961), 145–62.

———. *Storia economica e sociale di San Gimignano*. Florence, 1961.

———. "Stato di popolazione e distribuzione della ricchezza in Prato secondo il catasto de 1428–1429." *Archivio storico italiano* 123 (1965), 277–303.

———. *Demografia, movimento urbanistico e classi sociali in Prato dall'età comunale ai tempi moderni*. Florence, 1968.

———. "Sulle condizioni alimentari di Prato nell'età comunale." *Archivio storico pratese* 42 (1972), 3–26.

Forestié, Edouard, ed. *Les livres de comptes des Frères Bonis: Marchands montalbanais du XIVe siècle*. 2 vols. Paris, 1890–94.

Giani, Guido, *Prato e la sua fortezza dal secolo XI fino ai giorni nostri*. Prato, 1908.

———. *Ebbe Prato una zecca? esame storico critico della controversa questione*. Prato, 1915.

———. "Appunti e note sull'arte della lana in Prato: la colonia veronese del secolo XIII." *Archivio storico pratese* 1 (1917), 78–83.

———. "Per la storia dell'arte della lana in Prato." *Archivio storico pratese* 8 (1929), 97–113.

———. "Le pestilenze del 1348, del 1526 e del 1631–1632 in Prato." *Archivio storico pratese* 9 (1930), 49–63, 97–108.

Goldthwaite, Richard, A. "Schools and Teachers of Commercial Arithmetic in Renaissance Florence." *Journal of European Economic History* 1 (1972), 418–33.

———. "I prezzi del grano a Firenze nei secoli XIV–XVI." *Quaderni storici* 28 (1975), 5–36.

———. *The Building of Renaissance Florence: An Economic and Social History.* Baltimore, 1980.

———. "Local Banking in Renaissance Florence." *Journal of European Economic History* 14 (1985), 5–55.

Goldthwaite, Richard A., and Giulio Mandich, *Studi sulla moneta fiorentina, secoli XIII–XVI.* Florence, 1994.

Guasti, Cesare. *Il sacco di Prato e il ritorno dei Medici in Firenze nel 1512.* 2 vols. Bolgona, 1880.

———. *Lettere di un notaro a un mercante.* 2 vols. Florence, 1880.

Hatfield, Rab. *Botticelli's Uffizi "Adoration."* Princeton, N.J., 1976.

Herlihy, David. *Pisa in the Early Renaissance: A Study of Urban Growth.* New Haven, Conn., 1958.

———. "Direct and Indirect Taxation in Tuscan Urban Finance, 1200–1400." In *Finances et comptabilité urbaines du XIIIe au XVIe siècle.* Brussels, 1964.

———. *Medieval and Renaissance Pistoia: The Social History of an Italian Town, 1200–1430.* New Haven, Conn., 1967.

———. "Santa Maria Impruneta: A Rural Commune in the Late Middle Ages." In *Florentine Studies: Politics and Society in Renaissance Florence,* edited by Nicolai Rubinstein. London, 1968.

Herlihy, David, and Christiane Klapisch-Zuber. *Les Toscans et leurs familles: Une étude du catasto florentin de 1427.* Paris, 1978.

Hibbert, A. B. "The Economic Policies of Towns." In *The Cambridge Economic History of Europe.* Vol. 3, *Economic Organization and Policies in the Middle Ages.* Cambridge, 1963.

Hoshino, Hitetoshi. *L'arte della lana in Firenze nel basso Medioevo.* Florence, 1980.

Imberciadori, Ildebrando. "Proprietà terriera di Francesco Datini e parziaria mezzadrile nel'400." *Economia e storia* 3 (1958), 254–72.

Jones, P. J. "Florentine Families and Florentine Diaries in the Fourteenth Century." *Papers of the British School at Rome* 24 (1956).

Judges, A. V. "Scopi e metodi della storia dei prezzi." *Rivista storica italiana* 63 (1951), 162–79.

Kirshner, Julius, and Anthony Molho. "The Dowry Fund and the Marriage

Market in Early Quattrocento Florence." *Journal of Modern History* 50 (1978), 403–38.

Klapisch, Christiane. "Déclin démographique et structure du ménage: L'exemple de Prato, fin XIVe–XVe." In *Famille et parenté dans l'occident médiéval,* edited by Georges Duby and Jacques LeGoff. Paris, 1977.

Kotelnikova, Liubov. "Artigiani-affittuari nelle città e nelle campagne toscane del XV–XVI secolo." In *Aspetti della vita economica medievale* (Atti del convegno di studi nel X anniversario della morte di Federigo Melis, Firenze-Pisa-Prato, 10–14 marzo 1984). Florence, 1985.

Lane, Frederic C. "Investment and Usury in Medieval Venice." *Explorations in Entrepreneurial History* 2 (1964–65), 3–15.

Lane, Frederic C., and Jelle C. Miemersma, eds. *Enterprise and Secular Change.* Homewood, Illinois, 1953.

Lopez, Robert S. "The Trade of Medieval Europe: The South." In *The Cambridge Economic History of Europe.* Vol. 2. Cambridge, 1952.

———. "Hard Times and Investment in Culture." In *The Renaissance: Basic Interpretations,* edited by Karl Dannenfelt. 2d ed. Lexington, 1974.

Lopez, Robert S., and Harry Miskimin. "The Economic Depression of the Renaissance." *Economic History Review,* 2d ser., 14 (1962), 408–26.

Luzzatto, Gino, *An Economic History of Italy from the Fall of the Roman Republic to the Beginning of the Sixteenth Century,* translated by P. J. Jones. London, 1962.

Manselli, Raoul. "Istituzioni ecclesiastiche e vita religiosa." In *Prato storia di una città,* edited by Giovanni Cherubini. Vol. 1★★. Prato, 1991.

Martines, Lauro. *The Social World of the Florentine Humanists, 1399–1460.* Princeton, N.J., 1963.

———. *Lawyers and Statecraft in Renaissance Florence.* Princeton, N.J., 1968.

Martini, Anna. "La dedizione di Prato a Roberto d'Angio." *Archivio storico pratese* 27 (1951), 3–44.

Mazzi, Maria S. "Note per una storia dell'alimentazione nell'Italia medievale." In *Studi di storia medievale e moderna per Ernesto Sestan,* edited by Maria Mazzi and Sergio Raveggi. Vol. 1. Florence, 1980.

———. "I quadri ambientali della vita urbana e rurale." In *La Toscana nel secolo XIV caratteri di una civiltà regionale,* edited by Sergio Gensini (Centro di studi sulla civiltà del tardo medioevo). San Miniato, 1988.

McLaughlin, Terence P. "The Teachings of the Canonists on Usury (XII, XIII, XIV Centuries)." *Mediaeval Studies* 1 (1939), 81–147, and 2 (1940), 1–22.

Melis, Federigo. *Storia della ragioneria.* Bologna, 1950.

———. *Aspetti della vita economica medievale.* Siena, 1962.

———. "Aspetti della vita economica medievale (studi nell'Archivio Datini di Prato)." *Prato storia e arte* 7 (1963), 1–13.

———. "Il consumo del vino a Firenze nei decenni attorno al 1400." *Arte e mercatura* 4 (1967), 6–33.

———. *Documenti per la storia economica dei secoli XIII–XVI.* Florence, 1972.

———. *Mercanti e consumi: Organizzazione e qualificazione del commercio in Italia dal XII al XX secolo* (Il convegno nazionale di storia del commercio in Italia). Bologna, 1986.

———. *La banca pisana e le origini della banca moderna,* edited by Marco Spallanzani. Florence, 1987.

———. "La grande conquista trecentesca del 'credito di esercizio' e la tipologia dei suoi strumenti fino al XVI secolo." In *La banca pisana e le origini della banca moderna,* edited by Marco Spallanzani. Florence, 1987.

———. "Note di storia della banca pisana." In *La banca pisana e le origini della banca moderna,* edited by Marco Spallanzani. Florence, 1987.

Meyer, Paul. "Le livre-journal de Maître Ugo Teralh, notaire et drapier à Forcalquier, 1330–1332." *Notices et extraits des manuscrits de la Bibliothèque Nationale* 36 (1899), 129–70.

Meyer, Paul, and Georges Guigue. "Fragments du grand livre d'un drapier de Lyon, 1320–1323." *Romania* 35 (1906), 428–44.

Miskimin, Harry. *The Economy of Early Renaissance Europe, 1300–1460.* Englewood, N.J., 1969.

Modesti, I., S. Brami, S. Guizzalotti, "Tre narrazioni del sacco dato alla terra di Prato dagli spagnoli, 1512." *Archivio storico italiano* 1 (1842), 237–63.

Molho, Anthony. *Florentine Public Finance in the Early Renaissance, 1400–1433.* Cambridge, Mass., 1971.

———. "A Note on Jewish Moneylenders in Tuscany in the Late Trecento and Early Quattrocento." In *Renaissance Studies in Honor of Hans Baron,* edited by Anthony Molho and John Tedeschi. Dekalb, Ill., 1971.

———. Review of *The Building of Renaissance Florence,* by Richard Goldthwaite. *Speculum* 57 (1982), 884–91.

Molho, Anthony, and Franek Sznura, eds. *Alle bocche della piazza diario di anonimo fiorentino.* Florence, 1986.

Moretti, Italo. "L'ambiente e gli insediamenti." In *Prato storia di una città,* edited by Giovanni Cherubini. Vol. 1*. Prato, 1991.

———. "L'architettura." In *Prato storia di una città,* edited by Giovanni Cherubini. Vol. 1**. Prato, 1991.

Mueller, Reinhold C. "Les preteurs juifs à Venise au Moyen Age." *Annales E.S.C.* 30 (1975), 1277–1303.

Narrazione e disegno della terra di Prato di Toscana messa insieme e composta da Giovanni Miniati, cavaliere di S. Stefano, l'anno 1594. 1827. Reprint, Prato, 1966.

Nelson, Benjamin N. *The Idea of Usury.* Princeton, N.J., 1949.

Nicastro, Sebastiano. *Sulla storia di Prato dalle origini alla metà del secolo XIX.* Prato, 1916.

Nigro, Giampiero. *Gli Uomini dell'Irco.* Florence, 1983.

Nirrnheim, Hans, ed. *Das Handlungsbuch Vickos von Geldersen.* Hamburg, 1895. Reprint, Osaka, Japan, 1977.

Nuti, Ruggero. Il distretto pratese in un Plantario del 1584." *Archivio storico pratese* 7 (1927), 154–59.

———. "Inventario dell'Archivio dei Ceppi di Prato." *Rivista storica degli archivi toscani* 6 (1934), 136–46.

———. "Un mercante pratese in Ungheria nel secolo XV." *Archivio storico pratese* 12 (1934), 1–5.

———. "Famiglie antiche pratesi." *Archivio storico pratese* 12 (1934), 76–84, 112–22; and 13 (1935), 27–32.

———. *La topografia di Prato nel Medio Evo.* Prato, 1937.

———. "Mercanti e lanaioli pratese: I Marcovaldi." *Archivio storico pratese* 16 (1938), 169–79.

———. *La fiera di Prato attraverso i tempi.* Prato, 1939.

———. "La Cronaca di Sandro Marcovaldi." *Archivio storico pratese* 18 (1940), 49–69.

———. "Aspetti di Prato nel Medioevo." *Archivio storico pratese* 29 (1953), 25–48.

———, ed. *Inventario sommario dell'Archivio di Stato di Prato.* Prato, 1939.

Origo, Iris. *The Merchant of Prato.* New York 1957.

Pampaloni, Guido "Vendemmie e produzione di vino nelle proprietà dell' ospedale della Misericordia di Prato nel Quattrocento." In *Studi in memoria di Federigo Melis.* Vol. 3. Naples, 1978.

———. "Prato nella republica fiorentina." In *Storia di Prato.* Vol. 2. Prato, 1981.

———. "Artigiani e salariati a Prato nella metà del Quattrocento." *Aspetti della vita economica medievale* (Atti del convegno di studi nel X anniversario della morte di Federigo Melis, Firenze-Pisa-Prato, 10–14 marzo 1984). Florence, 1985.

———. "La compagna: Abitanti e agricoltura." In *Prato storia di una città,* edited by Giovanni Cherubini. Vol. 1*. Prato, 1991.

————. "L'autonomia pratese sotto Firenze, 1351–1500." In *Prato storia di una città,* edited by Giovanni Cherubini. Vol. 1✱✱. Prato, 1991.

————. "Popolazione e società nel centro e nei sobborghi." In *Prato storia di una città,* edited by Giovanni Cherubini. Vol. 1✱. Prato, 1991.

————, ed. *Inventario sommario dell'Archivio di Stato di Prato.* Florence, 1958.

Piattoli, Renato, and Ruggero Nuti, eds. *Statuti dell'arte della lana di Prato (secoli XIV–XVIII).* Florence, 1947.

Pinto, Giuliano. "Il personale, le balie e i salariati dell'Ospedale di San Gallo di Firenze negli anni 1395–1406: Note per la storia del salariato nelle città medievali." *Ricerche storiche* 4 (1974), 113–68.

————. *Il libro del biadaiolo.* Florence, 1978.

————. "Forme di conduzione e rendita fondiaria nel contado fiorentino (secoli XIV e XV): Le terre dell'ospedale di San Gallo." In *Studi di storia medievale e moderna per Ernesto Sestan,* edited by Maria Mazzi and Sergio Raveggi. Vol. 1. Florence, 1980.

————. "I livelli di vita dei salariati cittadini nel periodo successivo al tumulto dei Ciompi, 1380–1430." In *Il tumulto dei Ciompi* (Convegno internazionale di studi—Firenze, 16–19 settembre 1979). Florence, 1981.

Popovic, Mirjana. "La penetrazione dei mercanti pratesi a Dubrovnik nella prima metà del secolo XV." *Archivio storico italiano* 112 (1959), 503–21.

Portal, Charles. "Le livre-journal de Jean Saval, marchand-drapier à Carcassonne, 1340–1341." *Bulletin historique et philologique du comitè des travaux historiques et scientifiques* (Paris, 1901–2), 423–49.

Raveggi, Sergio. "Le condizioni di vita." In *Prato storia di una città,* edited by Giovanni Cherubini. Vol. 1✱. Prato, 1991.

————. "Protagonisti e antagonisti nel libero Comune." In *Prato storia di una città,* edited by Giovanni Cherubini. Vol. 1✱✱. Prato, 1991.

Repetti, Emanuela. *Dizionario Corografico della Toscana.* 1855. Reprint, Florence, 1977.

Rodolico, Niccolò. *La democrazia fiorentina nel suo tramonto, 1378–1382.* Bologna, 1905.

Rosati, Sonia. *Benedetto di Tacco da Prato Speziale, 1345–1392: Vita, attività, ambiente sociale ed economico.* 4 vols. *Tesi di laurea,* Facolta di lettere e filosofia dell'Università di Firenze, 1970–71.

Rutenburg, Victor. *Popolo e movimenti popolari nell'Italia del '300 e '400.* Bologna, 1971.

Sapori, Armando. *Una compagnia di Calimala ai primi del Trecento.* Florence, 1932.

————. *Le marchand italien au Moyen Age.* Paris, 1952.

———. *Studi di storia economica.* 3 vols. Florence, 1955–67.

———. "Case e botteghe a Firenze nel Trecento." In *Studi di storia economica.* Vol. 1. Florence, 1955.

———. "Città e classi sociali nel medioevo." In *Studi di storia economica.* Vol. 1. Florence, 1955.

———. "Economia e morale alla fine del Trecento: Francesco di Marco Datini e ser Lapo Mazzei." In *Studi di storia economica.* Vol. 1. Florence, 1955.

———. "Il personale delle compagnie mercantili dei medioevo." In *Studi di storia economica.* Vol. 2. Florence, 1955.

———. "L'interesse del denaro a Firenze nel Trecento." In *Studi di storia economica.* Vol. 1. Florence, 1955.

———. "Saggio sulle fonti della storia economica medievale." In *Studi di storia economica.* Vol. 1. Florence, 1955.

———. "La disciplina degli affitti delle botteghe a Firenze nel Trecento." In *Studi di storia economica.* Vol. 3. Florence, 1967.

———. "La gabella delle porte di Firenze, 1361 e 1364." In *Studi di storia economica.* Vol. 3. Florence, 1967.

Schiaffini, Alfredo. *Testi fiorentini del Dugento e dei primi del Trecento.* Florence, 1926.

Serianni, Luca. "Il dialetto pratese nel Medioevo." *Archivio storico pratese* 52 (1976), 3–29.

———. *Testi pratesi della fine del Dugento e dei primi del Trecento.* Florence, 1977.

Shahar, Shulamith. "The Regulation and Presentation of Women in Economic Life (Thirteenth to Eighteenth Centuries)." Paper presented at the annual seminar "La donna nell'economia," Istituto Internazionale di Storia Economica "F. Datini," Prato, April 1989.

Sivieri, G. "Il comune di Prato dalla fine del Duecento alla metà del Trecento." *Archivio storico pratese* 47 (1971), 3–57; and 48 (1972), 3–39.

Spallanzani, Marco. "Alcune lettere di credito con 'segnali' dell'inizio del Cinquecento." In *Studi in memoria di Mario Abrate.* Turin, 1986.

Spufford, Peter. *Handbook of Medieval Exchange.* London, 1986.

Storia di Prato. 3 vols. Prato, 1981.

Sznura, Franek. "Edilizia privata e urbanistica in di crisi." In *Prato storia di una città,* edited by Giovanni Cherubini. Vol. 1*. Prato, 1991.

Tangheroni, Marco. "La distribuzione al minuto nel medio evo." In *Mercanti e consumi: Organizzazione e qualificazone del commercio in Italia dal XII al XX secolo* (Il convegno nazionale di storia del commercio in Italia). Bologna, 1986.

———. "Il sistema economico della Toscana nel Trecento." In *La Toscana nel secolo XIV: Caratteri di una civiltà regioinale* (Centro di studi sulla civiltà del tardo medioevo). San Miniato, 1988.

Thrupp, Sylvia L. "Medieval Industry, 1000–1500." In *The Middle Ages*. Vol. 1 of *The Fontana Economic History of Europe,* edited by Carlo M. Cipolla. New York, 1976.

———. "The Gilds." In *The Cambridge Economic History of Europe.* Vol. 3, *Economic Organization and Policies in the Middle Ages.* Cambridge, 1963.

Travaini, Lucia. "L'organizzazione delle zecche toscane nel XIV secolo." In *La Toscana nel secolo XIV: Caratteri di una civiltà regionale* (Centro di studi sulla civiltà del tardo medioevo). San Miniato, 1988.

Trexler, Richard C. *Economic, Political, and Religious Effects of the Papal Interdict on Florence, 1376–1378.* Frankfurt, 1964.

———. "The Spiritual Power: Republican Florence under Interdict." In *Studies in Medieval and Reformation Thought.* Vol. 9. Leiden, 1974.

Usher, Abbott B. *The Early History of Deposit Banking in Mediterranean Europe.* Cambridge, Mass., 1943.

Vigo, Giovanni. "Real Wages of the Working Class in Italy: Building Workers' Wages (Fourteenth to Eighteenth Century)." *Journal of European Economic History* 3 (1974), 374–99.

Villain-Gandossi, Christiane, ed. *Comptes du sel de Francesco di Marco Datini pour sa compagnie d'Avignon, 1376–1379.* Paris, 1969.

Violante, Cinzio. *Economia, società, istituzioni a Pisa nel Medioevo: Saggi e ricerche.* Bari, 1980.

INDEX

account books, 114; content of, 63–64; entries in, 75; as evidence of usury, 98; land sales in, 85, 159n.78; ledgers, 65, 68; of Pratese tradesmen, 119–23; reconstruction of, 152n.2; supplementary, 67–69, 155n.19

accounting practices: of small entrepreneurs, 63–69

Albertis, 2, 3, 127n.9

Angevines, 3

Antonio di Cambio di Ferro, 29, 57, 141n.84

apothecaries, medieval, 43. See also druggists

apprentices, cost of, 46

Arezzo, registers at, 8, 131n.43

Arte del Cambio, 7

Arte della Lana, 51, 52, 53, 119

artisans, xii, 9, 35; in account books, 74; account books of, 86; business environment for, 34; conservative outlook of, 33; credit used by, 74; garden plots of, 20; in local economies, 117; moneylending by, 115; records of, 64–65, 66; women as, 40, 41. See also entrepreneurs

banchiere, 90, 161n.6

bankers (tavolieri), 90, 107; local, 106–7; and overdrafts, 109–11; as pawnbrokers, 161n.6; and reference to interest, 168n.39; in small business, 112; and third-party payments, 108. See also merchant bankers

banking: credit in, 101–2; deposit, 101, 165n.1; history of, 101, 165n.1; origins of, 101, 166n.2

banking services, in local markets, xv, 110, 168n.40

bank transfers, 109–10

barter system, 21, 72, 84

basket makers, 151n.24

Benedetto di Filippo (merchant banker), 32, 90, 106, 107, 167n.23; ledgers of, 161n.6

Benedetto di Tacco (druggist), 21, 22, 24, 26, 27, 31, 41, 42–43, 46, 47, 49, 66, 67–68, 73, 74, 75, 76, 80–81, 91, 92, 93, 95, 97–98, 110–11, 114, 125n.2; account books of, 103, 119–20, 153n.5; earnings of, 45; holidays observed by, 30; income sources of, 43–44; ledgers of, 85; records of, 110, 168n.43; religious customers of, 28–29

Biagio di Giovanni Bertelli (paper manufacturer), 22, 24, 36, 41, 122, 129n.34

Biblioteca Roncioniana, 52, 56

bill collectors, 78

Bindaccio de'Cerchi, bank of, 52

bishopric, for Prato, 2

Black Death, 46, 120, 128n.22, 154n.13; and medieval diet, 16; in Tuscany, 5, 23, 120, 154n.13

Black Guelfs, 4

blacksmiths, 7

bonds, modern, 102

Bonis brothers, 87

borrowers: characteristics of, 92, 115; women as, 93. See also loans

bread, 16–17; prices for, 17–18, 134n.2

brokerage transactions: commissions from, 55; records of, 56–57

brokers, 35, 116; account books of, 54, 123, 150n.21; for guilds, 52–53, 149n.7; independent, 52; operations of, 52–55

Library of Congress Cataloging-in-Publication Data

Marshall, Richard K.
  The local merchants of Prato : small entrepreneurs in the late
medieval economy / Richard K. Marshall.
    p.   cm. — (The Johns Hopkins University studies in historical
and political science ; 117th ser., no. 1)
  Includes bibliographical references and index.
  ISBN 0-8018-6057-1 (alk. paper)
    1. Small business—Italy—Prato—History—To 1500.   2. Prato (Italy)—
Commerce—History—To 1500.   3. Prato (Italy)—Economic conditions—
To 1500.   I. Title.   II. Series.
HD2346.I82P725   1999
338.6′42′094551—dc21   98-43545
                                                                                       CIP